ESSAYS ON
COUNSELING

ESSAYS ON COUNSELING

Jay E. Adams

Ministry Resources Library

Zondervan Publishing House • Grand Rapids, MI

Essays on Counseling
Copyright © 1972 by Jay E. Adams

Ministry Resources Library is an imprint of
Zondervan Publishing House, 1415 Lake Drive, S.E.,
Grand Rapids, Michigan 49506

Library of Congress Cataloging in Publication Data

Adams, Jay Edward.
    Essays on counseling.

    (The Jay Adams library)
    Originally published: The big umbrella and other
essays on Christian counseling. Nutley, N.J.:
Presbyterian and Reformed Pub. Co., © 1972.
    1. Pastoral counseling.   I. Title.   II. Series:
Adams, Jay Edward.   Jay Adams library.
BV4012.2.A27   1986   253.5   86-4135
ISBN 0-310-51171-2

Printed in the United States of America

86   87   88   89   90   91 / 10   9   8   7   6   5   4   3   2   1

Dedicated
to
The Faculty of the Reformed Episcopal Seminary
To whom I owe a debt that
I could never pay

PREFACE

The Big Umbrella is a selection of essays and addresses
adapted from lectures and articles. Most of the lectures have
been given during the past two years in colleges and theological institutions and before ministeriums. Others were delivered in more popular contexts. In almost every case they were
used more than once. All have been revised, some more extensively than others. Yet, in spite of revision, throughout I
have purposely attempted to retain the extemporaneous and
sometimes quite informal flavor of the original speaking situations.

The articles cover a variety of subjects, all in some way
having to do with counseling. While they are not presented
in order to explain methodology and technique, in not a few
places such information occurs, some of which is unique to
this book. A more systematic textbook for counselors is
presently in preparation.

There is some inevitable repetition in the lectures that was
necessitated by the need to orient different audiences to the
fundamental ideas of Christian counseling. This repetitious
material was included only because it could not be removed
without seriously damaging the fabric of the whole and requiring nearly a total rewriting of the chapter. This was not
possible. However, repetitious materials have been pared to a
minimum

With great pleasure I send forth this volume in hope that
the many encouraging friends who have asked me to make
one or another of these essays and addresses available will be
satisfied, and that others may find the same sort of help and
profit from them that these friends claim to have received.

I cannot conclude without thanking my family for the time
they have given to me to allow me to prepare and edit this
book. My warmest thanks and deep gratitude must be ex-

pressed to Mrs. David Crawley for transcribing most of the addresses from tape, and to Mrs. Richard Wagner for her cheerful typing and retyping of the entire manuscript.

Jay E. Adams
Philadelphia, 1972

CONTENTS

The Big Umbrella

During the last generation a big umbrella was opened. Beneath its huge, over-arching expanse you now find people with the most diverse problems and difficulties. Under its shadow they have been gathered together according to the novel idea that nearly everybody who is having problems, regardless of what his difficulties may be, is sick. The name of this umbrella is *Mental Illness*.

This umbrella was designed and opened by Charcot and Freud and others who worked with them. Until their time, "illness" meant physical illness. But they stretched the concept of illness until it pertained to nearly any and every sort of difficulty in life. I cannot review the historical reasons for this radical change, but if you want to learn more about how it came about, borrow Thomas Szasz's book, *The Myth of Mental Illness*, and read the first two chapters. You will find that he explains very plainly how this happened. What is of importance is that Szasz shows how Charcot and Freud used the medical model (illness) to declare those who previously had been called malingerers, to be sick. You will find this history most enlightening.

Regardless of the historical background, we are all aware that the umbrella is wide open today. Huddled together under it are people with organic problems and people with non-organic problems; people with perceptual difficulties and people with behavioral difficulties; people whose brains have been damaged and people who, to put it simply, have never learned how to get along in life. Those who are criminal or guilty or lazy have found escape beneath the umbrella together with those who are senile and those who have glandular problems. This is truly a most motley mob.

---

[1]This talk originally was delivered as a lecture to the student body of the Reformed Episcopal Seminary. Since then, it has been used at various ministerial gatherings (revised).

All sorts of people, then, have been labeled mentally ill. My thesis is that you who are ministers of the gospel must not be content with these current conditions. You may not condone the practice of confusing illness with behavioral deviation; such a position is clearly contrary to the Word of God. Instead, you must do something to alter this serious situation. You must take out of the rack an entirely different umbrella, a much smaller one, for that big umbrella is the product of a wholly wrong concept. It was manufactured according to non-Christian specifications and has been used for humanistic purposes. You must do all that you can to reduce the big umbrella to its proper size.

There is a much smaller umbrella that legitimately might be labeled mental illness; but it is very small, almost minute, in comparison to the Freudian umbrella. Many of those people who are now hiding under the shelter of the large umbrella will not fit under the smaller one. God makes no provision for them there. There are, of course, people who are mentally ill. If I were to raise a crowbar and bring it down squarely across your head, you would have—literally—mental illness; there would be no question about it. You would have an *illness* caused by physical, organic brain damage. Quite legitimately you could be declared "ill." In every genuine sense of the term you would be *mentally* ill. Some people whose brains have been injured by toxic substances have mental illness. It is possible that some genetic and some chemical problems may cause a physical or organic type of illness very similar to brain damage. All of these problems are valid instances of mental illness. But by comparison with the crowd under the umbrella, the number of people who have that kind of true illness or sickness due to some sort of organic mental malfunction is small.

Under the big umbrella are people who have difficulty keeping a job, who do not get along with their husbands or wives or children or parents, and who are irresponsible and undependable. In short, they are people who have learned all sorts of sinful behavior patterns that, in God's world, eventually get them into a peck of trouble. Although they are not, they have been erroneously *declared* mentally ill.

Now let me punch a few holes in the big umbrella. The new concept of Mental Illness, naturally, required a new sort of practitioner. Consequently, the profession of psychiatry was developed to work with these supposedly non-organically "sick" persons. In order to chalk out an area for his newly-spawned discipline, the psychiatrist moved into territory that once was inhabited by Christian ministers and by physicians. The larger amount of territory, by far, was usurped from the minister. The psychiatrist drove out pastors from the land of their forefathers, a land originally given to them by God. Pastors, you must recognize the fact that they moved onto *your* inheritance and stole *your* birthright. They now are situated firmly on that land as squatters. Asserting squatters' rights, they now have the audacity to defy ministers to move back. Yes, the umbrella has grown too large and its dimensions must be reduced.

To put it another way, I find it necessary to question seriously whether there is any legitimate place for the psychiatrist. Is there any territory allotted to him in the economy of God? Physicians, psychologists, ministers of the gospel, all have legitimate separate functions—but psychiatrists? Where is there room for a third person to stand midway between the physician and the pastor? Does some kind of mid-ground belong exclusively to him upon which neither a physician nor a minister can tread? What territory, what discipline is rightfully his, and his alone? Is there anything that he does that no one else has any right to do? I think not. My point is that in order to justify his very existence he has had to take a little bit of land from the physician and a great deal from the minister. Subsequently he fenced off this land and called it his own. And it is on this stolen property that he has posted "No Trespassing" signs!

One way to determine whether this is true is by asking the

question, "What does a psychiatrist do?" The more that you think about it, the more difficult it is to discover any function that he performs that gives him the right to claim that his work is a specialty of his own. For instance, a psychiatrist is not necessarily a medical man. In other countries (Europe, for example) the psychiatrist is not required to have a medical degree. Freud himself was very plain about this matter. He did not believe that a psychotherapist had to be a physician. He knew that his work was not really medical, and at times he was quite open about the fact. In this country, because of a prestigious alliance with the A.M.A., a psychiatrist is required to have an M.D. But you will soon agree that Freud was right if you read the articles written by some psychiatrists complaining about the necessity to take medical training that they never use in their work and soon forget. The point is this: there is nothing that a psychiatrist does with his medical training that a physician couldn't do just as well, or better. And the physician could do it in conjunction with a pastoral counselor. The psychiatrist may write prescriptions for tranquilizers or other pills now and then, but a physician does that all of the time. There is no need for a specialty in order to prescribe pills. So his medical training and work, you see, is not a specialty but merely an exact duplication of a portion of the physician's training and work.

What is it then that a psychiatrist mainly does if he does not do medical work, if he is not really a medical specialist? He talks; that is what he does. He spends most of his time talking to people about their problems (although some psychiatrists spend most of the time listening[2]). What does he talk about? People go to a psychiatrist because something is wrong: they don't feel right, other people say they don't behave properly, or they themselves recognize that they are not

[2]But see Jay Adams, *Competent to Counsel,* Nutley: 1971, pp. 87 ff., for a fuller discussion of Rogerian "listening," which I have shown is not listening at all.

making it in life for some similar reason. They go to a psychiatrist hoping that he will be able to get them out of trouble. They want him to show them the way to eliminate the pressures, the tensions, the difficulties and the terrible tangles into which their lives have been raveled. And this he tries to do, presumably *by talking.* Now that is not medical practice; there is nothing peculiarly medical about solving problems by talk. Indeed, if these people were really sick, it would seem to be a strange means of dealing with sickness and disease.

Preachers once were known as the people who talked to other people about their problems. They used to direct people to God's solutions as they are found in the Scriptures. But it is strange how modern preachers have learned to keep their mouths shut when listening to people's troubles. They have been willing to learn not to talk. They have been brainwashed by floods of propaganda into refusing to talk to these people. They have been taught, instead, to refer them to psychiatrists so that they may talk to them. But talk hardly makes the psychiatrist's discipline unique. It has always been the province of the minister to speak to men collectively and individually about the welfare of their souls (cf. Col. 1:28; Acts 20:31). Unless you pastors are willing to continue to close your mouths, when God has bid you to open them, you will be in conflict over the territory of talk.

"But perhaps the *content* or *end* of psychiatric talk is unique," you may protest. Fair enough; let us ask, what is it that psychiatrists talk about and what is it that they want to accomplish by means of this talk? Psychiatrists wish to change feelings and behavior; that is the end that they have in view. They are concerned to change attitudes and feelings, character and behavior; in short, they want to change the client's way of life in some fundamental way. They seek to alter behavior, attitudes, values, etc. But in accordance with what standard? According to their own goals and beliefs? According to those that the counselee may suggest? You see, this poses a fundamental problem that we must consider before we are through; obviously, the ends and goals envisioned in this purpose should be matters of great concern to us as pastors. They also constitute another area where you can see that conflict over territorial rights is inevitable.

Gentlemen, behavior modification and the discussion of values and attitudes is something that preachers have been doing ever since the beginning. As a matter of fact, that is a large part of what a minister's activity is all about. God has commanded us to talk to men about their sinful lives and their need for a Savior. We are commissioned by Him to be concerned with the way He regenerates and changes (sanctifies) them by the power of the Holy Spirit. Indeed, God has told us that it is the Spirit's work in their lives that changes sinful human character. He brings men to repentance and makes their lives fruitful in all the good attitudes and behavior mentioned in Galatians 5. Sanctification, the process of putting off the old man and putting on the new man (Eph. 4, Col. 3), involves just the sort of attitudinal and behavioral change that the psychiatrist also seeks to bring about. The two will be in conflict unless the Word and the Spirit are involved in both. But if they are, of what need is the psychiatrist?

So, I say that the psychiatrist has usurped the work of the physician, but mostly the work of the preacher. And he engages in this work without warrant from God, without the aid of the Scriptures (in almost every case), and without regard to the power of the Holy Spirit. Thus he seeks to change the behavior and the values of people in an ungodly manner.[3] Insofar as he succeeds, the results may be feared.

The work of changing men's lives belongs to the Christian ministry in particular and to Christian people in general; not to some self-appointed caste of humanistic priests that has moved into the Church's territory, and, by declaring hosts of

---

[3] Psalm 1:1, "Blessed is the man who does not walk in the counsel of the ungodly."

people mentally ill, has said, "We who are mental specialists alone can deal with these people." At every point the Word of God challenges this claim. Can you not see that there is something radically wrong when, after collecting a crowd under the umbrella of mental *illness,* the psychiatrist quickly throws aside all medical pretenses and instead starts *talking* about values and behavior change?

Szasz has shown that the whole thing began as a tragic fraud. Now, because so many well-meaning persons have been caught up in this fraud, it needs to be understood and exposed. That cannot be done here, since I do not have the time to punch any more holes in the psychiatric umbrella. But in the light of what has been said, let us consider five facts that are important for you as ministers of the gospel.

I. You have greater opportunities than you may think

There is a host of people who have been declared sick who are not sick at all. They may be sick *as a result* of their poor behavior,[4] of course, but I'm talking about the *cause,* not the result, of their problem. The cause is not sickness. The cause of their problem is, to put it generally, that they have not been living as God says man should. They are people with personal problems; that is what is wrong with them. They have not been making it in life because they are not doing what God says they must do in one or more life situations. Therefore, there is a great opportunity for you to help those people. They are not getting much help through psychiatry. The rate of recovery for psychoanalysis, Eysenck showed, is precisely the same as the spontaneous remission rate, i.e., the rate of recovery for those who did nothing about their problem. The psychoanalysts have had a rate of success that is precisely the same as if they did nothing. That is a pretty

---

[4]As, for example, ulcer patients who are physically sick because of the sin of worry or colitis patients who may be ill from resentment and anger.

poor record, especially when people have spent millions of dollars on psychoanalysis. Can you, a minister of the gospel, do any worse?

But more than that, let me remind you of the biblical commission to deal even with those people who are sick physically. They are not even exclusively within the physician's province. In James 5, God put you and me squarely in the business of helping people who are sick because of sin. He required the elders of the church to minister to such people. They must help bring such people to the confession of sin. The acknowledgment of violations of the Word of God, followed by thorough repentance, leads to changes that are in accordance with the Word and subsequent healing from God.[5]

Throughout the Scriptures, pastoral work is consistently described in terms of helping people who are in trouble. It is true that all Christians are encouraged to participate in this kind of work, but, par excellence, this is *pastoral* work. For example, in Colossians 1:28, Paul says when he is summing up his whole ministry: "We proclaim him" (speaking of Christ) "nouthetically confronting every man and teaching every man with all wisdom that we may present every man complete in Christ." There are two sides to the work of the ministry. A minister must (1) *teach* every man and he must (2) *confront* every man nouthetically.

Paul was a great teacher. We rightly think of him as such, for he was a tremendous teacher. He taught publicly from house to house (Acts 20:20). Everywhere he went and all of the time he taught. He taught by means of letters; he taught out on the streets; he taught in the synagogues; he taught wherever he had the opportunity, and when there was no opportunity, he made one. He preached the gospel and taught the Word of God. Yes, he was a teacher, but he did other things too; teaching, he himself says, was only half of his work.

---

[5]Cf. Adams, *op. cit.*, p. 107 ff. for a fuller discussion of this passage.

The work that he mentions first is "nouthetically confronting every man." The coin of teaching has another side. On the flip side, according to Paul, is nouthetic confrontation (whatever that might mean). But before we explain the term, let's look at another passage in which Paul again speaks about this question. In Acts 20 is recorded Paul's famous address to the Ephesian elders, where he says good-bye to them in that touching scene by the seashore. He urged the Ephesian elders to "be on the alert, remembering that night and day for a period of three years I did not cease to nouthetically confront each one of you with tears" (vs. 31). Note carefully these words: "night and day." That involves a large slice of time. "For a period of three years"; that represents the whole period that he remained at Ephesus. According to the New Testament record, Paul spent more time in Ephesus than in any other city. He may have stayed elsewhere for a longer time, but as far as the record goes, he was at Ephesus longer than anywhere else. Consequently, at Ephesus his work was more pastoral than at other places.

We usually think of Paul as a missionary, always on the move from one place to another. We picture his moving through Crete, stopping at this spot and that, leaving behind small groups of people as unorganized congregations. We read of his sending word back to Titus to appoint elders and organize the churches. Here is truly a man on the move. We may think of Paul on the move all of the time, and generally speaking, that is an accurate picture. But we must also take into account these three years where he labored as pastor. That he could do an intensive pastoral work during a three-year stay is easy for us to understand, since in many circles today a three-year pastorate is not at all uncommon.

He says also, "I did not cease," adding these words to indicate that the nouthetic activity was not confined merely to the first or second or third year. He did not do this work only part of the time or at certain seasons; he did not engage in nouthetic confrontation only in fall and spring campaigns; he did it continually throughout the whole length of the three-year ministry. Paul's words indicate that he might be engaged in such activities at almost any period of time on a given day of any year. Every day, night and day, then, he "did not cease to confront each one nouthetically with tears." So you can see that nouthetic confrontation was a large part of Paul's ministry.[6]

Now I suppose I must tell you something about the biblical idea of nouthetic confrontation. Fundamentally it means this: God using one man to confront another verbally about something that God wants changed for the benefit of the individual who is confronted. Many of the persons that Paul confronted doubtless would be labeled mentally ill today. Christian ministers must learn again to confront members of their congregations about the *sin* that lies at the root of many of their problems. They must learn again from the Scriptures how to use direct verbal confrontation. They, of course, must not do so apart from the power of the Spirit working by His Word. Let us then see what God has said about nouthetic confrontation.

The first element in the word *nouthesia* involves the idea that there is something wrong in the counselee's life that God wants changed. That means that known sin in the lives of the members of the church must not be winked at. It is a responsibility of those who have the rule over the flock to lead the sheep in the paths of righteousness as the Great Shepherd has directed. That will often involve confronting them when they wander into the paths of unrighteousness.

The second element in the word is that the change is attempted by use of appropriate verbal means in personal con-

---

[6]We must not think dichotomistically about the pastoral and evangelistic (missionary) ministry. The great commission (Mt. 28) is plainly pastoral, "teaching them to observe all things" That Paul did pastoral work not only at Ephesus but everywhere, seems plain. (Cf. I Thess. 2:11, 12 where it is clear that he worked nouthetically even in Thessalonica where he stayed so briefly.)

frontation. The idea of personal counseling is clear. The counselor does not attempt to change the person he is confronting by manipulating him in some behavioristic fashion, but he does so by personal counseling, by a verbal confrontation, by sitting down and talking through his problems with him, hopefully to reach biblical solutions to them. He uses a verbal confrontation and a verbal methodology; that is to say, a *counseling* methodology. Talk, the psychiatrist's methodology, was not given to him but was ordained by God for the work of the ministry. Yet it is talk of a specific sort. *Nouthesia* is plainly directive counseling; it involves the application of biblical principles to concrete life situations.

There is also a third element in that word: the confrontation takes place in order to change the man for his own benefit; for his own welfare. There is the connotation of loving concern in this word; the New Testament never loses sight of that element in the word. You see it emerge where the term is used in familial contexts. For example, this element is prominent when Paul told the Corinthians, "I do not write these things to shame you but to confront you nouthetically *as my beloved children"* (I Cor. 4:14). When he talks about the disciplining of a brother, he urges, "Do not look on him as an enemy, but confront him nouthetically *as a brother,"* or, "as you would confront a brother" (II Thess. 3:15). And in that family context in Ephesians after he has instructed children to obey their parents, he addresses their fathers with these words: "Bring them up in the nurture ('discipline,' or 'training,' as the word *paideia* means) and the nouthetic confrontation of the Lord" (Eph. 6:4). Parents must confront their children in the same way that the Lord confronts them as His children. And so the word occurs in these warm contexts, showing that it carries the idea of concern for the other person. Even in Acts 20:31 that note also is sounded strongly when Paul says, "I did not cease to nouthetically confront each one *with tears."* The deep involvement of Paul for each one of these believers, the personal attention and the "weeping with those who weep" is apparent. The words "each one" occur not only in Acts, but also in Colossians (cf. Col. 1:28). This personalized concern and the tears that it brought to his eyes show his love. Counseling must be done in love, and love must be "in the truth" (II John 1; III John 1).

Now the reason I have brought the word *nouthesia* over into English from the Greek New Testament instead of simply translating it "admonish" or "counsel" or "warn" or "instruct" or by some other term, is because none of these words in English has the depth and the fulness of meaning that is inherent in the Greek term. So far as I know, there is no English word that adequately expresses the three elements in the Greek word *nouthesia.* It seems important to note that whenever you do not have a word for the thing, usually you do not have the thing itself. Where you do not have a word to describe an activity adequately, it is normally because you are not engaged in pursuing it. Indeed that seems to be the fact in this instance. We do not have a word in English because the concept of *nouthesia* has not been explored fully in English literature and, therefore, not adequately worked out in the life of the church. We rarely see this kind of confrontation of church members; overwhelming concern for people that compels us to go to them and talk to them in order to change their lives is virtually nonexistent. We know little about nouthetic confrontation in our society. Everything else has been substituted for it, but true biblical nouthetic confrontation rarely exists.

And so, what I'm saying is that *you* have greater opportunities than you may think. You may open up the New Testament idea of *nouthesia* to your congregation. The very concept, put into practice, could make your ministry flower. The possibilities and opportunities that nouthetic activities offer for the edification of the saints are as unlimited as the need is great. As evangelical pastors who believe the Word of God, who want to follow it, and who want for your flocks all of the blessings of God, you cannot avoid this matter. So, to begin with, I want to urge you to consider the great potential for good that is wrapped up in *nouthesia*. Great change in the Church of Christ for good can be brought about by developing fully all that God says about this aspect of the work of the ministry. Let us not fall short of it.

But you might say,

"Perhaps so, but I'm not qualified; I can't handle people in all sorts of difficulties that you are saying that I ought to be handling. That psychiatric umbrella isn't too big for me. I'm glad to see most of those people under that umbrella. I'm glad to have someone to whom I may refer them. I'm thankful for psychiatrists and mental institutions. I'm glad I don't have to handle the people I can send on to them. And not only that, think of the damage that I might do if I tried to counsel such persons. Why, I might injure them for the rest of their lives! Excuse me; I simply am not qualified."

I want to assure you (secondly) that

II. You have greater qualifications than you may realize

Not only do you have greater opportunities than you may think, but you have far greater qualifications than you even may begin to recognize. We have seen that changing the lives of your people is not a psychiatrist's work. Rather, behavior and value change is the work of God's servants. You and I cannot escape our responsibilities so easily.

Look once again at your qualifications for the work. What training, for instance, is really best for the task of changing men's lives? Medical training? Psychiatric training? Training in some clinic or theoretical school of psychotherapy in New York or Washington? University training in psychology? What about a solid seminary training in the Word of God? Think— what is the *best* training and background for the work of changing the lives of other people? I maintain that a good seminary background is the best education for the work of changing lives. If that training is truly biblical, it will as a matter of course provide experience in biblical counseling. I insist that a seminary background (of the right sort) is the proper and by far the best means for training a person for that work. When you begin to think seriously about this matter, you also will begin to realize that this is a seminary's task. When we give a man the tools (Greek, Hebrew, hermeneutics, exegesis) so that he can study the Word of God for the rest of his life and find out what this Book has to say, we are giving him the background that he needs for counseling as well as for preaching. He must learn how to share the results of his studies with his people in both his preaching and in his counseling. His ministerial training should give him a basic foundation in the Scriptures so that he comes to understand the fundamental ideas, concepts and principles of God's Word. It is these that are needed to help people with personal problems. And in seminaries we must—though often we have failed to do so—teach prospective ministers how to communicate the Word of God concretely from the pulpit and in the counseling room. A good seminary training, in principle at least, ought to raise all of the matters that a minister and his people must face in life. It should show him how to use the Scriptures to help them find practical solutions to these problems. That is what seminary training is all about—or ought to be about—equipping future ministers with the tools and methods necessary to develop among the people of God a standard of living that is acceptable to God and a witness to the world.

People whose marriages are all mixed up need to know how to live *before God.* Parents and children at odds need to be brought together *in the Lord.* Apart from the Word of God (and the God of the Word) such goals can never be attained.

What are the fundamental qualifications for such work? Well, if you look at the passages that talk about nouthetic confrontation, you will discover what those qualifications are. In Romans 15:14, for example, Paul, speaking to the laymen in the church at Rome, says that they are "competent to counsel," or "capable of nouthetically confronting one another." He says he believes this "because I am convinced that you are *full of goodness* and *filled with all knowledge.*" In Colossians 3:16, where he talks about "nouthetically confronting one another" as well as "teaching one another," he speaks again of being filled with the knowledge of Jesus Christ: "Let the Word of Christ dwell in you richly." There he adds a third element: "with all *wisdom.*" These verses mention three things that qualify one for nouthetic activity: goodness, knowledge and wisdom. These are the three fundamental qualifications of a man who is going to confront others in order to change their lives.

He needs (first of all) to know God's Word well: the Word of Christ must "dwell within him richly." He needs to be "filled" with a knowledge of the Scriptures. I do not know of any university training in clinical psychology, or of any psychiatric institute that attempts to fill a man with such knowledge. I do not know of any psychoanalytical schools that prepare counselors so that they are richly endued with the knowledge of the Word of Christ. But theological education attempts to do just that. You men have had the best sort of training to qualify you for this work.

Knowledge has an experiential side that must not be missed; it is to "dwell within him"; i.e., become a living, vital part of the fabric of his being. Unfortunately, seminaries have not always stressed this fact.[7]

Secondly, the nouthetic counselor needs to be full of *wisdom.* Wisdom means (among other things) the practical application of that knowledge; the ability to apply a truth found in the Scriptures to a man's life at the place where he lives. Wisdom brings the Word of God to bear upon problems in

---

[7]Before ordination a man's qualifications for the ministry should be determined by the presbytery not only on the basis of his academic record or intellectual abilities, but also on the basis of these three factors.

pertinent and relevant ways. Again, it has an experiential side that says something about the man who possesses it (cf. James 3:13-18).

Thirdly, there is the essential quality of *goodness.* The word goodness probably does not refer so much to the goodness of the life of the counselor (though that certainly is involved in it and behind it) as it does to his goodness of attitude toward others. It is this quality that in loving concern motivates a pastor to take the time and make the effort to seek out God's answers to the problems of another. Such goodness toward others continually gets him involved in another person's life *for his good.*

Those are three basic qualifications that the Scriptures require of a counselor. Those are also basic requirements for a good minister of the Word. Certainly no man should be in the ministry unless he has those qualifications; which is to say that if a minister is not qualified to counsel, he is not qualified to be a minister.

To summarize: it is essential to have a *knowledge of the Scriptures* in order to evaluate man's problems and to discover God's solutions to them; to become *wise* in the ability to deal with counselees in personal confrontation (note use of "wisdom" in a similar connection in Colossians 4:5, 6); to have *goodness of heart* to motivate one to engage in the difficult task of confronting another and to condition his attitudes in doing so.

There is a *fourth* qualification that must be mentioned because it is the most basic of all and stands as bedrock beneath the first three. In Galatians 6:1 Paul says that if any brother sees another caught (or possibly catches another) in sin, he must restore him. This commandment is directed to those "who are spiritual." Picture a brother whose life is badly messed up. For all practical purposes he has ceased to function vitally as a member of the Church. Paul does not say that he may be referred to an unsaved psychiatrist or to an unbelieving marriage counselor for help. Indeed, he explicitly forbids Christians to obtain help from those who know nothing about Jesus Christ; the brother must be helped by another Christian: "Ye who are spiritual." When he wrote those words Paul was not referring to two kinds of Christians, spiritual Christians and unspiritual Christians. That is not the point of the distinction; such a consideration did not even pass through his mind. Throughout the book of Galatians (as also in his other letters) Paul clearly identifies men as belonging to two, not three, categories. For him the two kinds of men are the "spiritual man" and the "natural man" (cf. I Corinthians 2). The former is a man who has the Spirit, the latter a person who does not have the Spirit. All men are born natural men. But those who have been regenerated by the Holy Spirit thereby have become spiritual men. The Spirit dwells in them whom He has regenerated. So what Paul is saying in Galatians 6:1 is, "You in whom the Spirit dwells must be the ones to restore your brother." This prerequisite is a fundamental factor that disqualifies all but Christians.

Looking at these biblical standards then, may I ask who is qualified to do nouthetic confrontation if it is not Christian ministers? So, you have greater opportunities than you may have thought and greater qualifications than you may have realized. But let me also encourage you further by asserting that

III. You have greater knowledge than you may recognize

You say,

"I do not. I wouldn't know what to do if I had to confront somebody who is severely depressed. I don't know how to help a homosexual. Suppose somebody starts running down the street naked with a meat cleaver; I wouldn't know how to handle that!"

Well, maybe you should think further about what to do in such specific cases. But I believe that basically you do know what to do, even though you may not realize it. What I am trying to say is that I think you know a lot more about how to handle these and other kinds of situations than others do, or than you yourself may recognize.

First of all, you have inside information about man's fundamental problem. You can pull books off the shelves by the dozens that theorize about what is wrong with man, but *you* know that the answer lies in the third chapter of that Book on your study desk. That chapter shows how, as the result of man's sin, all sorts of tragic problems began to complicate his life. The dynamics of sin were exposed at the very beginning. Reconstruct the scene. Adam and Eve have sinned. God comes as usual in the cool of the day, the time when He used to walk with Adam. But instead of a joyful response to the presence of God, Adam runs in fear. It is apparent that something has come between them. Sin has driven a wedge between Adam and God. God comes and Adam hides; he has to be ferreted out of the trees. He finally emerges, still trying to cover his nakedness in the presence of the God before whom all is "naked and open." Adam tries to hide because he realizes now that the openness and frankness that he once enjoyed in God's presence no longer exist. They were once so close that nothing—not even clothing—came between them. But now he feels ashamed in the presence of God; there is a great gulf between them. He is a guilty sinner who has offended the holy God.

Notice what happens when God begins to deal with Adam in a nouthetic fashion. Adam makes excuses. What does Adam do? Does he say in repentance, "Lord, I have sinned, forgive me"? No. Not only do the basic problems that have come snowballing down through history already appear, but along with them can be seen the fundamental sinful response patterns that cause additional confusion and complicate the situation. They all began back there in the garden. In seed form, at least, every major problem that a counselor must handle today is found there at the beginning. The hundred different counseling problems that you encounter from day to day are merely variations on these basic themes. It was all there in the sin and the sinful responses of Adam at the beginning.

God confronts Adam with his sin: "Adam, did you eat of that tree?" Notice how Adam replies. In effect he says,

> "Now wait a minute, Lord. That woman that you gave me, *she* was the one who did wrong. I didn't do anything wrong. I mean, after all, I ate, sure. But look, *you* gave *her* to me. It's really your fault; after all, you gave me someone like *that* to live with. So, don't blame me."

There is no repentance in his reply. There is no feeling of personal sorrow about what he did. He does not assume responsibility for his sin. Instead, we see only blame-shifting, excuse-making, and even complaining; Adam attempts to throw the responsibility for his sin back upon God. Men have not changed. The Lord turns to Eve: "What about it, Eve?" She replies, "It was the serpent's fault, not mine." Again the buck gets passed. Not only has a wedge been driven between God and man, but you can imagine how Adam's blame-shifting also drove a wedge between himself and his wife. It all began right there, and every problem that you and your counselees have to face today is there in seed form.

In Genesis 3, sin leads to hiding, for instance. This hiding by Adam is the archetype of every avoidance pattern (no matter how sophisticated) that you will run into in counseling today. People still run from this and from that, but reflection upon the fact leads to this conclusion: just as all blame-shifting (ultimately) is blaming God, so all running is (in the end) nothing less than man running from God. You *know* that; as Christian ministers you already *know* that fact. You know, basically, what is wrong with man. He is a sinner who needs to be changed by the grace of God. Most of the hypothesizing, theorizing and speculating on the part of the psychiatric schools about what is wrong with man and how he got that way is useless chatter. There is only one right answer. And you already know the answer. You are way ahead.

"But," you say, "I still don't know what to *do* to help people." Yes you do. You know more than those writers who fill the libraries with the products of their speculation; you know a *lot* more (read again Psalm 119:99). What you need to do is to recognize how much you already know. You already hold to some basic biblical presuppositions just as every other counselor does. Every psychiatrist, every clinical psychologist, and every marriage counselor has his presuppositions. No one is neutral. You have yours (which, hopefully, are not yours but God's). Every person thinks and acts according to his presuppositions, whether he knows it or not, and whether he can articulate them or not.

What are your presuppositions? Well, to begin with, because you believe the Bible you know much about the counselee before he walks into the room. You have a great advantage in the fact that your presuppositions are founded not upon speculation, but upon the revelation of God. There is a sign in the Detroit airport that says something like this: "When you see a man reading the *Wall Street Journal,* you already know a lot about him." That is an interesting sign; it implies that there are a number of questions that you do not need to bother to ask a man if you see him reading the *Wall Street Journal;* that fact alone already tells you the answers to those questions. How many of you read the *Wall Street Journal?* You see, even the fact that we *don't* tells a lot about you and me. By means of the basic biblical presuppositions to which you are committed, you know a lot about any counselee before he walks through the door. The one fact that you need to know in order to answer dozens of questions is that he is a sinful son of Adam.

I was speaking to a woman in a counseling session recently whom I had never seen before, when twenty minutes into the first session she sat upright in her seat, looked at me aghast and said, "You know me; how do you know me?" The answer to that was, "God told me all about you in the Bible." It is that simple (and profound); really it is. You *do* know a lot about people before they enter the counseling room, far more than do those who speculate apart from God's revelation. The Bible is plain about man's sin and how it has affected his life. You must recognize that, gentlemen. You need a new confidence that the Word of God is sufficient and true. You need to believe that it is adequate both to describe and to meet man's needs.

You also know, for example, that according to the Scriptures, sinners, simply because they are sinners, develop sinful life patterns. These patterns, the Bible says, are hard to break. They are called the "old man" by Paul. These old ways of living need to be "put off" (abandoned) after a person becomes a Christian, and new patterns of living must be "put on" (developed). The new life styles that are according to the law of God, Paul called the "new man." The new man and the old man are not some kind of entities within the person (as if he possessed separate natures) but they are simply Paul's graphic way of describing two ways of life. The "old man" is called the "former manner of life" in the New American Standard Version (Eph. 4:32). By the way they respond to life's problems in difficult situations, sinners develop sinful patterns from the beginning of their lives. We should expect this because that is all that unconverted sinners can do. Those patterns may pay off for a while, but they will not continue to do so forever. The Scriptures speak of the temporary pleasures of sin (Heb. 11:25). Eventually, however, sinful living gets people into trouble. Sinful responses to life's problems begin to pile up and complicate the original problems. Problems grow, sometimes so much so that people don't know which way to turn next, and they give up, or blow up, or crack up. Now you know *that;* you *know* that! You are not so ignorant about people and their problems as you may pretend. You are far more conversant with all of this than the psychiatrist might like you to believe. By studying the Word of God carefully and observing how the biblical principles describe the people you counsel (not to speak of measuring your own heart and life by the yardstick of the Scriptures), you can gain all of the information and experience that you need to become a competent, confident Christian counselor. It will take time and study and prayer, but it is possible.

You know even more before that counselee walks through the door. In addition to what I have already mentioned, let me point out also that you know the goals for human life. You should read the conflicting suggestions in the books by the "experts" about the goals of counseling! The psychiatrists, the clinical psychologists and the pagan marriage counselors are having a hard time deciding what those goals should be. They can't agree upon what the final product should look like. They don't know what to do with the fellow who comes through the door. They ask each other, "What is it that we want to make out of him?" Take a clinician like Skinner who believes that he can manipulate people with a carrot out in front and a zap from behind. He says that he has the power to make just about whatever you might want to make out of a man by conditioning his responses to various stimuli. But the problem is, what do you want? Is it *Walden II?* That is a real problem for him and his followers. Indeed, Carl Rogers attacked him at this very point. But Rogers cannot avoid the problem either; he must opt for client-centered goals. Skinner may well ask him, "Why?" What do psychiatrists want to do to a "patient"? What are their goals? Where shall they get them? How can they agree upon them? They must ask,

> "Should my goals for another man be the same as the goals that I have adopted for myself? These are the goals that I *think* are best. Or should they be *his* goals?"

Who can answer their questions? It is a very subjective problem; no wonder that they get into hassels and debates over this matter. They do not even know where they want to go. The psychiatrist is like a man with a brand new automobile, but no place to go. He lacks the divine Road Map.

But before that man walks through the door, *you* know

what you want to do with him (or you *should*) because *God's* goals are set forth clearly in the Scriptures. You have the Ten Commandments that spell out the whole of God's will for man's life. You have the characterological goals that are described as the "fruit of the Spirit" in the fifth chapter of Galatians, which, incidentally (N. B.), are the fruit of the *Spirit.* (That is one reason why only a spiritual man, somebody who is indwelt by the Holy Spirit, can help a brother to produce and gather more of the fruit of the Spirit.)

His fruit must be produced by the Spirit himself; it cannot be produced by any other person. You cannot whomp up the fruit of the Spirit by human effort or techniques. That is why it is called fruit, rather than works. In contrast, Paul also refers to the *works* of the flesh. We can all produce works, but who else but the Spirit can produce His fruit? Fruit has to grow naturally in accordance with proper growing conditions. There are many conditions necessary for the growth of fruit. But the fundamental condition that is essential for the fruit of the Spirit is the Spirit's presence. How can we hope for love, joy or peace, for instance, in either the counselee or in the counselor, apart from the Spirit? Listed as part of the fruit is "self-control," one of the crucial elements that nearly every counselee so desperately needs. But how do we expect him to learn self-control in a Spiritless counseling session? Can you therefore justify referring a husband and wife who are having marital difficulties to a pagan marriage counseling center? How do you expect them to learn self-control or develop love apart from the Spirit of God?

I do not intend to limit the Spirit. I know that the Spirit of God may work in spite of our follies. If this is a Christian couple, the Spirit of God may bless them in spite of a godless counseling situation. But He who works when and where and how He pleases ordinarily does His work in conjunction with the Word which *He* has given. His means of working is through His Word. So if counseling ignores the Word of God, there is no reason to *expect* the Spirit to work through it.

The Scriptures must be the basis for all that is said and done in counseling. The Scriptures must strongly influence the content of all counseling. They must be the source of every goal, the authority for every purpose, and they must contain the principles behind every procedure. If the Scriptures do not permeate counseling, and if the Christ of the Scriptures does not emerge at the center of the counseling sessions, then you cannot expect the Spirit to do His sanctifying work. It would be extraordinary if He did work where His Word was neglected, because this is the means of grace by which He Himself has chosen to carry on such work. It was He who "moved" men to write the Scriptures for this very purpose. Why should we expect Him to abandon the means He took pains to perfect? In all nouthetic confrontation, then, the "Word of Christ" must be used "richly."

So then you know (1) what God's goals for counseling are, (2) how He effects changes by His Word, and (3) what kind of man the Spirit uses in the ministry of His Word. You do not need to study the answers to these questions in other books; you have all that you need to know about these fundamental aspects of counseling in God's Book. These matters have been plainly settled for you by God, and there is no need for confusion. Let me say again, therefore, that you have greater knowledge than you may recognize.

But you know still more; you also know the solutions to man's problems. You know that the basic solution lies in the redemption of Jesus Christ. You know that to enjoy the fruit of the Spirit a man must be saved. He needs to repent and believe the Gospel; he must have his sins forgiven. He needs to come to terms with God, recognizing that he has offended Him by breaking His law. He must depend upon the death of Jesus Christ on the cross to find this forgiveness. He must trust in Christ's bodily resurrection from the dead. Once a man is saved, the Spirit of God who gave him the life to believe, will continue to work in him. He works His sanctifying changes from the time He regenerates a believer and enables him to believe in Christ to the point where He makes him perfect at death. Those are the conditions for changing a man: regeneration (the new birth) and sanctification (growth by grace). Men grow by the grace of God toward perfection. God's grace, in part, comes to His children through the counseling ministry of the Word.

Brethren, *you* know all of these things. But that pagan marriage counselor knows none of them. This is the basic dynamic of change according to which God has called us to minister to the needs of men. How dare we refer the sheep to, or adopt the goals and methods of, unbelievers who know nothing of the biblical dynamic? Should we call ourselves Rogerians or Freudians, or eclectic? Why be something else when God has told us what to be and what to do? How can pastors who believe the Word of God preach it from the pulpit, go into the study, hang up their preaching hat (together with its authority) and put on a different (permissive) one? How can they close their Bibles and lay them aside as they close the counseling door? Can they say, in effect, "Now tell me your problems, and I'll 'ahum' and 'uhuh'? No longer will I tell you authoritatively (directively) what God says about your life."

How can conservative pastors do that? They can do so only (against conscience) because they have been brainwashed into thinking that this is what they should do. It is only because of a tremendous propaganda campaign that they have been sold on the idea that they have nothing to offer their people. It is only because of the big umbrella!

Evangelical pastors, you must awaken to the fact that Freudianism and Rogerianism are getting you and your congregations nowhere. Open the Scriptures and freely minister to your flocks out of the goodness of your heart. Help your people to abandon those sinful life patterns that are ruining their lives, and things will happen quickly; which leads to the next point.

IV. You can offer greater resources than you suppose

Think for a moment of the resources that you have by comparison to the greatest resources of a psychiatrist. What does he have? He has Freud, Adler, Jung and half a dozen others. If he buys the newer behavioristic schools, he has Skinner, Krumboltz and Wolpe. (Incidentally, behaviorism is catching on rapidly now and looks as if it will be the new fad and threat of the future.[8] The reason why I have mainly stressed Rogers and Freud is not because I fail to realize the tremendous influence of the behaviorist school, but because the Church as usual is behind the times and is still thinking largely in Rogerian and Freudian categories. Of course, many psychiatrists are just as far behind.) But give *all* of these to the psychiatrist, and what does he have? He has a grand mass of contradiction and confusion; the ideas of one cancel out those of another. He has very, very little; and most psychiatrists know it.

But what resources do *you* have? The Holy Spirit, who is called the "Comforter" (but better translated, the "Counselor") is at work in your ministry. He is the one who counsels through you, by you and with you. You never need to counsel alone. He is also there at work in the counselee. He works

---

[8]Nouthetic counseling is not simply biblical behaviorism. While it is concerned with behavior and deals with it biblically, it must be distinguished from behavioristic views that start with the non-Christian premise that man is only another animal and, therefore, may be manipulated as any other animal might in training him to do the tricks that his master wishes. Behaviorism involves such things as the denial of man's special creation in the image of God, a rejection of human responsibility (since environmental conditioning is thought to be at the base of everything), and a propensity to use manipulation rather than biblical persuasion. It by-passes personal conviction and cares nothing about one's relationship to the holy God of creation and redemption. It is plainly based upon a utilitarian or pragmatic and evolutionary philosophy. Meyer and Chesser wrote: "Behavior treatments . . . have as their primary aim the modification of behavior rather than an understanding of it." V. Meyer and Edward Chesser, *Behavior Therapy in Clinical Psychiatry,* Science House, N. Y.: 1970, p. 25.

through His Word, His church, and His sacraments. Don't undersell the Word of God and the Spirit working through that Word. Don't underrate the potential of a counselor rightly using the Scriptures, or the fellowship of the church, as imperfect and meager as that fellowship often may be. Even so, that body of redeemed people is a growing, learning group of people with whom one can find real fellowship on a level of depth and loving truth. As John put it in his second and third letters, "Whom I love in the truth," i.e., in the sphere and the realm of the truth that all Christians hold in common.

And don't forget that the Spirit of God is at work in *you*. He not only works in the counselee; He works also in you to make you a better counselor and to give you better insights into His Word (I Cor. 2). He gives you the wisdom that you need (James 1:5). You must be willing therefore, to step out by faith upon the promises of His Word. Tackle all of the problems that you can. Humbly admit it when you don't have the answers or can't handle a case. But instead of despairing, seek harder for the answers in the Word of God so that the next time that you meet a similar problem you will know what to do. Talk to other pastors; counsel together with them; compare cases. Read every book on counseling that is published—if it truly attempts to be biblical. In short, work hard to become as competent as possible. All the while, move ahead with prayerful confidence in the Word and the Spirit. God will watch over you and mould you and make you a more effective counselor. He *will*. Not only do you have greater opportunities, greater qualifications, greater knowledge and greater resources, but

V. You should have greater hope than perhaps you have

Indeed, you should have much hope. First of all, you should have hope for yourself. After all, you are empowered by the Spirit of God (think of that—God is at work in you!). But take another fact, for example—you are concerned about being men of God; you want to grow into the full stature of

Jesus Christ. You believe in taking heed to your ministry and to yourself. You want to become the right kind of person. I wonder how many non-Christian counselors work very hard at self-growth. Yet one's personality and example (not to speak of his values and beliefs) are universally acknowledged as of crucial importance in counseling.[9] And the more you grow into the right kind of person, and the more this concern permeates your life and thought, the more capable you will become.

You should have hope for yourself also because of the great truth that Paul revealed in I Corinthians 10:13: "There is no test (trial, problem, temptation) that has overtaken you but such as is common to man." There is ground for enormous hope in that promise. Have you ever thought about it? Paul is saying that there is really *no new problem;* there is no problem that you will have to face in a counselee that you or some other Christian counselor hasn't had to face previously. That is what I was saying earlier when I mentioned the fact that it is all—in seed form, at least—in Genesis 3. No one is going to present to you a unique problem tomorrow or next week. Of course, the specific features of each problem are unique; the way that it comes, the configuration that it takes, the intensity with which it appears, the rapidity with which it grows, naturally all of these things vary. And there are hundreds of subtle little details that differ, so that no two cases are ever exactly the same. But at bottom, when you boil off all of the fat, when you get down to the bones and meat, the problem is precisely the same as the problems that you must face or that anybody else has to face, or anybody in the future will ever have to face.

That is what Paul explains in the tenth chapter of I Corinthians. He was writing to Corinthians who lived in a cosmopolitan setting. The Corinthians thought of themselves as liv-

---

[9]Even behaviorists admit to the importance of what Meyer and Chesser call "therapist potency." *Op. cit.,* p. 208.

ing at a late date in history. He alluded to this when he wrote, "You upon whom the ends of the ages have come" (vs. 11). Writing to people in that historical situation, at the very end of the Old Testament era, he wanted them to know that all of the things that happened to the Israelites in the desert long ago when they were living a nomadic existence under *entirely* different outward circumstances than those in Corinth were nevertheless relevant. He said, in effect:

> You may find yourselves in cosmopolitan Corinth, the double seaport city of the Mediterranean, the place where both the North and South traffic moves across the Isthmus of Corinth, the city into which also much East and West traffic flows. Yes, you may live in such a city; a city into which every new idea and every new vice is sure to come, but your situation is not unique. You may live in a town where the Corinthian games are held and the famous Corinthian bronzes are manufactured. You may live in a cosmopolitan city, a world city, and a wicked city. (If you wanted to insult someone, you might call him a "Corinthian.") But what happened to the Israelites is also pertinent to you (vss. 6, 11).

What he meant was:

> Although you live at this late date in history, in those kinds of circumstances; even though you are so culturally removed from the Israelites, and despite the fact that you are so many generations removed from them, I want you to know that the things that happened to that nomadic group of people wandering through the desert on their way toward Palestine are written for *your* example.

That is why he stresses the point that, "There is no test that has overtaken you (in Corinth) except what is common to men." What happened to the Israelites is the same as that which is happening to you.

That is also one reason why the Bible has relevance to *us* today. This ageless relevancy is a reality even in this fast-

32

moving age of the generation lap (there is no generation *gap;* what we are experiencing is a generation lap or overlap. The generations are being compressed; they overlap. Longevity, modern communication, mobility, etc. have all had a hand in speeding up the process of change. There is no longer gradual change spanning several generations. For millennia each generation gently took the place of the preceding. As they did so, it was with a tender nudge. Now, they slam hard against one another! As a result, several generations' worth of change must now be handled by a single generation. That is the problem. Changes take place so rapidly that we don't know what to hold onto and what to let go of. It is like an accordion full of generations that have been squeezed together). But whether there is a generation lap or lag doesn't really matter. The rapidity with which problems come may differ but, at base, the problems are the same today as they were back in the time of Corinth or Israel, or Adam. A thousand years hence, if this world endures, this verse will still hold true. God is the same, sinful man is the same, the basic problems of human relations between God and man and man and man are the same. The Christ who was in the wilderness is still the same; in the wilderness of Sinai, Corinth or Manhattan. So take heart. There is hope for you as a counselor. The problems and trials that you have been overcoming in your life by the Word of God that have qualified you to be a minister of Jesus Christ, are at bottom the same as those of your counselee. You, therefore, know what you need to know and to share with another who has a problem.[10]

But notice that there is hope for him, too. Paul's words should encourage him to hope. He doesn't have some kind of

[10] In a booklet entitled *Christ and Your Problems,* Presbyterian and Reformed Publishing Company, Nutley: 1971, I have discussed I Corinthians 10:13 in greater detail. This booklet, written in popular style, is designed for counselors to use as a handout to counselees. It stresses hope and responsibility.

strange disease. There would be little hope then. When we try to be gentle and kind by euphemistically labeling sinners "sick," we really do them a cruel disservice. Labels tend only to categorize one for life; a counselee gets a label on his file and that is the end of it (and him). He is one of those for the rest of his life. He may come to half believe it too. He may think that he has some incurable illness and lose all hope. He is stuck with it for life. There is little hope in that approach. But there is great hope in calling sin "sin." Every Christian knows that God sent Christ to deal with sin. It is not an unkindness, then, to be clear about sin; the most kindly thing you can do is to tell the truth. It is not only unkind, but even cruel to label sin something else, because there is no hope for sin apart from the acknowledgment of it before God in true repentance.

A psychiatrist's openers through the years have sounded something like this, "Now you know we can't guarantee anything, and you know that this may take a long time—two, three, four, five or more years." Freud, in fact, said that psychoanalysis is never over. (I think on the basis of its presuppositions that he was right.) The counselee meekly replies, "Yes," as all hope vanishes. What a way to start counseling— "I can't guarantee anything"; "It may take a long while"! What a discouraging way to begin; what little hope! Obviously here is one factor that accounts for the failure of psychiatry; when you see how poorly such sessions begin, you should not wonder why more is not accomplished. When a counselee comes with little or no hope to begin with, and then hears that, his worst fears are confirmed. Hope is destroyed. Yet, to be honest, institutionalized psychiatry has had to confess its failure in such terms. Why should the counselee put forth any genuine effort? And when he comes back session after session, and nothing ever happens, except talk and more talk, when no change takes place and none of his problems are solved, hopelessness turns into despair. And if by some chance the psychiatrist thinks that now after months (or years) of talk something might be *done* about a problem, it is far too late to suggest this. If the revolutionary idea of taking action at the end of a long inactive period should happen to occur to the psychiatrist, he will hardly be able to achieve anything now after spending months convincing the counselee by session after session of inaction that he must expect no change.

In contrast, what should happen when someone goes to a Christian counselor? We say to him, "You know, this may take a long time; it might even take as long as ten or twelve weeks."[11] When he looks dubious, we respond, "Now don't get excited. Most people leave in eight weeks, but many leave sooner." Then we say,

> "We can guarantee you everything, everything that God promises. You can have it all if you are willing to do what God requires. We can guarantee that your problem can be solved, God's way. Indeed, if you don't go out of here changed to some extent *tonight,* then it is your own fault. You can be different *today* to some extent. Not every problem can be solved today, but you *can* at least take the first step in the right direction."

We expect to see change from the first week. We build into our pattern of counseling the biblical idea that change is not only demanded by God, but also possible. When counselees come each week, they don't know what is going to happen next; but they come expecting change (sometimes with fear and trepidation). One thing they know: something is going to happen. When they are ready for it, in the providence of God it usually does.

A missionary and his wife who had come back from the mission field because of her problems, for a year and a half went to see a psychiatrist-who-is-a-Christian (that's the best way I know how to say it). He dealt with each one separately.

---

[11]Of one hour sessions each week.

Each time they went they just talked and nothing happened, except that the problem grew worse. Eventually they were directed to us. The first thing they said was, "We've come here because we understand that this is the place where you get things done quickly." I replied, "Sit down, let's get started." Things did get done quickly. In the very first session the real problem came out, that during the previous year or more had not even been mentioned to the psychiatrist. She said, "I have never told anyone before, but the problem is that I do not love my husband." I think the main reason that she told us was that, in contrast to the psychiatrist, we offered hope. Yes, there is reason for much greater hope than you may now have. And that hope can be realized.

I have tried to challenge and encourage you. I haven't told you about many cases or explained principles concretely, or suggested techniques. [12] We could talk for hours on those subjects, but what is the use unless you are convinced that you can and should do the full work of counseling?

Let me say in conclusion, if you do have greater opportunities than you may have thought, if you do have greater qualifications than you may have realized, if you do have greater knowledge than you have recognized, and greater resources than you may have supposed, you can offer greater hope to your people than can anyone else. I challenge you to assume the responsibility of this great task which truly is yours. Open your own umbrella like a banner raised in the name of Jesus Christ, and invite suffering men and women to find shelter and help beneath its crimson protection. Ever widen that umbrella until you embrace all of those to whom your ministry should extend. Be sure your umbrella is fashioned according to biblical patterns and dimensions. A man who owns an umbrella and is too frightened to open it in a storm to help another for fear that it may be blown inside out will himself be drenched.

---

[12]This I hope to do in detail in a forthcoming volume.

Is Society Sick?

I am here to talk to you about counseling from the Word of God. To begin with, let me describe several cases. We shall then take a closer look at these cases later on.

Sylvia and her husband were referred to our center by a Christian physician. She told me in the initial interview that the physician said,

"There is nothing I can do for you; you're getting an ulcer, but it is not from any physical cause. Go to the Christian Counseling and Educational Foundation and get some counseling."

I encouraged her to tell me more about it. She continued, "I can tell you exactly why I am getting this ulcer." She reached down into what looked more like a shopping bag than a purse—though I think it was the latter—and pulled out a document about an inch thick, single spaced and typewritten on both sides of 8½ by 11" paper. She slapped it down on my desk and said, *"There* is why I'm getting an ulcer!" Well, I couldn't have read it in a month—or cared to—but I flipped through it, spot checking to get the gist of it. Immediately it became apparent what this was. In my hand was a record of thirteen years' worth of things that her husband had done wrong to her! "My husband," her thesis was, "has given me an ulcer."

A Christian girl, who had been a top student, during finals at college refused to take her exams and grew very touchy and suspicious about everything and everyone. She claimed to see flames shooting out of her wall, and said she heard voices. At one point she stripped herself and ran around the dorm. She became belligerent and so berserk that finally she

[1]Special lecture at Berkshire Christian College, Lenox, Massachusetts, 1970 (revised).

had to be locked up overnight until her parents could come to take her home.

Another incident: a young man 21 years old late one night jumped into a river trying to take his life. The only reason that he survived was that he was an excellent swimmer. At the last moment he panicked and just barely succeeded in swimming back to shore.

A high school girl ran away. When she was found, no one could make sense out of her explanations for leaving, so her family sent her to a mental institution. Here she was given a series of shock treatments, with no perceptible results. She was released and was home for only a few weeks when she ran away again, this time returning home dishevelled and totally incoherent. She was again committed to the mental institution, where she underwent more shock treatments.

A middle-aged woman, who had totally ceased to function as a housewife, came for counseling. She was no longer doing her ironing. It had piled up in huge piles in the family room. Green hairy stuff had begun growing in the refrigerator. The children were making their own lunches for school and dad was cooking meals for the family. She claimed that she was too depressed to assume her responsibilities. Instead, she spent her days lying around on the couch, watching an occasional TV program and eating chocolates.

What was wrong with these people, all of whom came to our counseling center?[2] There was one problem common to all of them. The same basic fault lay with each one. It was expressed differently in each case, but one underlying root problem was present. Would you state it in this way—"They were *sick*"? Isn't a person who tries to commit suicide sick? Isn't someone who runs away from home and babbles incoherently sick? Well, that is what many people think. In every one of these cases, family, physician or friends advised and

---

[2]Cases have been "flattened out" to make them unidentifiable.

acted on that basis first. This is to be expected because of the propaganda that has been spread successfully throughout our country. That propaganda inculcates the idea that there is a strange disease abroad that causes mental illness. This is a mysterious sickness; an illness that may be caught by almost anyone without warning, and there is nothing that he can do about it. It may strike any one of us suddenly, unannounced. About all that can be done is to send us to a mental institution or to a psychiatrist for the next several years. In rare cases people do seem to recover from this frightening illness, but there really isn't much hope. That is the picture that many people conjure up today when they think of counseling.

Images of counseling may differ, but generally they stack up to something like this: picture a counselee lying on a couch and a "therapist" sitting behind the counselee's head listening as he talks on and on, freely associating one idea with another in a stream of consciousness (or perhaps, unconsciousness). The counselor sits out of view jotting down a few notes. Perhaps now and then he utters an occasional grunt.

Another image of counseling might be that of a counselor behind a desk (or as a member of a group sitting in a circle) listening to the counselee who does all of the *significant* talking. This counselor talks more frequently than the first, but not significantly. He simply repeats everything that the counselee says. He sits there, as it were, with a mirror—reflecting the counselee's words (hopefully) in sharper focus (using different words but trying to say exactly what the counselee has first said). The idea behind this is to help the counselee to understand what he is thinking and come to deeper insight into his problems, their causes and solutions. All that is needed to do this lies within the counselee himself. In this type of counseling the counselee might say, "I've got a problem," and the counselor replies, "I see. You feel that you are in trouble?" "Right," says the counselee. He continues: "I really don't know whether I should marry Susie or Janie." The counselor says, "I feel you're torn two ways." "That's it," says the counselee. He then describes both girls in detail. "Now tell me," he goes on, "which one should I marry?" The counselor, still faithfully reflecting back everything, responds: "I see, you feel that I should tell you which way to go." He will give him no advice, no help; he won't tell him what to do. This is, perhaps, the other image that you have of counseling. And if either of those images came to your mind when you heard the word, you would not be far from wrong, because those two images of counseling do represent most of the counseling that goes on today. There are other methods that are rising rapidly on the horizon and that raise new and somewhat different problems for the Christian, but these two institutionalized models of counseling have been around for quite a while. Both presuppose that something has happened to the counselee for which he is not responsible. They both presuppose that he is sick.

But Christians must counsel people very differently. This is because we begin with an entirely different assumption. In every one of the cases that I have described, an entirely different problem was at the root. We must return to these cases and see what happened.

Take, for instance, the woman with her manuscript, a tome of one-inch typed script, that she slapped down on the desk and declared, "Here's why I'm getting an ulcer." Her husband was cowering across the room. What would you have said to her if you were her counselor? I could think of nothing better to say to her than, "It's been a long while since I've met anyone as bitter and resentful as you." She looked at me startled. Her husband looked also; both in stark unbelief. I went on to point out to her that no husband or child or mother or grandmother or anybody else can put an ulcer on your stomach by doing the things that she had listed in her manuscript. "Instead," I assured her, "it is you who have put the ulcer on your stomach!"

Indeed, it was the way that she had handled what her husband had done to her that was giving her an ulcer. Subsequent sessions showed that this was a very accurate record. The husband had his side to deal with, too, you see. Yet, as far as she was concerned, if we could have multiplied the items in that "book" until it was ten inches thick, it would not matter, because what was putting the ulcer on her stomach was not her husband's sins but the sinful way in which she was handling them. She was getting an ulcer because of her sinful behavior, not because of his. Contrary to what I Corinthians 13 says about love not keeping score, she had composed an accounts book. But that book was a record not only of her husband's sin, but it also was a record of thirteen years' worth of unloving bitterness on her part! There it was in black and white, and she could not deny it. That is what gave her the ulcer.

In Ephesians 4, God says, "Let not the sun go down on your anger." This woman had let many moons go down on hers. That is why she had an ulcer; it was not because she was mentally ill. It wasn't because others were responsible for this ulcer; but it was because of the sinful patterns of responding to wrongdoing that she had developed over the years. I do not want to minimize the difficulty of her situation for one moment. But she had handled this very difficult situation quite wrongly. Instead of doing *good* to the one who had despitefully used her, she became bitter and wizened and sour and resentful, and as the bitterness hardened, she suffered. Physiologically, that is very sound.

Take the case of the girl who abruptly stopped studying for exams, the one who became terribly suspicious and whose behavior suddenly became quite upsetting. This girl, it turned out, had remained awake for hours on end studying for examinations. She had stayed up for several nights with little or no sleep. She failed to consider the fact that the Bible has much to say about how we must handle our bodies. At least, she was not applying these biblical principles to sleep, and she certainly did not realize that significant sleep loss can cause all of the same effects as LSD. Incidentally, let me warn you right now that this. could happen to you! Students whose bodies suffer from significant sleep loss subject themselves to the same danger. The first sign of the perceptual difficulties caused by sleep loss is a growing touchiness and suspicion about others. It can even lead, after a couple of days of the loss of rapid eye movement sleep, to hallucinations. Persons with sleep loss may "see" strange things like bugs crawling over the floor (that nobody else in the room sees), or a blue flame flashing out of the sky, or may hear things that nobody else hears. Every sense of the body, depth perception, touch perception (you might run your hand along a piece of smooth wood and find that it feels furry), taste, smell—any or all may be affected. These perceptual difficulties result from lack of care for the body, which is sin. So again, it was a sinful pattern of life (abuse of her body by failing to get adequate sleep) that led to such consequences.[3] Her problem was not sickness.

Take the third case of the young man who plunged into the river at midnight attempting suicide. He was sick, wasn't he? No. His parents came to counseling with him. From the first they began by minimizing everything negative that he had to say about himself. They were telling him even as they walked through the door, "Now you know that isn't so, Bill." And he was saying, "Yes, it is too; I'm just no good!" But they wouldn't take him seriously. They refused to accept his evaluation as the real reason for his problem. They would not take him seriously about his sin. He kept on saying things like, "I'm not worthy to walk on the face of this earth; everybody would be happier without me. I'm no good." It was almost as if his parents didn't hear him; they kept on responding with words like, "Now you know that isn't true; you've been a *good* son, Billy." As soon as this pattern became apparent, I

---

[3]Cf. Gay G. Luce and Julius Segal, *Sleep,* Lancer Books: New York, 1967, pp. 81-100.

had to cut through all of that and say, "Wait a minute; Bill knows more about himself than anyone else but God." Turning to him I said,

"I'm inclined to believe you, Bill, that you aren't very good. Maybe you're *no* good. Maybe there isn't a worthwhile thing in your life. At any rate, I think you must have some pretty solid reasons for wanting to take your life; but I also think that suicide is the wrong solution to those problems. You may have some weighty reasons for trying to take your life, but that action was a very poor answer to your problems. Indeed, suicide is just another plank in the platform of failure that you have been building. It is another wrong non-solution just like the ones that you tried before. It will fail to solve anything, and you can't really escape by it; it will only bring you face to face with God. In the end, because it is sin, it can only cause untold heartache and sorrow."

The moment that I took him seriously about his sin, the whole story poured out. His parents had been trying to get the story out of him for two weeks; they could not because they minimized the severity of his problems. But in the first few minutes of this first session he poured it all out. Yes, and it was clear that he had some good reasons for his action. What he told us was a tragic, mixed-up story of interpersonal relations that eventually led to a place where he could see no way out. So he decided to run out. His reasons were sound enough, but his solution was not Christian. Therefore, it could only complicate but never really solve any problems. Sin was at the base. Today that young man is married and living a happy Christian life.

Take the third situation—the high school girl who ran away from home. Her parents brought her to the counseling center only after all other attempts to help her had failed. It turned out that the truth of the matter was that she was afraid she was pregnant, and, rather than face the reality and shame of that situation, she had run away from home. She was found and then sent to the mental institution. Rather than uncovering the truth, at the mental institution she was given shock therapy! When she came home, she ran away again, but this time she was picked up by an older man who assaulted and raped her. That's when she came back incoherent; she went back to the mental institution and back to more shock treatments. All of this had nothing to do with her real problem. Her problem plainly was that she was a sinner. She was a sinner who had not dealt honestly with her sin. When she sinned, she would not face up to it. Instead, she kept running from her sin and from its consequences, only to run into deeper and deeper problems. The complications of her unconfessed and unforgiven sin snowballed, as they always do. She was not mentally ill.

Take the last case, the deeply depressed woman who is the composite of a dozen or more women who appear for counseling almost every month. She may be a mother who is trying to avoid the responsibilities of a family over which she has lost control, or perhaps one who simply has never solved the problem of being a woman. She may never have learned the secret of doing her work as a housewife and Christian mother *joyously*.[4] Instead, she becomes depressed over that pile of ironing that must be done again; so she lets it sit. Possibly something else happens that day that she can use as an excuse to avoid her work. Or she may simply say, "Oh, I just don't *feel* like doing the ironing today." So she leaves it. Her feelings may be lulled temporarily by the excuse, but the pile grows higher. Then the next day when she looks at the ironing again, the pile has grown still higher, so she feels *less* like doing it. So she doesn't do it that day either. But then it grows higher and her feelings get lower, and so on and on and on. Depressing feelings of guilt escalate. And the first thing

---

[4]Cf. Proverbs 31:13b—"and works with her hands in delight" (NAS V).

you know, she concludes that the pile is much too high to tackle because her feelings are much too low. Indeed, by now they are so low that she does not feel like making the lunches for the kids, either. Now she concludes that she "can't" do that; she doesn't *feel* up to it any longer. And the next thing you know, she doesn't feel like cleaning the refrigerator, and the green hairy stuff starts growing. Before very long she is lying around on the sofa deeply depressed and nearly immobile.

Dynamics even so simple as these can bring on depression. A sinful life pattern of such irresponsible living is all that it may take. Christian women know that they ought to be living like that woman in Proverbs 31, who did her housework—and much more—with joy and enthusiasm. King Lemuel's ideal woman used all of the gifts that God had given to her for the glory of God and for the benefit of her family. Instead, depressed Christian women are often those who gripe and groan about their lot. They think, "My husband can get out during the day and get away from the children, but I have to stay around the house all of the time. What future is there in doing dishes or ironing day after day?" and so on and on—wallowing in sinful self pity.

In every one of these cases the problem was not sickness; it was sin. There are some people who are mentally ill. Let me make this fact very clear. If a beam in the ceiling of this chapel were to fall with some force across your head, if you survived, doubtless you would be mentally ill; literally so. That is a legitimate instance of mental illness. There are people who have organic problems, brain damage, chemical damage or malfunction, toxic damage or other kinds of organic causes behind some of their problems. Now it is not those people about whom I have been speaking.[5] As a matter of fact, the number of people who fall into that category is very

---

[5]Many of these people too wallow in self pity when they could get medical attention, or, if the problem is incurable, learn to live up to the capacity that they possess.

slight by comparison with the number of people who have been "declared" to be mentally ill but really are not. Instead, most persons who are depressed, suicidal, incoherent, or whatever, are like that for reasons similar to those behind the cases that I have just described.

I counseled for a summer at two mental institutions in Illinois. That experience was a revelation. Most astounding was the fact that when I got to know these people I found out that great numbers of them were there because of their sin. I should have known this from the Bible, but I too had been influenced by the propaganda that evaluates these people as mentally ill. Some were there because of sexual tangles; others had fled from the Income Tax people who were breathing down their necks. Many were there simply because it was easier to live inside than to assume the responsibilities that are on the outside. Largely, they didn't want to face this problem or that; they were running from something or someone. Some were taking a cheap vacation from the housework and children, lolling around on green slopes, letting the state pay their way. It was relatively rare to meet anyone who was there because of physical or organic reasons.

When you talked with these people several hours a day, you got to know them and what their problems were; you got to know the dynamic behind what was going on. It was startling to me to discover that the books on counseling that I had read that told me that these "patients" were victims of other people who had traumatically injured them, or that some kind of a mysterious mental "disease" had attacked them, were wide of the mark. Instead, I came to see what I should have known anyway as a Chrsitian, that the reason why numbers of people are in mental institutions (and the reason why most people outside are in trouble) is not because of illness but because of sin. That experience drove me back to the Scriptures to take a new hard look at this whole question. And that is what we have been doing in our Practical Theology department at Westminster Seminary ever since.

Over the past few years we have been trying to develop a truly biblical view of counseling. That biblical view begins with some assumptions about God and man.[6] Before a counselee tells his story, we know a great deal about him. We know that he was born in sin and that he is going to express this sin in a dozen different ways in life. We know that because of his sinful human nature, the easiest patterns for him to develop in response to life's problems are sinful self-defeating patterns. We know that there is no man (except Jesus Christ) who has not developed those kinds of sinful patterns. And we know that apart from Jesus Christ (unless there has been a saving transformation) men become more and more enmeshed in that kind of living. One sin leads to another (cf. Romans 6:19). We also know that even those who have been saved still retain a great many of the old patterns of life (which Paul calls the "old man"). And we know, therefore, that the use of the Word of God as the Spirit's prime means of grace in changing those patterns in the believer must be a life-long process. We know all of these facts, and many of the implications of them, and a good bit more, *before* we meet the counselee for the first time. And that knowledge will totally affect our counseling.

One's presuppositions determine what he will do from the outset. Take, for example, the Freudian model of counseling that I sketched earlier; because of the fundamentally different presuppositions behind it, it differs radically from our model of Christian counseling. Ask—*why* is it that men are counseled on a couch; *why* is it that a psychotherapist sits behind his head and (as one did) can peel and eat an orange while he listens to a counselee? Ask *why* the latter is encouraged to freely associate one idea after another according to the stream of consciousness format. Keep asking, *"Why* is that?" Keep asking, *"Why* does he use that methodology?" And if you ask

---

[6]Cf. the brief summary Note, "Sickness in the Scriptures," at the end of this article.

frequently and persistently enough, you will discover that what he does he does because of basic presuppositions (articulated or unarticulated; clear or unclear) about God and about man and his problems. That is why I insist that what he supposes is wrong with a counselee will inevitably influence the counselor with regard to what he thinks needs to be done to help the counselee out of his problem.[7]

Freud's most fundamental premise is that a man is not responsible for what he does. Instead, someone else is. If he behaves badly, the counselee must not be blamed for this. Peculiar, irritating, dangerous or bizarre behavior stems back to a constellation of events that have taken place in the past. Others have misused the "patient"; he is a victim. His maladaptive behavior is the direct result of what others, therefore, have done to him. Grandma has had a bad influence upon him, his parents certainly must have had a deleterious influence upon him, the church has been a baneful influence in his past and probably a variety of other influences (traumatic or otherwise) have made him what he is today. Because he is the product of these destructive influences, Freud's poor sick patient certainly is not responsible for whatever it is that he (as such) has done. He is a man *under the influence* of his past!

Freud's view is that such persons are ill, they are sick, just

---

[7] In counseling, as in every area of life, you usually find what you are looking for. Freud found sex behind all problems; Rogers discovers failure to live according to one's own best potential; Skinner uncovers bad training (conditioning). Since this is so, it is of utmost importance for the counselor to begin with proper presuppositions. What he assumes is wrong is what he will find wrong. How crucial it is then to examine one's presuppositions to be certain that they are biblical. Since proper presuppositions about God and man can be found only in the Scriptures, counseling based upon any other foundation cannot be trusted. Only the counselor who knows and trusts the Word of God can look for that which God wants him to find.

All methodology grows out of presuppositions: e.g., the questions that one asks of a counselee are determined by (and determine) the answers that he expects (and gets).

as truly as if they were invaded from without by a virus. And if you believe someone is sick, you treat him accordingly. When your husband catches measles, what do you do? Do you kick him out of bed and say, "Get to work"? No, of course you don't! So if a counselee is really sick because of what others have done to him, you don't begin to hustle him up to his duty and responsibilities or challenge him about the way that he is handling life. You sympathize with him; you bring him ice cream! According to Freud, the "mentally ill" are sick because others have built a too-strict conscience *(superego)* into the "patient," and this causes a conflict with his *id* (primitive desires of sex and aggression).

If he is sick (a presupposition), how do you help him? By psychoanalytic and psychotherapeutic methods. What are these at base, anyway? Well, to put it in very simplistic terms that nevertheless fairly state the facts, these methods are like taking an archaeological expedition back into the man's past in order to upturn every flat stone to discover any and all vermin that might lurk beneath it. The attempt is to uncover all of those baneful events and influences of the past in order to discover who did what to him. In other words, it is a blame-shifting endeavor. That is the first step.

Next, the therapist, through the process of "transference," helps the patient "relive" his past. This time, however, the therapist takes the place of those persons out of the past (mother or the church). But instead of being a cruel and harsh "authority figure" who says, "No, no, you must not do that," or "Thou shalt" and "Thou shalt *not*"—this time "mother" becomes very warm and the "church" quite permissive. In this way, the therapist resocializes the patient by chopping down to size the overly strict, victimizing conscience that his mother and the church and others have built into him. The therapist takes the stick out of the hand of the cruel policeman! Now the *Id* can freely stride forth without hindrance. No longer will conscience stand at the door of expression and bat it back with his nightstick.

Well, that is one view, but it is a totally non-Christian view. It is non-Christian because biblically, Christians must not side with their sinful desires. Why should we who know what the Scriptures say about the heart of man, want to trim down a man's conscience and release his inner sinful impulses? May we resocialize against biblical standards? May we alter the biblical injunction to read "put on the old man . . . put off the new man"? The Freudian view involves a totally non-Christian objective to be reached by a totally non-Christian methodology that flows out of a totally non-Christian presupposition, namely, that somebody else is responsible for a counselee's problems and poor behavior.

Now it is true that a child has tremendous influences exerted upon him. And it is also true that adults have terrible things done to them. But as a human being grows and begins to reevaluate his own life, he is responsible personally to accept or reject the views and patterns that others may have taught him; and also those that he may have developed on his own. God holds each one of us responsible for his life. Those who trust Jesus Christ and follow His Word can learn to handle any kind of wrongdoing in the right way. Jesus did not become bitter against those who drove the nails through His hands, or get an ulcer on the cross. Instead, He prayed, "Father, forgive them." He always did the best thing He could for those who wronged Him. There is a Christian response at every point which not only heals the body and makes the life more joyful, but is a righteous and a responsible response before God and man. It is a response in which a Christian does the will of God according to the commandments of God. Whenever we respond to wrongdoing in God's way, we bring about good consequences in the long run. Christians are never forced to sin by what someone else has done to them.

Then there is the Rogerian view of counseling and its method of reflection (repeating the counselee's words). What does that mean and how did that methodology come about anyway? Why do counselors do things like this? Why does the counselor become a wall off which the counselee bounces his ball? Well, one reason why Rogerian methods have been so rapidly and widely adopted is because of their simplicity and lack of risk. To learn and use them you do not have to know very much. That is probably the secret behind the rapid widespread acceptance of Rogerian methods. All that you have to learn is the relatively simple skill of rephrasing questions. I know that many Rogerians would disagree with that. They would say that there is so much more. For instance, one must learn to become empathetic; he must discover how to read the affective side of the counselee, and many other such things. Rogerian counseling, they say, requires great skill. But, frankly, I will not buy that. By comparison, with what it takes to do biblical counseling in which one painstakingly gathers data and gives advice helping the counselee to grapple with his problems in the light of the Word of God, Rogerian methodology is a snap.

But, more fundamentally, the basic presupposition of Rogers is this: man has all of the resources that he needs in himself. The counselor does not need to give advice to the counselee. Most of all, he must not impose the instructions of an authoritative Book; that would violate the personality of the counselee. In Rogerian counseling, there can be no message from God. Indeed, Rogers believes that man doesn't need divine revelation; he is autonomous. Rogers stresses human autonomy as essential to successful living. In fact, the sickness comes when one fails to assert this autonomy. The cure, then, must involve methodology that helps him to do so. In one of his most clear and revealing statements, Rogers says that the closer he gets to the core and center of a man, the more sure he is that there is something basically good in him. Well, that view of man is an absolute antithesis to the Christian doctrine of sin. And it is upon the fundamental presupposition inherent in that antithesis that Rogers developed his method. Rogers bounces and flashes ideas back to the counselee, because he believes that the counselee is entirely capable of solving his own problems himself and surely does not need God to tell him what to do or to believe. If the counselor keeps rephrasing the counselee's words, finally out of his own resources the counselee will respond not only with the insights necessary to understand his problem, but with all of the insights necessary to clarify and to solve that problem. Nothing could be further removed from the biblical position.

In spite of this fact, Christians ask me, "Can't we use this method of Rogers? *Can't* we forget about his presuppositions and use his method? Hasn't Rogers at least restored the idea of listening to us?" Absolutely not! Rogers, you see, *doesn't* listen. Rogers has been praised widely by those who know little about his beliefs as the man who taught us to listen. But such a notion comes from the use of Rogers' own defective concept of "listening." If you listen to *Rogers* carefully, if you listen to the *contents* of Rogers' books, you will discover that Rogers says that we must "listen" only for feeling, never for content. We may not listen to the man's *problem.* We must never get involved in the *problem.* We must only become involved with the *man.* We must never concern ourselves about whether he should do this or that. The merits of the issue are irrelevant. Forget all of that; instead, listen for the *intensity* of the problem. Listen only for the *emotional* side of the problem. So what kind of listening does Rogers do? The answer is that he does a kind of listening that is only partial and very unbiblical. Biblical listening means listening not only to emotional responses. Certainly it means that; but it means also listening to the *whole* man. God made us whole people; we cannot separate the emotions from the rest of the man. Surely man's intellectual side must not be ignored. Yet Rogers took a psychological axe and split man down the middle. Then he declared, "This part of you means nothing to me; I'll listen only to the other part."[8]

---

[8]Even Rogers' "listening" to emotions cannot be considered biblical; as he "listens" he will "hear" what he hears only as a non-Christian.

Long before Rogers, the Bible told us to listen. God chides us in the Book of Proverbs for jumping to conclusions. He insists that we must not make up our minds too quickly before we have heard both sides of an issue (Prov. 18:13). But notice, carefully, that the listening involves intellectual activity on the part of the listener. Listening of the right kind plainly involves listening to content and gathering data. Biblical listening is listening to the whole man; it is listening to the man's problem as well as to the ways in which he is affected by it. It is not Rogerian listening, but real listening. The two are as far removed from one another as is Rogers' fundamental presupposition from the biblical doctrine of sin and God's sovereignty.

And so, our answers to people's problems must come from the Word of God. They will not come out of textbooks by Rogers or Freud or Skinner or anyone else. They will come from God's textbook. It does not matter who says this or that or the other, if he does not say what the Scriptures say, his counseling cannot be called Christian. Biblical counseling will grow only from the soil of biblical presuppositions; from a biblical view of God's redemptive solutions in Christ. On the base of those biblical presuppositions must be built a biblical methodology that can rest upon those presuppositions because at all points it grows out of and is appropriate to them. There is no other way to develop biblical counseling.

In conclusion, therefore, let me suggest this: counseling, at its very center, is the work not of a preacher or a Christian counselor; it is the work of the Holy Spirit. He is the Counselor par excellence. The Scriptures call Him the "Comforter." The word is better translated "Counselor," as in some of the modern versions. Jesus said, "I will send you another Counselor." He was to be another Counselor *of the same kind* that Jesus had been to His disciples; one to train, advise and guide

---

Christians, when they listen for emotion, will do so from a biblical stance toward man that a non-Christian cannot take.

them. Isaiah's "Wonderful Counselor" counseled His disciples as He walked with them every day (Is. 9:6). He met their needs by instructing, rebuking and training them. In this New Testament era, the Holy Spirit whom Jesus sent to be our Counselor, does the same for us. The Holy Spirit works through His Word which He has inspired and given to us for this purpose (II Tim. 3:15-17). Where the Word of God is not used in counseling sessions, you can be very sure that there is something missing, and almost always what is missing is the Holy Spirit. I ask you, what is counseling without *The* Counselor?

Christian young people, let me urge you to consider the fact that you are here training to be leaders in Christ's church. Tomorrow that leadership will be in your hands. Do not fall into the errors of the former generation. You cannot, you must not, ecclectically sprinkle holy water on the systems of those who deny Christ. In every field you must examine presuppositions and build appropriate methodology from nothing less than a consistently Christian vantage point. Only when you stand there, firmly upon the Bible, will you be able to determine what perverted insights from other systems attained by the common grace of God, may be filtered, purified and used by Christians. In no area of thought has ecclecticism more strongly invaded the Christian camp than in that of counseling. You have invited me here because you read my book, *Competent to Counsel.* But what I wrote there is only a frail beginning. It is going to take dozens and dozens of us years and years to develop counseling that is fully Christian, clearly defined and articulated. It will take even many more man hours to discover the many methodological implications that will emerge from it. May God challenge some of you to take up the work, that in your generation there shall be across the length of this land Christian counselors who skillfully bring biblical principles to bear upon the needs of men and women everywhere in the name of Jesus Christ our Lord!

NOTE

SICKNESS IN THE SCRIPTURES

According to the Scriptures, there are three ways to become ill: (1) through organic causes such as diseases, injuries, chemical malfunctions and birth defects; (2) as the result of demon possession; (3) in consequence of sin (either as a direct or indirect judgment). There is no biblical category corresponding to the modern mistaken concept of mental illness.

It is disease in the etymological sense of the term (dis-ease, discomfort) with which the Christian counselor is concerned, particularly those discomforts of body and mind that are occasioned by sin, the third cause mentioned above.

Sin is the root cause of all such disease; if Adam had not sinned, there would have been no illness, sickness, pain or deterioration of the human body. Adam passed down not only guilt, but also corruption to all of his posterity with its consequences. The new body that believers will receive at the resurrection will be completely free from sin and all of its effects (Rev. 21:4; Rom 8:18-25). In this radical sense, sin is behind causes 1 and 2, as well as cause number 3.

But in a more immediate sense, individual sins (3) may be said to be the cause of sickness. Both the saved and the unsaved receive some judgment in this life (Prov. 11:31, cf. NASV, Berkeley). Sickness is sometimes the means that God uses in bringing such judgment (Ex. 9:8-12; I Cor. 11:30, 31). However, even in such instances, *hamartiagenic* (sin-engendered) sickness and dis-ease may itself come as a direct supernatural judgment (Acts 12:23) or as an indirect judgment of God in which He uses natural means (Ex. 15:26; cf. also S. I. McMillen[9]). However, it is not always possible to determine

---

[9] S. I. McMillan, *None of These Diseases,* Fleming H. Revell Company: Westwood, 1963.

whether a given portion of the Scriptures speaks of a direct or an indirect judgment.

It is important to observe that not all sickness and discomfort occurs as the result of God's immediate judgments (directly or indirectly administered) upon men for particular sins. The book of Job is a clear witness to this fact. Some may be sent as a test (James 1:2-4) rather than as a punishment. (Note the word "if" in James 5:15. James considers particular sins as the immediate cause of sickness to be so frequent as to specifically mention the fact, but by the "if" clause he also observes that there may be other causes as well. For further discussion of James 5, and especially with respect to anointing with oil, see *Competent to Counsel.*[10])

Consideration of psychosomatic (or better, *hamartiagenic*) illness and dis-ease necessarily leads to a study of such matters as the function of conscience and guilt, anger and hatred, worry and anxiety, and the effects of these upon the body. The understanding that there is a close relationship between the mind and the body is not a modern discovery. The Scriptures everywhere presuppose that this relationship exists. There are many biblical references to the question. For example, in Genesis 4:3-7 there is a pertinent passage concerning the consequences of Cain's sinful offering (Abel brought the first and best in contrast to Cain). When his offering was rejected, Cain became angry and depressed ("his face fell"—verse 5). God pointed to the solution: "If you do right, will it (your face) not be lifted up?" (Berkeley).[11] Proverbs 14:30 observes: "A relaxed mind makes for physical health: but passion is rottenness to the bones" (Berkeley). In Psalms 32, 38 and 51 the effects of unconfessed sin upon David's physical condition are discussed at length. There depression is

---

[10]*Op. cit.,* pp. 105-127.

[11]It is gratifying to notice that the NASV has corrected the vagueness of the KJV and other versions: "Will not *your countenance* be lifted up?"

shown to be one striking effect of unconfessed sin. Bodily anxiety reactions (such as dryness of mouth) and pain sometimes accompanied the depression. Proverbs 28:1 vividly pictures the effects of a haunting guilty conscience: "The wicked flee when no one pursues" (this phenomenon would in modern psychiatric lingo be called paranoia or a persecution complex; Proverbs notes the cause to be *hamartiagenic*).

Conscience is the God-given ability to evaluate one's own actions (Rom. 2:15).[12] When we sin, our consciences activate unpleasant visceral and other bodily responses to warn us to cease and desist and repent. God expects us to repent, confess our sins and become reconciled to Him. Our future behavior must be changed by the Spirit to conform to the Word of God. Conscience evaluates such an actual course of action as the proper one, and eases up on the unpleasant physical responses. Taking pills, using alcohol or other drugs in order to dull pain, anesthetize the brain or drown out memories, is

---

[12]Conscience *(suneidesis,* "a knowing together") is viewed functionally as self-evaluation in three ways in Scripture:

(1) As the *capacity* for self-judgment (as in Romans 2:15); the ability to evaluate and, therefore, excuse or accuse one's self.

(2) As the *rule* or standard by which the evaluation is made. (Cf. Romans 14 and I Corinthians 8, esp. vss. 10, 12.) Some consciences are "weak," i.e., poorly informed. The Scriptures are to be internalized into the heart (written upon the heart) as the rule or conscience by which one evaluates his own attitudes and behavior.

(3) As the *effects* of the evaluation. This is the emphasis in those passages in which one is said to have a "good" or "clear" (or by contrast, "bad") conscience (e.g., I Tim. 1:5, 19; 3:9; II Tim. 1:3; Heb. 13:18; I Peter 3:16, 21). Pleasant or unpleasant physiological responses (visceral and otherwise) are activated as the result.

The three aspects of conscience are analogous to the three steps in the process of trying a case at law. Conscience, at once, is the lawyers, the jury and the judge. Conscience argues the case (both *accusing* as the prosecuting attorney and *excusing* as the defense attorney), decides the case (as the jury) according to the law, and pronounces the verdict (as the judge) and thereby sets into motion any penalties. There is good reason, therefore, for the use of much legal terminology in the Scriptures such as "convict," etc. in conjunction with such processes.

60

one faulty solution to the problem that is widely followed today. The problem should not be handled by attacking the nervous system directly, since the unpleasant bodily sensations are not the result of an "emotional problem"[13] (the emotions are working all too well) but rather are the result of a behavioral problem.

Anger, hatred and bitterness are costly emotions to maintain. Anger in itself is not sinful (Mark 3:5), but its unwarranted, uncontrolled or uninterrupted venting is sin. Unlike modern psychiatrists, the Scriptures warn against ventilating hostilities (cf. Proverbs 14:29; 29:11, 20), and go so far as to direct a young man to avoid quick-tempered associates (Prov. 22:24, 25) lest he learn their sinful life styles. At the opposite extreme, anger must not be allowed to harden into resentment or hatred (cf. Ephesians 4:26). McMillen has written two very useful chapters concerning the *hamartiagenic* effects of anger (chapters 10 and 11[14]).

Worry and anxiety do not solve problems. Prayer and biblical courses of action do (Phil. 4:6, 7). In Philippians 4:6, the word "anxious" might best be translated "worried." Because God has commanded His children not to worry, worry is sin, and, therefore, harmful to the body (cf. also I Peter 5:7). According to Philippians 4:6-9, peace comes from: (1) casting our cares on God in prayer, (2) with thanksgiving (a key to verse 6; you do not worry about that for which you are genuinely thankful),[15] (3) focusing one's attention upon good

---

[13] A widely used confusing euphemism for sinful behavior, Christians should avoid the use of this erroneous designation.

[14] *Op. cit.*, pp. 65-75.

[15] In the light of Romans 8:28 Christians may be thankful for "all things." At the moment we may not be able to understand how seeming tragedies are working for our good, but by faith we may believe it and give thanks and look forward to the day when we shall know as we are known.

things rather than wallowing in self pity[16] (vs. 8), and (4) following the biblical teachings and examples of the apostles (vs. 9) in solving problems.[17]

Turning to psychiatrists and physicians for the cure of *hamartiagenic* illnesses is a mistake. While it may be necessary to receive medical help from a physician when one has worried an ulcer in his stomach, or begins to suffer from colitis due to resentment (96 per cent of colitis patients admitted to one hospital were dominantly resentful persons; cf. McMillen[18]), physicians and psychiatrists have no solution to the underlying cause of these problems. This is clearly seen in their widespread prescription of tranquilizers, barbiturates, amphetamines and other mood-enhancing drugs which admitedly may relieve symptoms and make life manageable but do not solve problems.

---

[16]Often this means talking about, praying about and searching the Scriptures for biblical *solutions* to problems, rather than wasting one's time by concentrating only on the problem itself. Worrying people are often lazy people; it does not require *action* to worry—only self pity (and ultimately self destruction).

[17]To sum up the solution for worry: (a) pray about problems with thanksgiving; (b) consider God's solutions to problems; (c) set out upon the biblical courses of action that God wants you to take to solve such problems.

[18]*Ibid.*, p. 71.

Grief as a Counseling Opportunity

Grief as a Counseling Opportunity[1]

A pastor does no counseling that is considered more exclusively his. own than the counseling of people in grief. If grief is peculiarly within the minister's province, all of you must be deeply interested in the nature of grief and what God wants you to do to help grief sufferers. As ministers, you and I need to do much thinking about grief, and it is also our task to speak and write definitively about the matter.

More Than A Technician

Yet, just because grief is your specialty, you must studiously avoid becoming technicians in death. If you should become merely that, you would be like the funeral director. His job is to handle death merely as a technician. He performs certain technical services, and that is that. Ministers who perfunctorily make two or three visits before or after death, and who perform expected rites and ceremonies at the funeral and at the grave, have become technicians in death. That is one way of handling the problem of grief. But such ministers are not true to their calling. If you have come here because you are interested in becoming (or in continuing to be) a better technician, then let me warn you that what I shall say will be a waste of your time. You will probably want to leave right now.

Today we shall take a hard look at grief. Even a casual acquaintance with the grief state indicates that grieving persons need the help of someone who will go beyond the work of a technician. They need the ministry of the Word of God. Nothing less than a word from God Himself can adequately meet the needs of a grief-stricken man or woman. That, then, is my concern today: to discuss some of the ways and means by which we may minister that Word in time of grief.

---

[1]Delivered to a ministerial conference at the State Mental Health Center, Norristown, Pennsylvania, March 16, 1971 (revised).

What Grief Involves

Grief may be called *a life-shaking sorrow over loss.* Grief tears life to shreds; it shakes one from top to bottom. It pulls him loose; he comes apart at the seams. Grief is truly nothing less than a life-shattering loss.[2] A mere technician can get a body underground, but a pastor who functions as such can never sew a severed soul together again.

Grief is a life-shaking sorrow, but usually grief is not *simple* sorrow. Plugged into the sorrow are other emotions. During grief, emotions of anger, guilt and fear often are involved. When anger, guilt, or fear become tangled together with the deep penetrating soul sorrow of such a loss, a pastor finds himself with a counseling problem of some magnitude. It takes more than a few perfunctory visits or ceremonies to handle this kind of problem. It will take more extensive counseling than usually has been offered.

Grief may be occasioned by a loss of any sort. Significant losses may shake persons dramatically. It could be the loss of a *person* by death, through a move, by a marriage, or because of a divorce. These other losses of a person sometimes can be just as devastating as loss by death. Often the complications that are involved in a divorce or at the marriage of a child are greater and more difficult to handle than those that occur at death. A child may leave the home and the community in anger (or perhaps while he remains bodily, he leaves psychologically; he may cut off the family as truly as if he had run away). Any significant loss of communion with a person may occasion serious grief responses.

Grief also may be occasioned by the loss of a *position,* as when one loses his job. We have begun to encounter this phenomenon more and more frequently today, now that the tight economic squeeze has come upon us. It is possible that

---

[2]Cf. the etymology of the interesting English word *bereaved.* To be reaved literally is to be broken up.

we shall see much more of this sort of thing in the near future. Loss of status also may lead to grief, as when, for instance, one loses his good name. So you see, it is not only through the loss of a person by death that grief occurs; loss of possessions, money, a job, house, or whatever a person holds dear, may be the occasion for grief.

You and I are called to minister (in a peculiar way) to persons in grief situations of every sort. We must not forget the broad scope of grief and the opportunities for counseling that this affords (and demands of us). But today I am not going to talk about all kinds of grief. Instead, I have been asked to discuss the limited area of grief caused by death.

Your Attitude Is Important

To begin with, if you wish to help persons in grief caused by death, you must have a proper attitude toward death. Now I must assume as a fundamental presupposition that a pastor whose own attitudes about death and grief are shaky will be unable to offer true comfort and help. Because of that uncertainty or ambivalence, he may be of minimal help only, or, as is more likely, he actually may become a harmful complicating factor in the situation. He may confuse the bereaved person more than help him; indeed, he may become a complication rather than a solution to the problem. Each one of us who thinks of ministering to a person in grief must first ask himself about his own beliefs concerning death. We cannot avoid expressing an attitude growing out of those beliefs; we cannot be neutral. This is because each one of us himself is involved in death. When he ministers to another's grief, a pastor thinks also of his own coming death. Since we think about these matters, we all have attitudes toward them. We shall minister out of those attitudes.

Those attitudes may be clearly articulated, or they may be very fuzzy or even unknown to us. Since I teach preaching at Westminster Theological Seminary as well as pastoral work, I

68

must discuss style (language usage) in my courses.[3] Students,
I have discovered, sometimes talk about "acquiring" a style as
if they were purchasing a brand new typewriter. The fact is,
the minute they first opened their mouths, they had a style.
The only legitimate sorts of questions about style are whether
one is conscious of it, whether it is good or bad, whether it is
canned or refrigerated, whether it is green and growing, etc.
What I mean is that those are the only legitimate kinds of
questions, since everyone already *has* a style. You would think
that students would know this, but frequently they have to
be awakened to the fact. It is not a matter of packaging something into an empty space; rather, in helping someone to acquire a good preaching style, the task requires repackaging
and retraining. The same is true about attitudes toward death.
You *have* an attitude toward death (and also toward grief).
Since this is so, you must become familiar with (and may find
it necessary to alter) your own attitudes. If you are not, you
may be doing things by those attitudes that you don't even
realize.

In framing a good attitude toward death and grief, it is
most important to settle your own theological stance toward
life, death, grief, sin, guilt and, of course, toward God. You
cannot avoid these issues. In fact, one's own personal relationship to God and his theological beliefs are central. If one's
theological beliefs and his life clearly come together at any
point, it is here. Here is the moment of truth for every preacher. Death and grief test a minister's true commitments. Each
one of you knows that he is going to die. What you believe
about death, the future, salvation and God will make a significant impact as you minister to a grieving person.

Today I can speak only from my conservative, Calvinistic
viewpoint as a Christian. I want you to know precisely where
I stand so that you will be able to evaluate what I have to say.

---

[3]Cf. Jay Adams, *Pulpit Speech,* Presbyterian and Reformed Publishing Company: Nutley, 1971, p. 111.

I happen to believe that what the Bible says about death is literally true. I believe that the God who created this world is going to do something for His people throughout all eternity, not just for the brief period of time that they live upon the earth. All that I have to say is influenced by the fact that I believe in sin and judgment, heaven and hell, the resurrection of the body, eternal life, and that redemption through Jesus Christ is the only answer to man's need. He died on the cross in the place of guilty sinners that through repentance and faith in Him they might have the forgiveness of sin and eternal life.

Now all of that has a large influence upon my attitudes toward life, death and grief, and, therefore, upon what I say and do when I sit beside someone who is going through a period of grief; indeed, it has an overwhelming influence. If you believe differently, what you believe also will have an overwhelming influence upon what you do at that time. That is why you must become aware of your personal-theological stance toward death and grief. If you do not have a biblical faith, I do not know what you will say to those to whom you seek to minister. The poverty of a skeptical or fuzzy faith is never more apparent than at the graveside.

Grief, Not Despair

There is a biblical distinction between grief and despair. Because I believe this distinction is fundamental, I try to communicate it to grief sufferers. Grief, on the one hand, is proper and good according to the Scriptures; despair, on the other hand, is quite wrong. In I Thessalonians 4:13, God revealed to Christians the basic information about death and the resurrection that they need to prevent sorrow from turning into despair: He spoke of "grieving" but "not as others who have no hope." The Greek word *lupeo* that is translated either "grief" or "sorrow" is simply the general word for "pain." Paul says that Christians should experience pain over loss, yet not as others who have no hope. He is interested in steering the true course between an unbiblical stoicism that stifles emotion and the despair that comes from lack of hope. Christian grief lies in between. This grief is a painful sorrow that issues in an honest expression of one's feelings; yet even in the midst of these intense feelings, the Christian may look with confidence beyond the tragedy to its solution in Christ.

Faith in the midst of grief looks to the *not yet* and says, "I believe that it *shall be.*" The Christian, therefore, has anticipation in the midst of sorrow. His tears only help him to see more clearly into God's revealed future. It is just this element of hope or anticipation that is lacking in despair. Indeed, faith and hope may grow tall in the soil of grief. Being mixed with grief, hope and faith are needed to give balance to it and to bring about the proper resolution of grief. It is precisely here that one's theological position makes all of the difference in the world (or out of it). If the ministry of the Word, then, requires a ministry of biblical hope, one must himself possess such hope.

To prevent grief from turning into despair, the pastor must share the Christian hope with the grief sufferer. He must remind grief sufferers that the Christian hope is firm, for it rests upon the death and resurrection of Jesus Christ. He must point them to that which is beyond death. He must show them again that there is more to life than physical life. He must remind them not only that there is a life after death, but also that there will be new physical life at the resurrection.

According to the Scriptures of both the Old and New Testaments, sorrow is proper. Every emotion is good. God has created man and gifted him with the capacity for expressing all of these emotions. Each is proper in the appropriate situation to which it corresponds. The loss of a loved one is a sorrowful event, so it is improper to hold back one's emotion of sorrow at the time of death. Yet, despair is inappropriate for the Christian who has God's sure word of promise to comfort him.

At the grave of Lazarus Jesus wept. His emotional responses were so apparent that others standing by commented about them. They said, "See how much he loved him." Sorrow expressed in the form of grief is, therefore, a very good and proper emotion that expresses one's love and shows that he cares.

Removing Fear From Death

But let us now consider the scriptural concept of hope. In I Corinthians 15, after discussing the resurrection of the body at great length, Paul closes his discussion with a quotation from the Old Testament in which (in a great apostrophe) he addresses death itself: "O death, where is your sting?" He acknowledges that there is a *sting,* that is, something *painful* about death.

The Greek word translated sting is *kentron.* This vivid word is used in other places in the New Testament. It is used, for instance, to refer to the sting of the scorpions mentioned in the book of Revelation. I don't know whether you have ever been stung by a scorpion or not, but I once had that unhappy experience in Texas. (Incidentally, I understand that the sting of our American variety of scorpion is not quite as painful as that of scorpions in Palestine, but that is hard to imagine!) I crawled into bed that night as a green northerner, not realizing that this eventuality could occur, and he had already blissfully gone to sleep in the bed before I got there. He must have resented my disturbing his nap, because he soon let me know it! For three days I walked around with a fiery red spot as large as a frying pan on my right leg. During the remainder of my stay, every time I got near a bed or a shoe or a shirt or tie or anything, I checked it out first before putting it to use. I immediately learned to respect scorpions because of their *sting.* The sting was painful, and I wanted to avoid it at all costs. Because of its painful aspects, I took every necessary precaution to make sure that I would not get involved in another similar experience. That is the picture in I Corinthians 15. Men shy away from death because of its painful aspect; they do not want to get near it or have anything to do with it.

The work *kentron* is used also of the goads employed to herd animals along the road. These goads were long sticks with sharp points on one end. The word occurs in the book of Acts (chapter 9). The risen Lord, addressing Saul said, "It is hard for you to kick against the goads." The picture here is of an animal that wants to go his own way. The herdsman is jabbing him with the goad to drive him back onto the path. But he is annoyed by this goading, so he gives the stick one good hard clout with his foot. The sharp point sinks deeply into his flesh and then he really gets the feel of the *kentron!* That pain is so severe that he will never kick it again. He has learned to respect it; he will avoid it at all costs *because of the pain* that it inflicts.

So in I Corinthians 15 Paul says to death, "Where is your sting? Grave where is your victory?" He continues, "The sting of death is sin and what gives sin its strength is the law." In other words, Paul notes that people are afraid to die. They fear death because of its *painful* aspect. They are afraid to die because they know that they are sinners, that they have not kept the law of God, and that they must face God at death as lawbreakers. So men avoid death because it is painful.

Paul's words, however, indicate that one need not fear death. He himself was able to address death without such fear. For him the painful aspect was missing. Christ has conquered death and removed its stinger. The Lord Jesus Christ came to die for sinners. Although His people had broken God's law, He bore the penalty for their sin. Death held no such fear for early Christians, then, since it was their firm conviction that death's stinger had pierced Another; it came loose on the cross. So the great specter is powerless and the fearful scorpion who once held the keys to death and hades has had them snatched from him (Rev. 1:17, 18). Jesus Christ now says to His people: "Fear not."

That is the Christian viewpoint toward death. While the

sorrow of loss remains, the hope of eternal life, the resurrection of the body, the anticipation of the reunion of believers, and most of all the hope of living in the personal presence of Christ also share space with it. Indeed, they should triumph over it.

The biblical view is found also in Hebrews 2:15. There the writer says that the Lord has released from bondage those who "all their life long were held in the bondage" of the fear of death. Christ's first sermon was preached from Isaiah 61:1-2. That passage predicts that He would come to comfort all who mourn. He came to deal with this question of death. His coming "brought life and immortality to light through the gospel" (II Tim. 2:10).

The pastor who believes this biblical teaching will bring the balancing note of victory into the milieu of grief. He will not find it possible to sound that note of victory at all times and in all places in the same way, but if he believes with Paul that "to die is gain" (Phil. 1:21), and that it means "to be with Christ, which is far better" (Phil. 1:23), all that he says and does will convey this viewpoint. It was only the victory of Christ over death that allowed him to speak to death as a defeated foe. It is that same fact that makes the great difference between hope and despair; it is the only hope that can make such a difference.

Using the Grief Process

So much, then, for the attitude of the pastor toward death and grief. To be helpful, a pastor must understand, evaluate, confront and learn to use the grief process. Again, it seems necessary to take a closer look at these matters through Christian eyes. Much has been adopted wholesale from the studies of psychiatrists. The work of Eric Lindemann, who made the classic study (1944), has been the basis of most of the discussion since. This study had severe limits, yet very few acknowledged those limits. Geoffrey Gorer is an exception. For twenty years, nearly everyone accepted Lindemann's view as the description of the normal grief process. But Gorer, in his book, *Death, Grief and Mourning,* challenged this assumption.[4] He has charged that the use of Lindemann's study made by most subsequent writers is invalid. Gorer points out that most of the mourners in Lindemann's study were bereaved through war or the disaster of the Coconut Grove fire. The husbands of the surviving widows had all been fifty years old or younger at the time of their death. Gorer observes that it is possible that grief over a death that is considered more "natural" (e.g., due to age and infirmity) will differ from the patterns occasioned by sudden unexpected deaths. Some of the elements Lindemann noted in the grief experience when the death is premature, may be missing. Gorer challenged Lindemann's findings because they differed markedly from his own. Since the results of his studies differed significantly from some of the conclusions to which Lindemann came, Gorer has cautioned, rightly, that there may be good reasons why Lindemann's description of the grief process should not be considered the norm or standard. Because of the failure to recognize these facts, the model of mourning in most of the existing scanty literature is very heavily biased toward premature and unexpected bereavement. Gorer found, in contrast, that hostility was not always present in more "normal" deaths.

It would seem important to ask the kind of questions that Gorer has asked. It is time to take many second looks and to ask many more questions. There may be some facts about the grief process that can be learned from Lindemann and from others. I am suggesting that subsequent writing almost monolithically has been based upon Lindemann's work. Much work needs to be done, therefore, in the study of grief. This should be the conclusion of anyone who has studied the literature in the field. Certainly the last word has not been spoken; I shall

---

[4]Geoffrey Gorer, *Death, Grief and Mourning,* Doubleday and Company, Inc.: New York, pp. 141-152.

not speak it today. It may be necessary to revise most of what has been said so far.

Christians ought to ask questions from the distinctively Christian viewpoint. Basic questions like, "What were the researcher's assumptions?" and, "What were his basic presuppositions?" have not been whispered. Yet those kinds of questions really are vital. What one looks for usually is what he finds. And every finding is evaluated from the vantage (or disadvantage) point at which one stands. What can Christians do by working from Christian presuppositions? The study of grief from a biblical viewpoint will elicit entirely different results. For example, Paul himself insists that the Christian faith will make a difference (I Thess. 4:13 ff.); he distinguishes between two kinds of grief. He speaks not merely of one, but of (1) a grief in despair, and (2) a grief in hope. For instance, Edgar Jackson, in his book, *For the Living,* cites some interesting studies that may have to do with this very question. He notes that there has been a difference in the rate of recovery between those who have hope and those who do not.[5] The distinction between those who have hope and those who do not also will influence the manner in which one approaches a grief sufferer. As Christians, we should not accept at face value the results of any studies that are based upon non-Christian presuppositions. Instead, let us who believe the Scriptures take our stand there and look at what others have said from that vantage point and also ask the questions that must be asked. Preachers too readily "buy" what psychiatrists and medical doctors say. There is another viewpoint, another stance and a whole new dimension to be brought to the problem. The Scriptures give us that perspective. Although we may learn much that is valuable and useful from others (if we know how to evaluate their work by the standard of biblical principle) we must not be intimidated by them into conforming our

---

[5] Edgar N. Jackson, *For the Living,* Channel Press, Des Moines: 1963, pp. 78, 79.

ideas to theirs. What we do and say must not conflict with the Scriptures. Why should we twist the Word of God?

Prepare for Grief

Turning now to how we may help our congregations, first let me note that much can be done by pastors to *prepare* others for the grief that inevitably will overtake them. So often we have failed our congregations by not preaching and speaking frequently enough about death and grief. We hear much today in churches as well as elsewhere about the facts of life. We teach courses, hold conferences, engage in studies, and publish books and pamphlets about the facts of life. We encourage young people's groups to discuss the subject. But where is there a course, a book, a study or anything else on the *facts of death?* Everyone of us will face death; not everyone will have something to do with the birth of a child. Death is more universal than the begetting of life, and yet we say virtually nothing about the facts of death.

Previous instruction concerning death and grief helps. Indeed, it helps immensely. That is why Paul wrote I Thessalonians 4:13 ff. Notice how he opens the passage: "I would not have you to be ignorant brethren concerning those who are asleep." Then he offers detailed information calculated to bring hope out of despair, to give answers to problems, and to give comfort in the time of sorrow. He closes that section with the words, "Comfort one another with these words." So information, detailed information, is crucial. I do not think that our congregations hear enough of this information. No wonder that there is often so little comfort. We have failed to prepare people for death and grief beforehand. Hope that will carry them successfully through the time of grief must have time to mature. It cannot grow fast enough in the overly rich soil of grief alone. There must be a mix. Grieving is affected by hope or the lack of it, and hope is affected by information or the lack of it. Hope does not grow out of misunderstanding and ignorance. Hope is based on information.

Grief should be discussed beforehand. Why not discuss the subject of grief with a young couples' group? These couples have parents who soon may die. As a result, they soon may face grief. In such groups the subject may be discussed at some length with great profit.

When I teach beginning Speech to students who have had no Speech courses at college, one of the things that I must explain is the process of stage fright. I talk to them in detail about it to help them understand the dynamics of what is happening and, *through understanding,* to alleviate the fear of it. If a speaker's mouth dries up like cotton, his tongue sticks to his jaw, his heart begins to pound, his hands get clammy, his knees knock, and he feels butterflies in the stomach, he is likely to become frightened by these bodily responses unless he understands them. When I explain that these are normal anticipation responses, similar to those of pilots before they take off for combat duty, that they are the same kind of responses that football players experience before going out on the playing field, and that they approximate the responses of people starting off on a long trip, students are helped so that they rarely develop stage fright. The feelings that I have just mentioned are the sensations associated with mobilizing the body for a challenging experience ahead. They indicate that the body is souped up for that experience. What you feel in your stomach, for instance, is not butterflies of course; it is the cessation of the comfortable peristaltic movements of the stomach that move your food along. When these cease, you get that hollow feeling in the pit of your stomach. All of these changes take place in order to *prepare* the body, and that is exactly what a speaker needs. He does not want to be so completely relaxed that he drapes himself all over the pulpit; that would show a lack of concern for his subject and his audience. But if he stands up keen and prepared, anticipating what he has to say and able to bring a full concentration of all of his forces (both mental and physical) upon his topic, he is ready to speak. But the anticipation response of the body is all part of what makes him ready to speak or preach. He should welcome this bodily change, not fear it. When you explain this to a student, it makes a tremendous difference to him. If sometime later he begins to feel a cottony mouth, he is not likely to become as upset about it as if he did not know these facts.

The same is true with grief. In fact, in C. S. Lewis' book, *A Grief Observed,* this very point is made. In this book Lewis records his own grief as he experienced it at the death of his wife. Note how he begins; listen to his very first words: "No one ever told me that grief felt so like fear." He says, "No one ever told me." Perhaps some of the problems that he experienced in that period of grief against which he rebelled so strongly, that he found so difficult to handle and that caused him so much fear, might not have occurred if someone *had* told him. I think that we must take a cue from C. S. Lewis and start talking to people about the process of grief itself.

The Process Itself

It is time to take a look at that process of grief. But we must look at it differently from the way that some others have. We shall consider it not as "grief work" that has to be done. This is the standard approach of Lindemann and the many who have followed him. We shall not discuss grief merely as so many things that have to be done in such and such a way in order to get through this process successfully. Those who adopt the "grief work" view think of the process as fairly uniform so long as one is certain not to short circuit it or delay it or divert it into some wrong channel. They have conceived of the grief process too mechanically and too uniformly. We must learn to understand the process and use it for the welfare of the one who is suffering grief.

The various stages of the grief process may be divided in different ways; for example, some see four stages, others three, etc. Three stages, at least, must be distinguished. All studies show at least three stages in the process. For the sake of convenience I shall call these three stages Shock, Disorganization and Reorganization.

SHOCK

The first is *Shock*. The length of this period variously has been computed as lasting from one to two hours. This is the period from when you hang up the phone, having been told "He's dead," to the time when you come to your senses and say, "Yes, he is dead." During that period one may experience numbness, the feeling of being stunned, hysteria, a near or an actual paralysis and bewilderment. Some persons, however, take such news quite coolly. One biblical example of a very strong reaction to the shock of the news of death may be found in I Samuel 4:19-21. Ichabod's mother was still carrying him as an unborn child when news reached her concerning the capture of the ark of the covenant. She was told that in connection with that sad event, her husband and her father-in-law had died. In shock, she gave birth to the boy, named him Ichabod and died on the spot. What a dramatic and forceful account of the initial shock period in grief! The combination of factors was overwhelming; too much for her body to stand.[6]

The pastor during this period sometimes may be more present than active. This is something that you hear all of the time, of course. I hesitate ever to say that about a pastor, and yet this seems to be the one place where we have to say it. The pastor normally ought to be far more active as a counselor than many believe he should. But here is one of those rare occasions where frequently there simply is not too much that he can say or do. He can handle discussion at this point only to the extent that it is possible to do so. But again, what he

---

[6] It clearly demonstrates that there is no uniform grief response. Cf. also Zechariah 12:10, where the mourning over an only son is distinguished as particularly bitter.

does will depend upon the particular individual involved and how he or she is reacting.

If the pastor enters the picture during this early stage, either during shock or during the next few hours as the sufferer moves into the second stage (Disorganization), sometimes he may be subjected to harsh treatment by the sufferer. Not everyone is likely to respond in this way, but now if the bars are down, the restraints have been removed, and the first glimmerings of what has happened begin to sink in (and particularly if there are other problems like hostility or guilt mingled with the sorrow), some sufferers are likely to spill their feelings upon the pastor or others who may be among the first to enter upon the scene. The pastor should be aware of this possibility.

This kind of a response needs to be handled properly. What does a pastor do? Well, to begin with, he must not think merely of himself. He should neither let his feelings be hurt, nor respond in anger, nor turn on his heels and walk away from the situation. He should not begin an argument or attempt a discussion. Instead, he can do at least two things. First, he can give a gentle, corrective rebuke in which briefly he may explain that he does not think that the charges that have been made are correct and that at a later time he would like to take up the matter. This leads naturally to the second point. *Later* (the pastor should refuse to discuss the matter at this point) the pastor may raise the issue. It is wrong to avoid the problem or to let the matter drop. Something came to the surface that needs to be dealt with. Postponement will provide a good opening for later counseling about the anger or fear or guilt that may have slipped out when the sufferer's defenses were down.

DISORGANIZATION

Let us now turn to the second stage: *Disorganization.* There is much that needs to be discussed about the questions of length and duration and even about the concept of stages itself, but I cannot do so today. The second phase may last from seven to ten days. Let us take a look at the symptoms that *may* occur during this period. All of these (as in the period of Shock) may not appear in every case. I do not think that in every instance they should. Certainly a devout Christian and an unbeliever should respond differently.

Physical distress may come in waves of bodily discomfort down deep inside. There might be twenty minutes worth of this, then a break and then more in an hour or so. Such feelings may include a tight feeling in the throat and a feeling of being suffocated. A number of people have talked about deep sighing. The sufferer may not even realize how often he sighs. He might go around saying, "Oh, my" or something like that. A sensation of desert dryness may plague him. He could possibly suffer from limpness of the limbs and little mobilization of the muscles in general. Then there is likely to be a drained emotional state, emptiness of feeling and a sense of unreality on the part of the person in grief. Perhaps at times he will wander off into a dream world. A "This can't really be true" attitude may begin to grow; whatever he is doing, his heart is likely not to be in it. There is loss of spirit, zest, joy, initiative and motivation. He may do things mechanically. He may become very stiff and formal during this period, even to his closest friends. He might appear standoffish (seeming not to care about others) or be discourteous. He may not give much thought to manners and courtesy or care much about tact. Now, of course, if he gets a good bit of sedation during this period of time (which may be very unwise), the whole process might be prolonged or altered. It might be wise even to chat with the physician about this matter. If you notice such a problem, you might alert him.

Guilt and Grief

If guilt is plugged into the picture, serious problems may arise. For example, if a bad relationship existed between the sufferer and the person who died and attitudes had become bitter and hardened with much resentment between the parties, most likely there will be added complications. It will be your task to discover such matters during grief counseling sessions. If necessary, you should probe directly into the question. This matter must be dealt with by confession and forgiveness and a subsequent change of life pattern.[7] May I say

---

[7]See general remarks in *Competent to Counsel* concerning confession. The difference here is that confession must be made to God alone. Since no confession may be made to the deceased, the pastor may experience a dissatisfied attitude on the part of the repentant confessor. If that is encountered, the problem may be due to the fact that there is no opportunity to experience reconciliation with the deceased. A new relationship cannot be established as when one confesses to a living person. Two things may be done, however, to meet this problem: the pastor may urge the counselee to (1) do whatever can be done to right continuing wrongs (cf. David's kindness to Mephibosheth, II Samuel 9:1-13); (2) consider other relationships in which the same patterns may yet exist. He must do all that can be done (Rom. 12:18) to be reconciled and to establish proper relationships to these persons. Part of the dissatisfaction may come in such instances from requiring an inadequate form of repentance that demands confession but no "fruits" (changes in the repentant one) appropriate to repentance. Such change must be effected wherever possible.

The friend of a young girl who was killed suddenly sought help. He said that he had failed to use many opportunities to witness to her about Christ. Now it was too late. He had become deeply depressed over this matter and had come to believe that he was guilty of sending her to hell. Nothing anyone could say would relieve the depression that had developed. Help came in the form of three things that had to be done: (1) He needed to repent and to confess his sin of failure to witness. Truly he had sinned against God and against the girl. He was guilty of this and had to be called to repentance. (2) He needed to get his theology straightened out. He was not responsible for the eternal destiny of that girl, although he was responsible for witnessing to her. She did not go to hell (if she did) as the result of his sin; she went to hell for her own sin. *She* was responsible to God for her sin; *his* responsibility was to witness to her about it and about her need for a Savior. Each was guilty of separate sins. Truly his sin entered into the question of her eternal state, but she would suffer eternally for her sin, not for his. (3) He could do nothing about the past, but to repent, yet genuine repentance would lead to fruit fitting to repentance: if his repentance over the sin of failure to witness was sincere, he would do differently in the future. As a matter of fact, genuine relief came only when he made a list of persons

that in counseling every week I find that there is much bitterness and resentment between people? Let's face this fact: many of the problems that we have with others never get resolved. Instead, they usually end up as hardened bitternesses; cast iron resentment. When someone dies with that kind of relationship still existing between the two of them, the survivor may have a hard time handling the problem of grief. God may use the death to bring about genuine repentance. But it will be complex, not simple as it might have been if repentance had occurred prior to the loss. The way of the transgressor is hard. Mixed together are the feelings of sorrow and guilt over the fact that this relationship was never resolved and now cannot be resolved. The resentment, if not dealt with before God, may continue. A genuine pastor will call the grieving one to repentance. This may seem cruel or harsh, but in truth it is the kindest act of all. Simple sorrow over loss is hard enough; it can become unbearable when complicated by unresolved guilt.

Perhaps the problem of telling the patient that he was dying had been solved in an all too typically unchristian manner: by lying. For two or three months, or even a longer period, the family knew that he had what is so coldly called "a terminal illness." Everyone had been informed that he was expected to die, but the physician said, "Don't tell him." Because the family agreed to this cruelest lie of all, they did not tell him, and a false, artificial relationship (everyone was always afraid that he might find out) began to grow. Most dying persons know anyway, but everyone (all around) was afraid to broach the subject. No significant communication between husband and wife or children and parent took place. The problem got in the way every time they were together. They could never really talk about the expected death or about what was going to happen after death. Fear grew in the

---

to whom a witness was long overdue and began to do what he could to make up for lost time.

one who was to be left that the deceased might have been able to relieve by his wise help and careful planning during those last few months. On the other hand, a vital ministry of love and help was withheld from the dying loved one who was effectively cut off from everything he needed. The physician and the family meant well, but because they violated God's law, they destroyed all that might have been good. They could not plan together for the eventuality of death. There could be no last words to the children.

This terrible situation so often exists today. One person dies and the family is left with *that* as the last memory. They remember the lies, the hard days, the emptiness and fear. There was no *grieving together before death* possible. Nothing relieves and helps grief more than this. This is hard for all. But it is particularly difficult for the bereaved, since much of the heartache of grief could be removed by proper Christian communication prior to death. If a husband and wife discuss the expected death beforehand, grief can be lessened by open exchange, reconciliation (if necessary), planning, preparation, warm moments and honest joint prayer and ministry of the Word. There can be pleasant memories of these last weeks or months, in contrast to the empty dread that accompanies the lies. Children can be challenged to duty and devotion as they were by the dying patriarchs. When people need one another so desperately, why should lies drive them apart?

The dishonesty and guilt of non-discussion doubtless is one serious cause of complication in grief. We must question seriously the whole matter of lies or even silence about possible death. Certainly lying about it is taboo for you as God's shepherd.[8]

---

[8] I hope to discuss this question at greater length in a forthcoming book on pastoral work. Pastors should warn congregations well in advance that they intend to tell the truth. The warrant to do so, in spite of family or physician, comes from God. The pastoral relationship demands a truthful ministry of the Word. The possibly dying parishioner

Resentment also may arise over the death itself. "He's left me now just at this time when I needed him so much," one bitter woman may say. "What will happen, now?" another asks in fear. Fear of the future may be mixed with anger. The survivor may become angry at the one who died, and yet be sorry that he has died. Trust in the providence of God alone can solve such problems. The ministry of hope stemming from the conviction that God is sovereign is needed at such a time. In the third stage, that hope will be intensified as the pastor helps a fearful lonely sheep plan for the future according to biblical principles.

Because grief tends to knock down defenses, the grief sufferer may seem to become a quite different person than you have ever known before. When inhibitions are removed, the real person may emerge. The real person may be very different from the manifest person that previously has been seen day by day. The sufferer has been able to hold under his real character until the life-shattering experience shook down the walls. His neighbors and friends and even his family may have thought him to be a very fine person. But now that the lid is off and he becomes outwardly everything that he was inwardly, he may not be very pleasant to have around. Fear may drive him to desperate means; he may speak harsh or foolish words or take irrational actions. The pastor's ministry of the Word may be extended markedly if this occurs. Possibly kindly admonition and rebuke may be called for.

Preoccupation with the image of the deceased (so often mentioned by Lindemann and sometimes by others) which may be very vivid, may possibly occur. In the daydreaming inner world into which he may retreat, this image may at

---

is not only a member of a family; he is also a member of Christ's Church for whom you and the session have a pastoral responsibility. It is important, however, to speak of preparation for the *possibility* of death, for no one knows when another will die. Many surprising recoveries have occurred in God's providence when a patient was all but pronounced dead.

times be so vivid that the bereaved person himself may even think that he has seen or heard the dead person in a visitation. Where this occurs as a problem, the pastor must steady the sufferer with sound biblical doctrine. He may wish to push beyond the problem itself to see if it is connected to a complicating difficulty like unresolved anger or guilt toward the deceased. He should inquire also about possible sleep loss. Two or more days of significant sleep loss (of R. E. M., or rapid eye movement sleep) can cause any or all of the perceptual difficulties associated with L.S.D. In every instance, it would be wise to urge adequate sleep. Sin against the body by pushing it beyond its limits can add unnecessary heartache, confusion and fear to the grief period. Grief can readily lead to sleep loss, so keep this important question in mind.

During this period of disorganization, you will be watching a very unpleasant thing. You are involved in helping a member of your flock through a very difficult period. It will not usually be pleasant. It is hard to watch a life come apart at the seams; it is heartbreaking to see the stuffings come out; it can be disillusioning to go through the wall behind which this person lives day by day and discover him for what he really is. It would not be pleasant for us or them if others were to look behind our walls. Yet that is often what you will see happening during this period. When one is be-reaved, the old ways are being destroyed. This is truly a period of disorganization. Old fields are being plowed up; old roads are being re-routed and old buildings are coming down. The old factors that seemed so secure now come crashing down around the grief sufferer and all is becoming rubble. He realizes that there must be radical changes, that he can no longer go on as he once did. Now that her husband is gone, now that his wife is dead, the survivor recognizes that much of life necessarily will be entirely different. A new life has to be built; he knows that. The old patterns will no longer suffice. But what will the new be like? The uncertainty may cause acute fear where faith is small or lacking. It will also take time for the transition to take place. The period of Disorganization is itself the first part of the transition period. It is the negative side that must come first.

A period of disorganization is a *negative* period, because it is the time when things come apart. It is a time of falling down, tearing up, and uprooting. But it is a necessary and important period: the remnants and the rubble of each collapsed building must be cleared before something new can be built on that same plot of ground. The pastor may help enormously in this process. A break has to be made with the past, and Christians must see to it that in every way this is a *clean* break. The unsettled sin of the past must be dealt with. The ground must be readied for the future sowing of seed and the building of new edifices. If they are to be good crops and sturdy buildings, all must be readied first.

Disorganization is just that; a life-shaking experience has disorganized the grief sufferer. It has shaken his life apart. He has lost his moorings; he is adrift on the sea of life. During this period, one's whole life comes under review. He takes a new look at himself; he can't help it. Here is where the pastor can be of real help. It is not so important (as many of the studies have insisted) to get grief sufferers to talk about the deceased.[9] Instead, what you need to do is to encourage the grief sufferer to talk about his *own* relationship to the deceased. It is really his life that is cracking at the seam; the other person is gone. If he wants to discuss the deceased,

---

[9]Particularly if the last weeks together have been open, honest and warm. Where unreconciled conditions remain at death, indeed, this must be discussed and handled biblically (even then the emphasis is not upon the deceased but upon one's own relationship to him). But assuming that has been done, or that the grief was simple (not complex) to begin with, then what I am about to say follows. The concept of grief work from which the idea of talk about the deceased emerges, is erroneous. Talk alone does not solve problems; indeed talk may serve only to intensify grief if that talk does not issue in biblical courses of action calculated to solve the problems discussed.

good, but also very soon you should move that discussion to the matter of his *relationship* with the deceased. And you can hardly do that without also talking about his relationship to God, and without talking about his own coming death. These are all pertinent subjects because a grief sufferer inevitably thinks about them. He will be thinking frequently about his own death during this period.[10] He will also talk about the kind of life style that he has led up until this period. This is important and it will usually grow naturally out of the discussion of these other topics.

Such a look at himself, in which he re-evaluates himself from top to bottom, may reveal that he has been an *angry* person. The pastor may need to point out how he has expressed anger toward God, against his relatives, or concerning someone at work. He may still be angry at the one he has lost.

The pastor also may need to show him that he is a *guilty* person. He may have great guilt over this anger and the bad relationships that he has sustained to the deceased and others. There may be guilt over other things that he has done in the past that come to him with renewed impact during this period of re-evaluation.

He may discover that he is a very *fearful* person, with little or no trust. As a wise pastor, you will take note of fear, particularly fears arising from uncertainty. A widow may say, "I depended so much on him, how can I go on into the future? What will happen to the business? What will happen to the children?" Here is a person filled with fear. You ought to be looking for this. When you spot it, you will want to plan to deal with this problem, especially looking forward to the next period in which you will help to allay many of those fears by stressing the faithfulness of God to His own, and offering concrete help from the Word of God. Since this is a period of breaking with the past, the goal for the pastoral counselor (as

---

[10]This fact should awaken pastors and other Christians to the possibility for evangelism that exists in the ministry to those in grief.

I said) ought to be to help the grief sufferer to make a clean break with the past. He must help him to deal with patterns of living that he has fallen into over the years, not only by righting all wrongs between himself and God and others, but by sorting through the rubble to discover these so that he may then help him to build something entirely fresh and new for the future.

Counseling in Disorganization

What I am calling for probably means a good bit more counseling than most pastors give to their people during the time of grief. But it is needed to do this job properly. It is well worth it. Rarely at any other time do you see a person in this condition. Rarely do you see a life come apart so completely. Rarely can you help one pick up so many pieces and put so much back together to form such an entirely new picture. Grief providentially affords one of the greatest opportunities to help persons to finer living for Jesus Christ than they have experienced before. Remember that this is the opportunity for ministry that God affords you every time a death occurs in your congregation. At this period you ought to seize the opportunity; move in on it with all of the resources of God and allot all of the time needed to do the job well. See if you can get his agreement to meet with you for a series of eight or ten weekly counseling sessions, if at all possible. Listen; ask questions about the recent past and then move backward. Always take a grieving person very seriously about his sin and guilt. Do not minimize his negative evaluations of himself. He is likely to be more open and honest than at any other time. Agree that he is sinful, but thwart depression by pointing to the biblical solution to each sin. Then help him to move in that direction. If necessary, you may have to help him to confess his sin to God and to seek forgiveness from God. You may need to stress reconciliation with God and others. It may be necessary to sit down with two or three members of the family and work out some matters between them. Instead of this becoming a time of squabbling and fighting over who is going to get what after dad has passed on, at this point a wise pastoral counselor may be able to *reconcile* estranged relatives. This could be the very period of time in which those members of the family who have been so far apart for so long can be brought together again. The opportunity exists as it hardly does at any other time. So let me suggest the idea of bringing *families* in for counseling. Deal with the members of the family who are intimately involved and who will live in intimate relationship in the days ahead and counsel them *as families.* This point could be vital.

Certainly during this period you will counsel the grief sufferer(s) not to make hasty decisions. The widow should wait, if at all possible, to decide about selling the business or moving. If she says, "I could never live in this community being reminded of John by everything," caution her to get some perspective on this matter. Say,

> "Wait until you've built the structure for a new life; then make those decisions. Don't make them now. So often people have sold everything and moved to Florida and four months later they remembered that all of their friends are back in Norristown. Because of a decision made before they were *ready* to make it, they have lost their church fellowship and good friends. The people and things that really mattered are irretrievably lost. They are sorry that they made that move."

One talented soloist, at the untimely death of her son, resolved that she would never sing again. She might have kept this hasty resolution if it had not been for the wise caution and encouragement given during this period in counseling by her pastor and the elders of her church. Today, her greatest joy is to sing of the victory of Christ over death. It is very important to advise people not to make weighty decisions until the period of disorganization and disorientation has passed.

REORGANIZATION

At the end of that seven to ten-day period, or whatever time it might cover, comes a third period or stage in the process of grief. I have called it *Reorganization.* This is the most neglected period of all, and yet it is the pastor's most opportune one. It is really the flip side of Disorganization. It is the positive side of grief. Yet this is the time when everybody begins to forget. By this time friends, neighbors, relatives and usually the pastor as well, disappear from the scene. They have all been very solicitous during the seven to ten-day period following death, but now that has ended. And rightly so; most friends can't continue to spend the same kind of time with the grief sufferer that they did before.

But what is deceptive is that since the grief sufferer now seems to be getting over it, since he can go back to work and begin to function fairly well again, everyone thinks that the grief process has ended. That is false. This third period is in one sense more crucial than the second. It is during this period, when he is forgotten by everyone else, that the grief sufferer usually, on his own, has to undertake the hardest task of all. This is a huge order, usually too large for somebody who has just come through an exhausting and disorienting life-shaking experience. It is too difficult to handle alone. He now must plan, lay the foundation and begin to build the structure for a brand new life; that is his work during the next few weeks. He must make many decisions; he must start up forces that may continue to work throughout the rest of his life. Everyone has forgotten him. Yet, he is very tired, sometimes very confused, and often fearful. He is still looking at everything very closely, and yet at this period he has to begin to make long-range decisions; he has to put his life together again. It is hard to get perspective alone. How important, then, to conduct regular counseling sessions from the earliest point following the death through the next two stages. If the time periods for stages two and three vary greatly among individuals, that will not matter, for if sessions were set up initially after the death, they would carry you well into this period no matter when it begins.

This is a very opportune period because this is the period of planning and building. This is the positive period. This is not the look back, but if the break has been a clean one, the pastor can help to make this a marvelous and often exciting period of growth, fresh and new. He can help him to look into God's future with faith and to plan a revised life style according to the Scriptures. During this period, radical change will take place; it must. So you may reckon on the fact that the bereaved is prepared for radical change; he knows that it must come. That big gapping hole in the home is there, so there must be radical change. Where he depended on her, he can no longer do so; change there must be. If radical change must come, here is the pastor's opportunity to point to the radical changes that *God* requires. The person is *ready* for radical changes, he *knows* they must be made, and he *will make them.* How important, then, that he make the right changes. You must move in to help him to do so; you can be of life-long help to him if you can help him to love and serve his Lord more dearly than before.

Change

It is important when we think about change to realize how change takes place. Change does not take place through talk alone. So much of the advice about counseling has centered (wrongly) upon talk. No one must be opposed to talk; talk is important. But talk *alone* can be very harmful; it can be destructive. Talk alone simply confirms the fact that there is a serious problem that is yet unsolved. Much talk that goes for counseling does far more harm than good. If that talk in the end does not issue in biblical courses of action, it is counterproductive. Change is a situation that grows out of talk that is oriented toward seeking and implementing biblical solutions to problems. Talk that does not only amplifies the problems.

Don't just talk, then; rather, talk through the problem to a solution. Otherwise, talk can be like tearing off a scab and poking your finger around in the bloody mess. That makes a wound all the sorer. That is what talk alone may do. A counselee may feel relieved for twenty minutes because he has got the pressure off his chest, but at the end he takes another hard look at it and he says, I just see more clearly how difficult the problem is. We've reached no solution; we've talked about nothing to do. So when you talk, always talk to a person about *change* and talk in concrete terms of *what* God says must be done and *how* to do it. Then, you will truly bless men's lives.

How can you best help the bereaved through this period? Here is one basic suggestion: you can help him to lay plans prayerfully. To do so, you may begin (1) by helping him to set biblical objectives for the future.[11] Then (2) you may help him to list his problems, specifically those difficulties that he must overcome in order to reach those objectives. It is good policy to *list* problems so that both of you know specifically what you are talking about. Also, in the process of writing, a person has to formulate and define problems more clearly. Sometimes the answers come as a result of the writing. In days ahead, progress may be judged by the list as he is able to scratch off one here and another there. When he sees the list diminish, he gains hope. Then (3) you might discuss and decide upon the biblical solutions to those problems. But, as I said, you may never leave it there. Quickly (4) help him lay out a course of action to take, including the scheduling (by date) of the initial steps to take to solve those problems and the means for checking up on him to make sure he is doing it.

If this and similar help is given, you are not likely to run into the kinds of difficulties of which so many of the studies speak. If people never get over their grief, or are sidetracked,

---

[11]Always with the holy caution of James 4:13-16 that delights in God's blue-penciling.

or a variety of other such tragedies occur, perhaps one reason is that pastors have failed to minister in a thoroughly biblical and, therefore, adequate manner to those who suffer grief. Why not resolve that by the grace of God you will enter into the opportunities and meet the needs?

Evangelism in Counseling

I was invited to talk to you only by default. You see, the Invitation Committee first visited a local establishment where they train Freudian therapists, and asked some Christians studying there if they would talk about counseling and evangelism. Even though they were Christians, they didn't believe you could evangelize in counseling, so nobody would accept the invitation. Then the committee went next door to the Rogerian counseling center and found some Christians studying there too, but to a man they all said you shouldn't do evangelism in counseling. So they could not get anyone to speak. After a considerable amount of rummaging around through the various 'ologies, 'erapies and 'isms, they could find only one person who was willing to say anything about evangelism in counseling. So they were stuck with me, and here I am.

Those first few facetious words are calculated to move directly in on my main theme, which is that if your counseling is biblical you will evangelize, and if you will not evangelize in counseling, your counseling is not biblical. If your counseling does not begin with the Bible, but with Mowrer or with Glasser, or with Maslow, or with Freud, or with Rogers, or with Skinner or with any other than God Himself, you will soon conclude that you cannot evangelize in counseling.

Evangelism in counseling presupposes that you start with a sovereign God against whom men have sinned, a God who has declared that He will punish sinners in hell. There are few Freudians, etc., who accept these biblical presuppositions about man and God. They are more likely to conclude that such ideas will cause (not cure) what they call "mental illness." Nor would they accept the foundational principle that apart from Jesus Christ all help is temporal and temporary,

---

[1]This address was delivered at the Reformed Presbyterian Seminary, Pittsburgh, Pennsylvania (revised).

mere bandaid work, when that which man really needs is radical surgery. Rogerians would insist that any attempt to evangelize in counseling would constitute a prostitution of the counseling situation, inasmuch as it would involve the authoritative (shudder) interposition of commandment into what they believe should be a permissive atmosphere in which the counselee is encouraged to resolve his problems by the use of his own resources. Evangelism would violate his autonomy. And so you can see why that committee was really up a tree. That is why I agreed to try to do my best to get them out of the jam.

The topic that they gave me was Evangelism In Counseling. I must admit that I feel very much at home with that topic, because I do counseling and I do evangelism all of the time— and I do each in conjunction with the other. I do not feel that I have to make an artificial division between the two. When I don the hat of an evangelist, I do not have to remove it and put on an entirely different hat in order to do the work of a counselor. God gave Christians a many-hued hat. I do not have a bifurcated view of counseling and evangelism, and I do not think that you will find one in God's Word. So this is my first point: a system of counseling that will not allow you to do evangelism as a part of that counseling is not biblical. On that criterion alone (even if you had no other) you can determine whether any given system of counseling is biblical.

When you stand in the pulpit you say, "Thus saith the Lord." But what happens when you walk down out of the pulpit into the study and close the door? Do you tell the counselee, "All right now, *you* talk?" For the rest of the hour do you sit there with your mouth shut except for a few imperceptible grunts coming through closed lips? Are your most intelligible utterances, "Good-bye, come again next week"? If so, again something is wrong. And this is what it is—that whole approach just isn't biblical. It isn't what Paul did; it isn't the way that Peter handled people. It certainly doesn't look like anything you can find in the New Testament.

But what do we find in the Scriptures? I'd like to begin the study of that question with the first two verses of the first chapter of the book of Acts. Luke, writing his second book to Theophilus, speaks about "the former work," the Gospel of Luke, and compares its contents to the contents of the book of Acts. He says that he composed the first account (the Gospel) about "all that Jesus *began* to do and to teach until the day that he was taken up." The interesting fact about this verse that easily might be missed is that in the second clause the word *began* occurs in an emphatic position in the original. This means that Luke intended to stress the word *began*. When the Greeks wanted to emphasize they used word order to do so. Since they had case endings to identify the exact import of each element in a sentence, they could move words out of their more normal order and place them in a different order to show where the stress should fall. That is what Luke does in this first verse; he puts the word *began* at the beginning of a clause in order to underscore it. So when you read these words, you ought to read "all that Jesus *began* to do and to teach." The Gospel of Luke tells about all that Jesus began to do and teach; the book of Acts is a further account of what Jesus continued (through his church) to do and to teach. This pivotal verse between the Gospel and the Acts tells us that Jesus Christ is still at work; He is still doing and teaching. These words refer not only to His personal ministry, but also to His subsequent ministry through the Holy Spirit. He sent the Spirit to be "another paraclete" (i.e., counselor). The term indicates that He is "another of the *same kind.*"[2] The book of Acts, then, is the story of what Jesus continued to do and to teach.

It is instructive to look carefully at the conjunction of those words "do" and "teach." Contrary to what some seem

---

[2]John 14:16, 17. The word *allos*, not *heteros*, is used.

to think, Christ's ministry was not simply a ministry of teaching; it was a ministry of *doing* and teaching. Indeed, at one place His entire ministry is summarized in this way: "He went about *doing* good" (Acts 10:38). That very succinct summary also is very accurate. He did good not only through the works He performed, but also through His teaching. The passage refers to His works of miracles and all else that He did. The book of Acts records the good that He continued to do through the Spirit working in His church. So it is plain that the ministry of Christ was not simply a ministry of teaching (though it certainly was that, too). The two are inseparably coupled.

This same double emphasis occurs, for instance, in the fourth chapter of Matthew. Matthew chose to group his materials rather than to follow exact chronology throughout his Gospel. Incidentally, Luke makes the point that he will write "in orderly sequence," i.e., precisely in the order that events happened (Luke 1:3). Matthew, of course, has the same overall chronology, but when it comes to details, it is evident that Matthew groups his materials topically. Matthew 4:23 and 9:35 are almost identical. Jesus is pictured going about in all of Galilee teaching in synagogues and proclaiming the gospel of the kingdom. There is the one side: *teaching,* a general use of the term that includes both teaching in the narrower sense and preaching (proclaiming). On the other hand, Matthew also stresses the *doing:* "and healing every kind of disease and every kind of sickness among the people." So the materials grouped in Matthew 4:23 through 9:35 describe Christ's dual ministry of doing and teaching. The same words appear at the beginning of this section in Matthew and also at the end, showing how Matthew has structured his materials.

This section is then subdivided into two smaller groupings. (1) In chapters 5, 6 and 7 there is a sampling of the teaching of Jesus. (2) In chapters 8 and 9 there is a grouping of healings and other "doings" of Jesus. He is shown as the healer of every kind of disease, sickness and demon possession and even as the raiser of the dead. Matthew groups other materials later: e.g., the parables of the kingdom in chapter 13, and eschatological materials in chapters 23, 24 and 25. But notice that in this first grouping Matthew, like Luke, combines the doing and the teaching. There is no dichotomy, but rather a combining of the two as a summary of His total work. These two elements, the teaching and proclaiming on the one hand and the healing and the doing on the other hand, constitute the pre-crucifixion ministry of Jesus.

Now when the Twelve were sent out, like their Lord they went out to *do* and to *teach,* not merely to teach (Luke 9:2, 6). He sent them to proclaim the Kingdom of God and to heal. Accordingly they went about among the villages preaching the Gospel and healing.

In the next chapter, Luke records Christ's charge to the Seventy: "Whatever city you enter, if they receive you, eat what is set before you and *heal* those that are sick and *say* to them the Kingdom of God has come near to you" (Luke 10:9 [emphasis mine]). Their commission also was to heal and to teach.

These passages show that there is a continuity between the ministry of Christ and the ministries that He gave to His church. Your ministry, too, like that of the disciples and the Seventy, is to be patterned after the ministry of Jesus. That does not mean that you are able to raise the dead as He was (such extraordinary gifts have ceased), but there is still the necessity to do as well as to teach. These two elements are always linked in all of these passages. Jesus spoke about that continuity in explicit terms when He said, "Believe me that I am in the Father and the Father in me, otherwise believe on account of the works. Truly I say to you, he who believes in me, the works that I do he shall do also and greater works than these shall he do because I go to the Father" (John 14:12). He makes it clear that it is not the disciple, himself, who performs these works, but it is the Son of God who empowers the believer to do His work: "Whatever you ask in my name, that will I do, that the Father may be glorified in the son. If you ask me anything in my name, I will do it" (John 14:13). Jesus said that *He* would do these greater works through them. Jesus is still at work doing and teaching.

Of course, those works were not greater in kind; surely there has been a reduction of intensity in the kind of works that we do. We do not raise people from the dead, as Jesus did. So when He said, "greater works," He could not have meant greater in *kind* (i.e., greater as to their nature), but rather greater in *extent.* His work was limited to a very short space of time, to a very limited geographical area and to one nation. The extent of His works (I'm not talking now about His atoning work, of course, but rather about the extent of the healing ministry in which He engaged and about which He is speaking in this passage) was very small in comparison to all that the church as a whole could do. The church would now carry the message to the whole world, so that simultaneously in a thousand cities the gospel message could be preached. How does that take place? Well, the answer is in verse 12: "Greater works than these shall he do *because I go to the Father."* In John's Gospel, Christ's going to the Father is viewed as His going there *in order to send the Holy Spirit to us.* He is speaking here very clearly of the work of the Spirit. He says, in effect, "If I don't leave you I can only perform these works in a very limited way. I will go away so that the One who comes after me can come to spread my message and do my works throughout the world. Through Him you can do my works on a much vaster scale than ever before. The church of Jesus Christ now does a world-wide work among all nations (Matt. 28) rather than a localized work among the lost sheep of the house of Israel. So Christ, in linking His work to the work of His church, has urged us to follow not only in teaching, but also in doing, teaching *and* doing, for this is the summary of His ministry. And it was about the doing that He was speaking at this very moment (cf. Paul's response in Romans 15:18).

A closer look at the works of Jesus Christ shows that these works were inseparably linked to evangelism. The healing ministry of Christ was not merely a healing ministry in-and-of-itself for the good of the person's body. Certainly Christ is concerned about the body. He did not make a dichotomy between soul and body as though the body were evil and the soul were good. The Scriptures look upon man as a being who was created perfect. There is nothing wrong with matter and nothing wrong with the body. Indeed, the resurrection of the *body* is a great hope of the Christian faith. Since Christianity does not demean the body in any sense, certainly I do not want to do so when I say that Jesus' healings were not merely intended for the welfare of the body. Instead, I want to insist that they *were* performed out of concern for the body, but at the same time I must insist that He had more than that in view.

Christ, for example, says that His healing ministry enabled people to believe: "Believe that I am in the Father and the Father is in me; otherwise believe *on account of the works themselves*" (John 14:11). Luke says that Jesus was attested to be God by His works. He uses three words that speak of miracles. The works of Christ are described as signs, wonders and powers. These terms make a clear link between the evangelism of Christ and the works that He performs.[3] It seems plain, then, that evangelism is connected with more than teaching and the *work,* the teaching and the *doing,* are linked together as essential elements in the summary of Jesus' evangelistic ministry. They seem to be inseparably intertwined. Other passages in the Gospel of John say virtually the same thing, e.g., John 10:37, 38; John 20:30, 31. In the latter, where the purpose of the Gospel is stated, the "signs" are said

[3]Acts 2:22. "Power" speaks of the mighty nature of the work itself; "wonder," of its effect upon those who observed; "sign," of its intention. The intention is clearly greater than the welfare of the body.

to be *the* crucial evangelistic agency: "Many other signs . . . but these have been written *that you may believe.*"[4]

These two elements (teaching and doing) also may be shown to be intertwined in the ministry of Christ in specific instances. In Matthew 9:2, for instance, Matthew was concerned about the doings as over against the teachings as we have seen. If ever there were a place where you would expect to find the two set off against each other, it would be here. Remember, Matthew divided his materials distinctly into a sub-group of doings and a sub-group of teachings. Matthew 9:2 does not occur in the teaching sub-group but rather in the doing sub-group. Chapters 7, 8 and 9 contain a list of doings. Yet even there where Matthew intended to show what Jesus *did,* because he had to be true to the facts, he could not help but say a great deal about what He taught. This is because the teachings are so closely connected with, grow out of, and are a part of the doings.

Matthew describes how Jesus got into a boat and crossed over the lake (Matthew 9). When He came to His own city, a paralytic carried on a bed was brought to Him. Seeing their faith, Jesus said to the paralytic: "Take courage my son, your sins are forgiven." The religious leaders began to grumble about these words. "The man is speaking blasphemy," said the Scribes to themselves. "How can he forgive sins?" they asked. Jesus knew their hearts and replied, "Why do you think these evil things?" Then He asked that penetrating question, "Which is easier to say, 'your sins are forgiven' or 'arise and walk'?" Of course, they were thinking, "Anyone can say your sins are forgiven; that is easy enough because nobody

[4]It is true that the word "sign" alone is used in John 20:30, but since John's Gospel also contains many of the long discourses of Jesus as well as the miracles, it is possible that John subsumed both under the term. However, note that it *is* the miraculous works that are individually singled out as "signs" and that led to belief through the manifestation of His "glory" as Messiah (John 2:11, 23).

knows whether they are or not. Now if he would miraculously heal this man, that would be a different story."

Actually, the more you think about the question, the more you realize how mistaken they were. That kind of reasoning, like all sinful thought, is backwards. But in order to confirm His *teaching,* Jesus performed the *work.* (Matthew puts it this way: "that you may know that the Son of man has authority on earth to forgive sins.") Jesus said to the paralytic, "Arise, take up your bed and go home." So you see what I meant when I said that the healings were not *merely* for the sake of the body. That is only a part of the picture; there is more involved. The works confirm the word. In order to substantiate His teaching, Jesus said, "I shall heal this man." He loved the bodies of men and wanted to see them whole. But what He emphasizes here is something more.

There is an incident recorded in John 9 of the healing of a man who was blind from birth. After Jesus healed him, his parents disowned him and he was excommunicated from the synagogue because he defended Jesus. First came the *doing.* Later, Jesus found him, and taught him what he needed to know. In doing so, He used blindness as an illustration to teach him and to rebuke the Pharisees. The whole discussion takes off from the healing of the blind man and moves directly to the healing of a blind soul. Analogously, the blind of soul are the Pharisees who will not come to Jesus for healing. The doing and the teaching once again are related.

Take the story of the evangelization of Nicodemus. The account moves from the miracles to the teaching. ("No man can do these miracles that you are doing unless God is with him" [John 3:2].) The event in the third chapter of John follows a discussion of miracles in the second (John 2:23). As a matter of fact, the third chapter actually should begin with verse 23 of John 2. The chapter headings and the verse demarcations were not inspired; please don't think I'm taking liberties with the text. These demarcations were made hundreds of years after the Bible was written, and some were done while riding on horseback. There are times when the divisions look as though the horse stepped into a pothole.

If verse 23 of chapter 2 is really the beginning of the account in chapter 3, there is a background for Nicodemus' visit that explains his opening words. When Jesus was in Jerusalem at the passover during the feast, many believed in His name, because of His miracles. All through the book of John, that is the thrust of the gospel: behold the signs and believe.[5] It is in that context that the interview with Nicodemus took place. He was in Jerusalem at the passover during the feast, "and many believed in his name, beholding the signs which he was doing (there again is the *doing*); but on his part Jesus was not entrusting himself to them, for he knew all men." He knew the innermost thoughts of their hearts. Many of these people were following Him only to get their stomachs filled. Many cared for Him only as a *doer,* and cared little for His teaching. In the confrontation with Nicodemus, it is apparent that Jesus sees right through the man. He also "knows what is in" Nicodemus. The story is a specific illustration of this general principle. And it is possible that the fourth chapter also offers additional evidence of that principle. There we see Him "knowing" what was in the woman at the well.

Nicodemus comes talking about the *works.* He comes to Jesus secretly at night as a representative of pharisaical authority. *"We* know," he says. It is interesting to follow the I's and the we's and the you's (the singulars and the plurals) here in this third chapter. Jesus dealt with Nicodemus both as a representative of the Pharisees and also as an individual. Jesus talked about Himself individually and also about Himself and John the Baptist collectively. I think these changes explain the verse concerning the water and the Spirit. Jesus spoke of John's baptism of *water* and His own baptism of the *Spirit;*

---

[5]In accordance with the stated purpose in John 20:30, 31. These signs were given to evoke belief. The first miracle (chapter 2) helped the disciples to believe (John 2:11).

one negatively representing the washing away of sins and the other representing the positive things that come through the Spirit. But this is no place to get into that question. In speaking with Nicodemus, Jesus goes far deeper than Nicodemus' lead question. He had said, "We know that you have come from God as a *teacher,* for otherwise you could not *do* these signs." The words "teacher" and "signs" are combined in Nicodemus' thinking. There is more hope for him than for others who separated the two. Christ moves from the signs to his inner needs: *"You* must be born again." Signs lead to the evangelistic encounter.

Much counseling today (as I said in the introduction) is not biblical because it is not so coupled with evangelism. Indeed, some theories of counseling are incompatible with evangelism. Freud's basic presupposition is that man is not responsible for his problems. His parents, grandma, the church, society in general may be responsible. If people are mentally ill, they are not responsible. You can't be held responsible for sickness. Ultimately this shift of responsibility puts the blame on God. That is what Freud's position really boils down to: blame your problem on God. The ethic of our contemporary society says don't punish an offender; don't jail him. Rather, get a sharp lawyer who will employ psychiatrists as "expert witnesses" to show how someone else is responsible. If the lawyer is clever, he will know how to refer to past environmental problems, traumatic experiences that his client suffered in boyhood, the common guilt of our whole society, etc., and will get him off. Then, instead of sending him to jail, the court will ship him off to some nice green place where he can lie around on the hillsides and watch the clouds scud by. Instead of working, other people on the outside can work to support him. And if the basic presupposition that man is not responsible for his sins is true, then we cannot evangelize in counseling. The gospel, instead, becomes a gospel of medicine. Instead of a Christian evangelist, the "patient" needs a medicine man, a witch doctor, or a psychiatrist. His "counselor" will be a man with a certain esoteric expertise.[6] Together with his specialized mumbo jumbo he has a bagfull of long terms to glue onto file folders, mystical ways of interpreting dreams, etc. Such mystical expertise *may* help, but, of course, he can *guarantee* nothing. Whatever else may be said, one thing is sure: there is nothing for the counselee to do with reference to God. Certainly the last thing a psychiatrist may do is to tell him that he is a sinner who needs to be forgiven. If people are not responsible for their attitudes and behavior, ultimately that means that they are not responsible to God and do not need to be evangelized.

A minister who was the chaplain of a state mental institution where the people of my congregation would have been sent, once told a group of local ministers:

> "These are morally neutral people down here. They can't help it. Their behavior in this institution may seem like sin, but behavior as blameworthy is taboo in a mental institution."

His position was clearly Freudian.

Well, what about Rogers? Carl Rogers doesn't think that man is all that bad. As a matter of fact, he thinks that people are responsible. His basic presupposition is that man has all of the resources in himself. Rogers says that "the more I deal with people, the more I realize that in the core of their personality there is really something solid and good. All we have to do is to dig down deeply enough and pull it out." That is why Rogers developed his reflective methodology. He wanted to help counselees to gain self-insight. The Rogerian counselor,

---

[6]Interestingly, psychiatrist E. Fuller Torrey concluded from a study of the goals and methods of witch doctors, in which he observed them at work around the world, "I found I was using the same mechanisms f >r helping my patients as they were." He continued, "Moreover, the techniques used by Western therapists are on exactly the same scientific plane as those used by witch doctors . . ." in "Psychiatry. It's Just Charisma," *Medical World News,* March 26, 1971.

therefore, is a pump primer, who helps the counselee to bring his own resources bubbling up like a fountain. When this happens, any man can solve his own problems. His sickness stems merely from not doing so. Man is autonomous and we must never violate that autonomy in any way. Because man has the resources in himself, counselors dare not impose the requirements of a sovereign God upon him. If you say to him, "You are a sinner, you need to repent of your sin and put your faith in the Lord Jesus Christ," you will violate that autonomy. You must not say that to him because to do so would mean bringing outside resources into the picture. Man would no longer be autonomous because this approach would make him very dependent upon God. And you, as a counselor, would have to become very authoritative; you could no longer merely reflect back to him his own ideas and thoughts. You would have to bring something authoritatively from the outside to him from God. You would have to insist that he submit to God. That is harder to do; it takes knowledge and courage and places a measure of responsibility upon the counselor as well. And, what happens to all of this basic goodness anyhow? If man is basically good in the core of his being, no Savior is needed. No Savior is possible with Freud; no Savior is needed with Rogers.

Biblical counseling, in contrast, assumes that problems stem from sin. All problems, without exception, organic and non-organic, go back to the Garden of Eden. The everyday non-organic problems, mistakes, broken relationships, personal hurts, running from problems and people, taking the course of least resistance rather than following the patterns of the Scriptures; all are due to sin. Biblical counselors assume that counselees are responsible for these problems. This fundamental assumption that man is a sinner makes evangelism an indispensible ingredient of counseling. A sinner is a responsible person who has offended a holy God by violating His righteous commandments. God alone can break the bondage of sin. It is not the kind of sin of which Mowrer speaks, which isn't really sin at all. By "sin," Mowrer means social unacceptability. All he needs to do is to teach and persuade the counselee how to fit into society. Whatever society's norms at a given time may be does not matter; today they are this and tomorrow they may be that. Whichever way society goes, Mowrer will teach you how to fit into it. The kind of sin of which Mowrer speaks is not sin at all. It is merely horizontally maladaptive behavior, and, therefore, Mowrer's approach does not require evangelism. Biblical counseling postulates an absolute unchanging standard of holiness and righteousness: the law of God. It is this law that man has broken, and it is against the God of that law that he has sinned.

Biblical counselors, then, must speak of forgiveness of sin. When people ask for a prescription for a pill or two, they tell them instead that they must lie down on the operating table for radical surgery. If a counselee is not a believer, he needs to hear the gospel. If he is a believer, the task of counseling is to help the counselee in the work of personal sanctification. That is what counseling is all about. And really, much of the counseling that is done with an unbeliever is evangelistic precounseling, a prelude to the actual work of counseling. Counseling cannot really begin in the fullest sense until a man becomes a believer in Jesus Christ; until the Spirit of God has entered his heart, opened his eyes to his sin, and has given to him the faith to believe the gospel. Truly successful counseling at a vital level of depth and permanence cannot be given to an unbeliever. Only a man who possesses the Spirit of God can understand spiritual things (I Cor. 2). Thus evangelism is not merely ancillary to but rather is *basic* to full-orbed Christian counseling.

The fruit of the Spirit (Gal. 5) is impossible apart from the Spirit, who alone produces it. You cannot structure the fruit of the Spirit into anyone's life. You can structure something that might look like it, or outwardly may seem to resemble it, but if you do so, what you get (in the long run) is always something other than the fruit of the Spirit. The "fruit" (of the Spirit) is the "result" of His work. The qualities mentioned in Galatians 5 are obtainable only as the result of the Spirit's work in a believer. That is what fruit means. The carefully chosen word "fruit"[7] also indicates that it cannot be manipulated into one's life. Fruit must grow. If you don't believe me, then—as someone once said—sit down some rainy afternoon and try to put together a watermelon. You cannot construct a cantaloupe, or a tomato, or a grape. Fruit must grow. Structure, if it is biblical, can provide the conditions for growth in a believer's life, but the fruit grows as a direct result of the work of the Spirit within.

But combining evangelism with counseling is dangerous, you say. There are all sorts of dangers, are there not? Yes, surely there is danger. For example, it is always possible that people will seek the help only to get over some hump in life and be insincere about the gospel. They may divorce the doing from the teaching. That is exactly what we find people doing in the time of Christ. "Where are the nine?" He asked. Ten lepers were healed, but only one was concerned about the Healer and His message. The other nine cared only about the doing, the work. The danger is there. But everything good is also dangerous. And such dangers did not stop Christ from combining the two. In counseling it is necessary to warn against this sort of thing. As far as possible, counselors must see to it that the person is sincere about what he is doing before God.

I would like to spend much time explaining what biblical counseling is all about, what we have called Nouthetic confrontation, but I have done that in print elsewhere. Let me conclude, therefore, by summing up what I have said.

Biblical counseling drives the Christian counselor to evangelism. It drives him to evangelism because as he talks to counselees whose whole lives are being destroyed by their

---

[7]Contrasted with the *works* of the flesh (vs. 19).

sinful ways and their guilt, he knows that the gospel is the basic answer to their problems. Problems that are the result of the entangling web of sin can never be solved apart from the gospel. What counselees need is Jesus Christ. No other approach is adequate; all other approaches are unbiblical. The counseling situation itself drives the pastor to evangelism. Consequently, I want to urge every one of you to understand that by your participation in and continuation of the "greater works," you must engage in the proclamation of the good news that "Christ died for our sins, according to the Scriptures, that he was buried and that he rose again on the third day, according to the Scriptures" (I Cor. 15:1-3).

Demon Possession and Counseling

The possession of human beings by demons (fallen angels, frequently also called "unclean spirits") is set forth in the Scriptures as an actual phenomenon and not, as has been alleged, a primitive explanation for madness, epilepsy or other mysterious afflictions and diseases. Nor is it merely a figure of speech. The Gospel writers, and notably Luke who was a physician (and, whose writings show what was probably a professional interest in the matter), were always careful to distinguish demon possession from sickness that is caused by disease or injury (cf. Luke 4:33-36, 40, 41; 6:17, 18; 9:1, 2; Matthew 4:12, 13; 10:1; Mark 1:32). Moreover, the record of the entrance of demons into a herd of swine is explicit evidence not only of the belief of the New Testament writers in the objectivity of demons, but also of their power to possess not only human beings, but animals as well.

While demon possession is everywhere distinguished from illness and madness as such in the Bible, it is nevertheless identified as one of several separate causes of both. Disease or injury (organic problems), sin and demon possession are viewed biblically as the three discrete causes of madness and illness. The symptoms of demon possession are closely related to maladies that result from various convulsive and perceptual disorders. In this regard, Matthew's words are especially interesting: "They brought to him all who suffered from various ailments and pains—demoniacs, epileptics and paralytics. And he healed them" (Matt. 4:24, Berkeley). According to this classification, demon possession is considered to be one among several possible causes of disturbing or painful ailments. When a demon is cast out, the formerly possessed person, therefore, is said to be "healed" (cf. *Supra,* Luke 8:2, etc.) or "in his right mind" (Mark 5:15). The healing or righting of the mind clearly refers to the obvious symptomatic effects of exorcism, not to the alleviation of disease or madness as the cause of such symptoms.

115

Symptoms of madness and illness due to demon possession include convulsions (Mark 9:18, 20, 26, cf. Berkeley translation), self-injury (Luke 4:35; Mark 9:18, 22), bizarre behavior (Luke 8:27), isolation and withdrawal (Luke 8:27—demons are thought to have been called "unclean" perhaps because of their association with ceremonially unclean tombs[1]), and deafness and dumbness (Mark 9:17-27). When Jesus was accused of possessing a demon, he was at the same time declared to be insane (cf. John 7:20; 8:48ff; 10:20, 21; Mark 3:21, 22, 30).[2] In our day, when we have begun to understand that the same perceptual symptoms that lead to bizarre (insane) behavior may arise from various distortions of bodily chemistry resulting from the use of hallucinogenic drugs, from significant sleep loss or from bodily malfunctions, there should be no difficulty in believing that bizarre behavior may also stem from other causes, including demon possession. Moreover, in a day in which the effects of hypnotism are so well known that its use as a therapeutic and anesthetic technique has met scientific approval, surely there should be no *a priori* arguments raised against the possibility of the control of one personality by another.

But is demon possession an obscure question, hardly worth discussion? Recent wide-spread interest in the matter has made discussion of the question mandatory. Far from being an isolated issue infrequently alluded to in the Scriptures, demon possession is mentioned 52 times in the Gospels, and, in addition, there are references to it in the Book of Acts. Why should this subject occupy so large a proportion of space in the Bible? There is good reason. In His earthly ministry,

---

[1]However, it would seem plausible that the designation has to do with their own sin. By designating them as *unclean* spirits, the Scriptures plainly distinguish them from clean spirits (the angels who did not sin, and preeminently the Holy Spirit).

[2]Thus showing a clear association of demonic possession with madness. N. B., the association was that of cause and effect; the two were not confused, but differentiated.

Jesus Christ directly confronted (and was confronted by) Satan's kingdom (Daniel's world empire). In this confrontation, simultaneously the Evil One was attempting to thwart the redemptive work of Christ, and the Savior was revealing His messianic glory as the King at whose coming Daniel's world kingdom would be shattered. This confrontation was manifested outwardly mainly by Christ's exorcism of demons. The comments of the demons who regularly recognized Jesus as "the Son of God," indicate this, and also that they feared His ministry as the beginning of the end of their kingdom (Matt. 8:29). Jesus rejoiced over the expulsion of demons by His disciples as the "fall of Satan" from "heaven" (Luke 10:17, 18), and directly related the casting out of demons to the coming of the "kingdom (or empire) of God" and to the "binding" of Satan (Matt. 12:28, 29; Mark 3:20-27).[3] Thus the frequent reference to demon possession in connection with Christ's ministry of exorcism is not incidental, but central to the Gospel writers' purpose. It is to be understood in eschatological terms as evidence of the messianic identity of Jesus, who came not only to preach about the kingdom (Mark 1:14, 15) predicted by Daniel (chapter 7), but also to establish it (Matt. 28:18, 19; Acts 1:3).

Paul predicted that extensive demonic activity would characterize the last days of the Old Testament era (I Tim. 4:1). It was during this period that John predicted that Satan's rage would be intensified because he had been cast down upon the earth (Rev. 12:13). There is reason to believe that this was fulfilled in the overlapping period of time dealt with in the Book of Revelation. There are good reasons also for believing that when Satan was bound (Rev. 20) and bruised (Rom.

---

[3]It is strange that some who think (rightly) that Satan is bound today, seem also to think that his minions are not similarly restricted. To postulate widespread demon possession in our time is to fail to understand biblical eschatology. To "bind" and "hinder" Satan is obviously to limit his activities, whether carried on directly by him or indirectly by means of his demonic forces.

118

16:20) by the full coming of the kingdom that this short intervening period was curtailed.[4] This curtailment or restraint (II Thess. 2) upon Satanic power and influence necessarily involved the virtual cessation of such activity by his demonic forces. This accounts for the rare incidence, if not the entire absence, of demonic possession in modern times. It is possible, of course, that demonic activity is still being curtailed *as the gospel penetrates* new and previously untouched communities of the world.

Significantly, at the end of the millennial era (which extends from the ascension of Christ to a point shortly prior to His second coming) Satan will be released to "deceive" the Gentiles again as he did throughout the Old Testament era (cf. Revelation 20). During the present "times of the Gentiles" the empire of God has been spreading (like a stone growing into a large mountain) throughout the world so that some from every tribe, tongue and nation shall become part of His empire. Looking forward to these times, Zechariah predicted that the "unclean spirits" would be removed (Zech. 13:2, cf. NASV). The present restraint that Paul declared would be imposed upon Satan (II Thess. 2:1-22; n.b. vss. 9-22) prohibits wholesale "deceit" by direct demonic activity. Yet Paul, with John (Rev. 20), predicted that this restraint will be lifted just before the return of Christ, thus bringing about another brief period of intensive demonic influence (cf. also Revelation 16:14 with II Thessalonians 2:9-12 and Revelation 20:7-10) that may be characterized by renewed incidents of demonic possession. The eschatological timetable and the nature of the present millennial era adequately account for the failure of the modern church to encounter demon possession as a common daily contemporary phenomenon.

Christians have differed about the fact of demon possession

---

[4]Cf. Jay Adams, *The Time Is At Hand,* Presbyterian and Reformed Publishing Co., Nutley: 1970, pp. 17, 22 ff., 42 ff., 83 ff.

today, and indeed some missionaries have cited instances of supposed possession. John L. Nevius, in his classic, *Demon Possession* (recently republished), has set forth the most systematic statement of this position. Yet the book, like most of the accounts by individuals, is unsatisfying, since it tends to accept pagan testimony and categories along with personal experience as the standard for determining what is a case of demon possession rather than applying biblical criteria. Such an approach to the matter may not be accepted. An adequate study of the biblical data has not yet appeared.

Modern Pentecostalists and others have gone beyond the Scriptures in claiming to be able to distinguish a second phenomenon that they call "demon *oppression*" from demon *possession*. Demon oppression is said to represent a strong and even controlling demonic influence over Christians. In such cases, intensive prayer or even exorcism may be necessary, as in cases of actual possession. In fact, while zealously distinguished from possession, the symptoms said to be connected with the phenomenon of oppression seem to be nearly identical. This distinct category takes its origin from a misunderstanding of Acts 10:38, where part of the work of Christ's ministry is described as "healing all that were oppressed by the Devil." However, there is no warrant for supposing that this summary statement looking back upon Christ's ministry as a whole refers to anything other than the work of casting out demons about which the Gospels speak continually (and exclusively). It would be strange, indeed, for Luke thus to introduce in the Book of Acts a brand new element of Christ's ministry about which he and all of the Gospel writers were utterly silent. The fact that this is a general summary rather than an explicit statement about a specific and distinct sort of Satanic influence is clear from the use of the word "devil" rather than the word "demon." Here all of the individual cases of possession by specific demons are viewed collectively as the work of the evil one who stands behind them. The term *katadunasteuo* means "to oppress, dominate or exploit," and may be applied aptly to the whole Satanic enterprise of demonic exploitation, domination and control of possessed persons.

There is no biblical reason to think that demonic possession (or oppression) can occur in the life of a Christian. The simultaneous presence of the Holy Spirit, who dwells within every true child of God, and an "unclean spirit" is impossible. This is clear from the utter antithesis of the two noted in Mark 3:20-30. Here also (3:30) Jesus warns that it is unforgivable blasphemy to attribute the work of the Holy Spirit to a demon.

This, and the other considerations about the cessation of demonic activity mentioned above has important implications for Christian counselors. More and more frequently failure in counseling has been attributed to the fact of demon possession. In the light of biblical theological eschatology, it would seem that a heavy burden of proof belongs to the one who retreats to demon possession as the cause of bizarre behavior. Counselors, in this present era, have every reason to expect that the cause of the problems with which they will deal in counseling will be other than demonic possessions. In more instances than one, I have seen incompetence in counseling excused by resorting to the diagnosis of possession by demons, sometimes with very damaging effects. If, for example, one's problems are the result of his own sinful behavior, and they are instead charged to possession by an evil spirit, those problems may be complicated rather than solved by efforts to cast out the demon. Not only will such efforts fail, leading often to hopelessness and despair, but they will shift the focus from the counselee's own responsibility. He will be viewed as a helpless victim rather than as a guilty sinner. The results are likely only to confirm him in his sinful life patterns, and the frustrations of counselors who are reduced to fruitless prayer and pity are likely to encourage deeper depression and even despair. It would seem vital to effective biblical counseling to presuppose that a counselee is free from such direct demonic influence in this era.

Pagan and Jewish ideas that demons were the shades or souls of departed wicked men (cf. Josephus, *The Wars of the Jews,* 7:6:3) must be rejected as foreign to biblical teaching. However, the Septuagint uses the word demon to describe pagan gods, as Paul also seems to do in I Corinthians 10:20, 21 and possibly I Timothy 4:1 (cf. also Psalm 106:37, Berkeley, NASV). The connection between pagan idolatry, demonic deception (and possession) is not hard to see.

You Are Your Brother's Counselor

The subject you assigned me is "Christian Faith and Counseling." I was asked to speak about counseling during this series because recently I have been doing a good bit of counseling and speaking about it. I asked if I could choose a different topic for a change, but the invitation committee said "No, you must talk about counseling." In asking, I thought that perhaps I might discuss a more relaxed issue, but the more I pondered what to say, the more I think the committee was right in insisting on the subject; today counseling is a very crucial matter. So I am not only willing to talk about counseling, but I am happy to do so. However, I must warn you that what I am going to say involves *you*, every one of you. In fact, in order to stress this I have taken the liberty to change the title of the series to "You Are Your Brother's Counselor."

To begin with, I'd like to give you a word association test. You know how a word association test works, don't you? I shall speak a word and you must note what that word immediately brings to mind. Let's try a dry run; are you ready? Here's your word: "dog." Some of you thought of fleas, others of bones, etc. That's the way it works. All right now, this time is for real. Here is the word: "counseling." Now what comes to mind? Although I'm not going to ask you to do so, it might have been interesting to take a poll of your thought associations; but you know what came to your mind first. Perhaps it was some experience you had in counseling and you pictured yourself sitting there sweating it out. Possibly you conjured up the vision of a couch, somebody lying on it and a bearded one behind his head listening to the man on the couch drone on. Maybe you could see in your mind's eye a youthful counselor behind a desk making unhuh sounds.

---

[1]Part of the Westminster Lectures delivered in 1971 to the joint congregations of Orthodox Presbyterian Churches in North Jersey (revised).

You could practically hear his grunts and groans. Now and then he would repeat the counselee's words, never coming to grips with the problem by giving advice or making suggestions. You may have thought of someone in dire straits, very seriously in trouble, sitting in a group therapy session. Or there may have come to your mind the rolling green lawns of some spacious mental institution. Well, whatever it was, some image appeared that may frequently come to mind whenever you hear the word "counseling."

But have you ever thought—that association (whatever it was) is either a Christian association or it is not? That is a very crucial point, isn't it? You may have in mind a non-Christian concept of counseling. I find that most people do, and it is precisely for that reason that I think that it is important to discuss this question to try to decide what the Bible says about counseling, so that when you take the word association test again (or perhaps the deeper test of an actual need for counseling) you will think of counseling as God wants you to.

There are many mistaken notions about counseling. You might say, for instance, that counseling is for other people, it's not for me. But if you as a Christian say that, you are wrong; you are very wrong. Every last one of us needs Christian counseling—literally, *every* one of us. God says so, so the fact is indisputable. That is one matter that we must consider in this lecture. But the reason you may have said "Well, counseling is not for me," or, "I'm glad there has been no need for me ever to be counseled, and I hope that there, never will be," probably is because your basic picture of counseling is so distorted and unbiblical.

Let us try to straighten out a few things at the outset. The first question we need to ask is, what is Christian counseling? Is it in any way akin to the Rogerian reflective counseling which has so permeated the practice of Christian ministers, social workers and other Christian workers? You know what Rogerian counseling is like, don't you? That's the kind of counseling I mentioned before where you say unhuh and reflect back the counselee's every thought in words similar to his own. It is all done with mirrors. The picture, remember, involves a counselor sitting behind a desk (or at a table or in a circle) with a verbal mirror. The counselee comes in, sits down and begins to talk. He says, "I have a problem." And the counselor says, "I see; you feel that you are in some sort of difficulty." "Yeah, that's it," says the counselee. "You see," he continues, "I love two girls, Mary and Susan." The counselor says, "I see that you feel torn two ways." "Exactly!" responds the counselee. "Now my problem is," he continues (getting to the core of the question), "which one should I marry?" And at that point the crucial test comes for the counselor, because he has been asked the direct question:

"Which one should I marry? Give me some help. Help me to decide whether Mary is the one or Susan is the one, or whether neither of them is for me. Give me some help. Please tell me how to go about finding out which one is the right one."

But here the Rogerian founders, for all that he may say is, "I see, you feel that I can help you to decide which one you should wed." He may change the word "marry" to "wed" or something else, but the exact words are of no importance, for in whatever he says he will merely try to repeat the question and say the same thing. He will stress what the counselee "feels" and avoid what he says. And right about that point is when the counselee ought to get up and leave, because, you see, there hasn't been any counseling going on at all. There has been no help because *no advice has been given.* Counsel, if biblical, necessarily involves giving advice from the Word of God.[2]

All the while, the Word of God has been lying on the desk

---

[2]For a biblical understanding of counseling, cf. Isaiah 40:13 (Berkeley, NASV) where counseling is defined in synonomous parallelism as directive instruction.

in plain sight but closed because Carl Rogers says (and here is his basic presupposition with which every Christian must take issue) that man has within himself all the resources that he needs to solve his problems. That is a fundamentally non-Christian presupposition. And it is because Rogers believes this that he advises counselors (quite authoritatively and directively) to act in the same way. In very strong terms, he and those who follow him insist that counselors must never violate the personality of the individual by giving advice, telling a person what to do, or persuading him to take a certain course of action. With the solemnity of a divine oracle, Rogerians command us never to use an authoritative revelation from the outside. We must not urge counselees to study and obey this infallible Word of God. Even if the counselor knows that God prohibits marriage with Susan because she is an unbeliever, he may not say so. Down inside of the man is all that he really needs. A counselor helps others only by using his verbal mirror. By means of it he enables them to see what they themselves are already thinking. He is permitted perhaps to sharpen or focus the thought a bit, but never to inject a foreign idea, for the counselee himself will soon come to his own adequate solutions. He has the resources and there is no need for outside help. That is the basic Rogerian view.

Christians can have none of this, because they believe that every person who is born into this world is born a sinner who is in desperate need of something from the outside. He is in desperate need of the regenerating power of the Holy Spirit to give him new life in order that he may believe in Jesus Christ as his Savior. Once he believes, he needs the Word of God to direct him how to change his life in every way. And he needs the continued power of the Holy Spirit to enable him to effect those changes. All of that is an outside job; none of it comes from the man himself; all of it comes from God. The doctrines of grace are diametrically opposed to the principles of Rogers. And so if his basic presupposition falls, the whole system upon which it is based and out of which it grows must collapse with it. Instead of doing it with mirrors, a Christian counselor will help the counselee to make his decision about Mary or Susan on the basis of biblical principles, which he may have to explain to the counselee. Counseling involves both instruction and persuasion from the Word of God.

What about the couch; what about Freudian psychoanalysis? The psychoanalyst sits where he cannot be seen (there really isn't much purpose for that except that Freud began counseling that way because he didn't like to look at the counselee, so he put him on a couch and sat behind his head where he wouldn't have to look him in the eye), taking a few notes now and then, making a few inquiries, but generally listening to ideas freely associated in a stream of consciousness pattern. The counselee talks about whatever comes to his mind, and that leads to something else, and that to another, and that to a third and so it goes. It is something like an hour-long association test of the sort that I gave you at the outset. And after a long, long while (possibly years) of this, of talking about dreams and so on, perhaps the analyst will at last consider himself to be in a position to begin to do something for the counselee. But first he must go way back into the past, hopefully as close as possible to prenatal years. When finally the counselee has told all, maybe (just maybe) something can be done for him. He is interested in all of this information about the past because he believes that the things that happened to him as a child made the counselee what he now is. His church, for instance, shaped him wrongly and gave him problems, or his parents treated him traumatically by spanking him and forbidding him to do various things, thus building within him a superego or conscience that is far too strict. This conscience now is the source of his difficulties. When he discovers just who did what, the blame can be placed where it really belongs (certainly not on the counselee), on these other people and on society in general as it has affected him.

The reason for that treasure hunt into the past is that

Freud's basic presupposition is that man is not responsible for what he does. Man is not responsible; other forces or other people are responsible. Of course, there is an inherent contradiction there, you see, since on this basis there are a number of people who are responsible for what the counselee did wrong *until* the counselor gets *them* on the couch; then, presumably, they are no longer responsible. It is amazing how a couch can remove responsibility! But that is an internal contradiction that we are not supposed to notice.[3] Nevertheless, somebody else is always held responsible for whatever I do wrong. Whenever I act in a strange way or whenever I behave immorally, or whenever I get into somebody's hair, I am entitled to blame my behavior on someone else. Our courts and our society (indeed, all aspects of our culture) are permeated with this kind of thinking. And in many instances, it is not even the individual that is said to be sick any more; we now throw it back another step; we live in a sick *society,* we live in a sick *world.* Everything is sick, sick, sick. A sick man or society is not held responsible and urged to assume those responsibilities. People make allowances for the sick; they let sick persons off the hook.

Then there is a third view: the Skinnerian view, growing rapidly in our time. Skinner has been followed, amplified and modified by various people who are writing today in the behaviorist tradition. Skinner believes in a view of behavior modification that says that man is simply an animal and that we must treat him as such. Man has all of the resources in himself, says Rogers; man is not responsible for what he does, says Freud; he is but an animal, says Skinner. And if he is but an animal, let us manipulate him, let us mold him, let us train him in whatever way that we want. "All that we have to do is to put him in my Skinner box," says Skinner. "I put a rat in a Skinner box and I can train him to do whatever I want; all

---

[3] Actually you can see that on this basis no one is ever really responsible; the entire idea of responsibility is destroyed.

that we need for man is a larger more complex box." The way Skinner changes men is akin to the Communist brainwashing techniques. For Skinner and company, all that the counselor must do is to zap the counselee with an electric current from behind (punishment) and hold a carrot out in front (reward) and he can teach the counselee to run any maze that he wishes.

Because Skinner considers man to be nothing more than an animal, he fails to see the believer as a child of God and he refuses to acknowledge that man was created in the image of God. Man is, for all intents and purposes, little more than a very complex rat. Obviously, the denial of the image of God in man leads to the use of manipulative techniques that bypass persuasion, conviction, conversion, and the Spirit and His Word.

Christians, who also believe in the biblical concept of reward and punishment, nevertheless regard rewards and punishments quite differently because of their views of man and God. Skinner's basic presupposition that man is only another animal means that he too has devised a methodology growing out of this assumption and that, therefore, cannot be ecclectically borrowed and used by Christian counselors.[4]

Yet all of these views have found their way into the counseling done by Christians. All of these views are behind the kinds of methodologies that may have come to your mind when you thought about counseling. But not one of them is based upon a Christian view of counseling and, for this reason,

---

[4]Eg., James Dobson's book, *Dare to Discipline,* Tyndale House, Wheaton: 1970 (which has become the current classic in some Christian circles), while placing a needed emphasis upon discipline by structure, is based upon this non-Christian ideology. It is basically a godless humanistic book. The discipline advocated is behavioristic (Skinnerian). According to Dobson, a child is to be "trained" as one would train his dog. The methodology does not differ. The presupposition (not stated, but underlying the book) is that man is but another animal. There is no place for the work of the Holy Spirit in conversion or sanctification. Change takes place strictly on the horizontal level.

every one of them must be rejected. Instead of those views of counseling, the Scriptures present another view that is very important for Christians to understand. There is a word that occurs in many places in the New Testament that speaks of biblical counseling. The Greek word is *nouthesia* (verb, *noutheteo*). That word is a word with which we are going to have to become better acquainted. *Nouthesia,* in the full-blown sense of that word as it appears in the New Testament, is not something that we run into day by day in our churches; but we ought to.

What does the word mean? *Nouthesia* has at least three elements in it. They are always there though one or the other of these might be uppermost in a given context. Always there is the idea of something wrong that God wants changed in the person who is confronted. Secondly, *nouthesia* speaks of making an attempt to effect the change by the use of appropriate verbal means. Thirdly, the change is contemplated for the benefit of the one who is confronted; his welfare is always in view. *Nouthesia* contains the idea of a deepseated interest in the person, a loving concern for him. That is why it is used consistently in the New Testament in familial contexts. The family relationship shines through. In that family passage in Ephesians 6:4, fathers are told not to "provoke their children to wrath" either by arbitrarily overemphasizing their authority in the home or by neglecting their authority in the home. (You know, you can provoke your children to wrath most easily by not being consistent and by not enforcing rules. By your doing one thing today and something quite different tomorrow, and on the third day doing something else, a child eventually gets angered, gives up and says, "What's the use?" He throws up his hands and says, "I might as well go my own way; you can never depend on what my parents may do." So you can provoke your children to wrath not just by a heavy hand, but also by a hand that is too light and shifty. What the child needs to know is that he can depend upon getting the *same* punishment *every* time he commits the same offense.) In contrast Paul urges fathers to bring up their children in the nurture and *nouthetic confrontation* of the Lord. He means, "Confront your children in the deep love of *nouthesia* the way the Lord does when he confronts you as His children." That is the picture of Christian counseling. The word for counseling, *nouthesia*, speaks of confronting a person when there is something wrong in his life in order to change him by verbal means so that the person himself is able to walk more closely with Jesus Christ.

It is interesting to relate these three elements in the Word to the three non-Christian views that I have mentioned. Each element of the biblical notion strikes at the heart of the unbiblical one. *First*, if there is something that God declares to be wrong in an individual and about which he is to be confronted, it is obvious that the counselee is held responsible for what is wrong in his life. Out goes Freud. *Secondly*, if verbal means like warning, advising, instructing, admonishing, exhorting or encouraging, are used in order to effect the change, clearly God expects a Christian counselor to bring something from the outside into the counseling situation. Out goes Rogers. And *thirdly*, if all men are looked upon as in the image of God, and God, with loving concern, considers those who have trusted in Jesus Christ as His dear children, and deep care and concern of one brother for another is to be manifested in *nouthesia*, Christian counselors cannot merely manipulate counselees by the shock/carrot method as though they were animals. So, out goes Skinner. It is very interesting that the three prevailing views of our time so radically disagree with the three elements in the biblical concept of counseling.

What is the place of such counseling in a Christian church? It may not, first of all, be used as a substitute for preaching. A number of clergymen have tried to substitute Rogerian counseling, or Freudian psychoanalysis, or group therapy, or half a dozen other variations or conglomerations of these for preaching because they claim that preaching is extremely ineffective. There are even conservatives today who believe that preaching is on its way out. They have said so openly. Of course, it is strange that today, when more people are getting up on soap boxes, before TV cameras, out on the streets, as well as everywhere else, that people should declare that preaching is passe. It is very strange, indeed, that they should choose this unlikely time and place to say it. Nevertheless, we must declare with God's Word that preaching can never be passe. Preaching has been ordered by God, and it will continue until the Lord Jesus Christ returns. I am not talking about all forms of preaching, of course. There are types of preaching that we all would rather see disappear as rapidly as possible. But preaching of a biblical sort, adapted to the man in the pew in his language, preaching of the kind that we find in the Scriptures, will always remain.[5] The Word of God must be proclaimed.

So counseling can never replace preaching, though some have made very strong attempts to substitute it for preaching. Nor should preaching be turned into mass counseling as Fosdick attempted to do. Fosdick thought that preaching ought essentially to be counseling on a broad scale. He tried to counsel his whole congregation from the pulpit in the way that he counseled them individually in the office. While preaching cannot be divorced from counseling, neither should the two be confused. Preaching is larger than counseling; it involves more than counseling. Preaching is the official public proclamation of the Word of God. Whereas counseling is largely remedial, addressing itself to problems that have arisen in individual lives, preaching is often preventative, dealing with potential problems by seeking to guide the Christian away from life shoals. The counseling note will always be present in good preaching; indeed in *good* preaching it cannot be avoided, but preaching is not counseling. Preaching includes the exposition of the Scriptures and there must be exposition

---

[5] For more on this subject, viz. Jay Adams, *Pulpit Speech,* Presbyterian and Reformed Publishing Co., Nutley: 1971, Ch. 1.

in biblical counseling, but the *emphasis* in each differs. So when Fosdick or Norman Vincent Peale try to turn preaching into counseling, they distort preaching and counseling as well. Counseling is not a substitute for preaching, but biblical counseling fits together with biblical preaching; because they are both biblical, the two always go together.[6]

In the first chapter of Colossians, Paul speaks about proclaiming the Word of God and the mystery that had been hidden in past ages. This mystery has now been manifested. The riches of God's glory will be given to the Gentiles, as well as to the Jews. This glory was exhibited in Jesus Christ. Paul then sums up what he has said in verse 28: "We proclaim him (Christ) nouthetically confronting every man and teaching every man with all wisdom that we may present every man, complete in Christ." See how the two go together? Teaching and nouthetic confrontation are wedded. They are two sides of a whole; two sides of a coin. They must be kept together in order to proclaim Christ properly. You can't really have the one without the other. Preaching involves the public proclamation of the Word, whereas counseling also involves a private proclamation: "we proclaim *(katangello)* him . . ." Both involve proclamation. Both center upon Jesus Christ. Preaching raises questions, makes points, convicts men of sin. Such preaching often drives one to the pastor's study for counseling. Look at John the Baptist. Notice the results of his preaching (Luke, chapter 3). John came preaching the baptism of repentance for forgiveness of sins (Luke 3:3). He preached judgment for sin. He demanded that converts bring forth fruits in keeping with repentance (Luke 3:8). What happened?

---

[6]The nonbiblical counseling of Fosdick, Peale, and others that they substituted for preaching, stands far off from preaching. Biblical counseling, in contrast, overlaps biblical preaching; the two are not widely separated. Many of the problems in previous discussions of the subject have not really been pertinent to our discussion, since the discussion did not center around the relationship of preaching to a *biblical* form of counseling.

136

The multitudes began to question him, asking, "What shall we do?" (Luke 3:10). That kind of preaching brought them to John for personal counseling. Insipid preaching that fails to stress hell and repentance and the necessity for changed lives has no such results. They said to John, "What must we do? We've heard you preach about repentance and changed lives, but specifically what does this mean in our lives?" They came for advice, help and personal counsel from him. To some of them who were tax gatherers, John counseled: "Collect no more than what you have been ordered" (Luke 3:12). He did not reflect their words. He did not go all the way back into their past history to their cribs. Instead, he dealt with the issues that were pertinent and gave them clear direction from God: "Collect no more than what you have been ordered to." In other words, repentance demands a change: you can no longer steal. You must now live by God's commandments. Some soldiers questioned him, saying, "What about us; what shall *we* do?" He said to them, "Do not take any money by force, and do not accuse anyone falsely, and be content with your wages." John's counsel centered upon the abuses that were prevalent among the tax collectors and the soldiers of that day. So it is evident that preaching and counseling paralleled one another in the ministry of John.

Take as another example the story of Nicodemus. The public preaching and healing ministry of Jesus raised questions among the Pharisees. They wanted answers to those questions, so they sent Nicodemus to talk with Jesus at night.[7] Nicodemus was particularly troubled in his own heart about Jesus, and since he was unable to reach conclusions about Him on his own, doubtless he readily agreed to find out the answers they (and he) sought. The counseling session that resulted is recorded in John 3.

---

[7]Cf. John 3:1, "a man from the Pharisees." Jesus addressed Nicodemus both individually (3:3, 5, 7, 11; note singular "you") and in his representative capacity (3:7, 11, 12; note plural "you").

In response to Peter's great Pentecostal sermon (Acts 2) the listeners were pricked in their hearts and said, "What must we do?" They asked for help. Paul often received the same response to his preaching (cf. Acts 19:18). Again and again in the Scriptures, the right kind of preaching leads to counseling. The two go together: preaching initiates counseling; counseling is the natural followup to effective preaching.

As a preacher sits face to face with another individual and learns to recognize concretely the human needs of which the Bible speaks, as he sees how sinful living rips life into shreds, his preaching cannot help but be affected. He will preach differently than when he was in seminary. Counseling, then, is fundamental to good preaching. A counseling preacher reads the Scriptures with a heavy heart because of the broken lives of the man and wife who just left the study, but he also preaches with triumph when he sees the grace of God bring harmony and joy to destroyed lives. If he truly is a nouthetic counselor, he weeps with those who weep and rejoices with those who rejoice (cf. Paul's words in Acts 20:30: "Night and day, for a period of three years, I did not cease to confront *each one* of you nouthetically *with tears*"). Deep involvement and concern grow through counseling. When a preacher counsels in that way day in and day out, it affects his preaching. The preaching takes on an air of authenticity and congregations reverberate to it. They know that he is bowling down their alley. They think: "He knows; he knows *me.*"

So, the two go together; that is the picture through all of the New Testament. In Ephesus, where Paul was more of a pastor than a missionary, where, as far as we know, he spent a longer period of time than anywhere else, night and day for the whole period of three years he did not cease to confront each member of his congregation nouthetically. These words indicate that such activity must have been a very large part of his ministry. How could he have said so more plainly? We think of Paul as an evangelist, primarily, not primarily as a pastor; yet it is he who summed up his ministry in Colossians

1:28 with those two words: nouthetic confrontation and teaching. Side by side they stand as the two essentials. Nouthetic confrontation never takes the place of preaching, but finds its place side by side with it, the two affecting one another as parts of the one work of presenting men complete to Christ.

Who needs counseling? If Christian counseling is *nouthesia,* then Christian counseling is a very large part of the fellowship of God's people. Who needs it? Look again at Colossians 1:28. There Paul says, "We proclaim him, nouthetically confronting *every* man and teaching *every* man with all wisdom that we may present *every* man complete in Christ." Remember, as I said before, we *all* need counseling. Every one of us needs counseling from another at some time in his life. Paul confronted "*every* man." Acts 20:31 says "each one" was confronted. If there is a Christian who has never been confronted nouthetically by another, he is to be pitied; for doubtless he lacks something. If somewhere along the way he does not receive Christian confrontation, when he is ready to face Jesus Christ he will be incomplete. You notice Paul speaks not only of nouthetically confronting every man, but also of teaching every man. Certainly we believe that Christian instruction is important and essential for every believer. Indeed, we believe that we get all too little Christian instruction. We need it week after week; we need it daily. Christian instruction is essential. But along with it in the same verse Paul speaks also of nouthetically confronting *every* man. He says they *both* are essential in order to present *every* man complete in Christ. Yet, have we looked on our activities in the church in that way?

You may say,

"But counseling as you have described it is different from what I first thought about when you gave the word association test. I never thought that every Christian needs counseling. I thought counseling was for people whose marriage was on the rocks, or who were deeply depressed, or who had ceased functioning or something like that."

Certainly those are valid occasions for counseling. But there is a great deal more than that involved in *nouthesia*. The kind of nouthetic confrontation (or counseling) that the Bible envisions is something far richer, far more important, far more basic than merely taking care of crisis issues in which lives have been torn to shreds. It also involves the care of persons before their problems ever reach that stage. That is what God provided for in the concept of counseling that we see in the Scriptures. This kind of counseling should keep marriages from ever reaching the breaking point. Two members of a congregation cannot sit on the opposite sides of a congregation and not speak to one another for six years if nouthetic confrontation is going on. *Nouthesia* rarely allows problems to grow that large. It does not wait until the elders resort to fisticuffs at a session meeting in order to step in.

The kind of counseling that the Bible talks about is a continual daily ongoing process. It is something that is happening all of the time, something that is taking place consistently and regularly. Everybody, it seems, gets involved in it somehow, somewhere. As a matter of fact, in the Scriptures all of the saints of God are to become involved in the work of nouthetically confronting one another, as we shall see later. The pastor does become involved in a particular way, as we have seen. But for now, notice that nouthetic counseling exerts a far richer, far greater, far more pervasive influence than other modes of counseling. It is essential to the very fellowship of the saints, to the health of the individual congregation and to power in conducting the ongoing program of the people of God. *Nouthesia* brings people together and welds them together. It provides a method for handling problems that unites instead of driving apart. It is God's provision for every one of us, and every church.

Don't you agree that such activity is rare in American Christian churches? Instead, we see all sorts of loose ends, all sorts of problems between people, all sorts of headaches and heartaches and troubles that are sapping the strength of the church of God. Day after day, week after week, the strength of the church seems to be waning. What is tearing it down? Not so much the external attacks as the internal failures. Parents and children who do not get along, husbands and wives who talk only on a superficial level, and feuding church members are squeezing life and power from the church. This is tearing down the Christian church more than anything else. Heresy has made a terrible onslaught on the Christian church, it is true. But why don't Reformed, orthodox Christians who are free from such heresy have more power? Why don't they forge ahead? One reason is that they are so hung up on problems between each other. And one major reason why they are so hung up is because they fail to do mutual counseling.

The daily solving of problems among all of us, all of the time, in a loving warm Christian manner is virtually unknown. But a fellowship among the saints on a deeper level than we now know, is possible because it is commended to us in the New Testament. It is not just in extreme cases, then, that counseling is needed, but, of greater importance, it is counseling that will keep the extremes from occurring that we need. Counseling in such cases, where difficulties are dealt with at an early time, will keep matters from deteriorating.

Everyone needs such counseling; even the disciples needed it. Jesus counseled them daily. And when He left them, He assured them, "I am not leaving you alone, but I am going to send you another Counselor (the word "comforter" ought to be translated "counselor"), another counselor who is just like me." If they needed that kind of counseling, so do we.[8]

You should seek counseling whenever you find you are unable to solve your problems alone. Whenever you find that by the normal and ordinary means of study and discussion, seeking reconciliation (or whatever the objective may be) cannot be achieved, you should go quickly to your pastor or to some

---

[8]Much more could be said about the total life counseling that Jesus provided for His disciples.

other Christian brother and ask for help. You should ask him
for advice, or ask him to step between you and the other person to help to bring the two of you back together again, or
for whatever help is necessary to solve the problem. There are
times when every one of us needs counseling, and God has
provided for these needs by the practice of biblical *nouthesia,*
about which I must now say a good bit more.

We have been trying to stress that all believers in Jesus
Christ need counseling. Colossians 1:28 and Acts 20:31 em-
phaisze this point. Those two verses make it plain that such
counseling is not just for a few people who happen to run
amuck, or for a few people who get off to a bad start, or for
a few people whose parents treated them traumatically, but
rather that this counseling is for all Christians. God, in His
providence, has provided *nouthesia* for every one of His children. The definition of the biblical term sketches a picture of
counseling that is much broader and more pervasive than the
usual picture. There is a particular specialized counseling ministry given to the pastor above and beyond the counseling
ministry that is expected of others, but this ministry is not
confined to the clergy alone. If *nouthesia* is something that is
going on all of the time, and if the minister is involved in it
(as Paul was) day and night throughout the whole of his ministry, then this all-pervasive *nouthesia* is a possibility.

But the pastor cannot do the work alone. And this is what
the New Testament record clearly shows—Paul did not do it
alone either. Paul expected every Christian to join him in this
work. The picture described in the New Testament shows that
God expects an all-pervasive contact among the people of
God, contact where brethren are brought close together in
Christ. This picture is of people who have come to know one
another deeply and intimately in the things of the Lord. They
have developed such a deep concern for one another that Paul
says they are members of the same body. When one weeps,
the rest weep with him; when one rejoices, the rest also rejoice. There ought to be a kind of spontaneous reverberation

among the people of God; but that is a concept that we don't know much about today. When something happens, it should either rock or bless the *whole* church.

That usually is not how things are. We ought to be like the springs in the old mattresses. You know how the salesman demonstrates the superiority of his newer product by contrasting it with an old coil spring mattress. He shoves down on one coil and way over there on the other side of the mattress a glass of water spills. But if you buy the product with its independent springs, the salesman shows you that you can push here and over there, or almost anywhere, and you can't even spill a glass of water filled to the top unless you push on the coil directly beneath it. Well, that's the kind of situation we have in our churches today; push out a family (or a Christian) here or there and it hardly affects the congregation. The water doesn't even ripple! Others may not know that anything has happened at all. And it really doesn't matter too much, does it? Well, it should! A Christian congregation ought to be like that old coil spring, where if you touch any part it affects the whole. That is the biblical concept of the church of Jesus Christ.

This unity comes hard, however. <u>It comes only to those who are willing to pay the price, and that price is to become vitally involved in each other's lives.</u> *Nouthesia* demands that very sort of involvement. The Scriptures speak of provoking one another to love and of stimulating one another to good works. This involves regular daily contact on a level of depth.

We saw that involvement and loving concern was a prime task of the evangelical pastor. A large share of his pastoral ministry was concerned with *nouthesia*. But going a step further, let us see from the Word of God how the biblical stress is not only on the pastor's getting involved in this work, but also upon every member of the church of Jesus Christ becoming involved as well. The pastor must take the lead, and the eldership must be very prominent in such work, but *all* must participate in it.

Two very important passages may be selected from among others to demonstrate this point. Paul, writing to a church that he had never seen and about which he had only heard by word of mouth, says,

"Concerning you my brethren [he is obviously not writing to elders alone], I, myself also am convinced that you, yourself are full of goodness, filled with all knowledge, and able also to confront one another nouthetically" (Rom. 15:14).

There it is, every believer in the church of Rome is expected to become involved. There may have been an exception here or there, but, as a whole, Paul considered the believers in that church to be "competent" to confront one another. And in the letter to the Colossians, the very letter in which we have seen that he stressed his own work of *nouthesia* as a minister of Christ (Col. 1:28), Paul also commanded the whole church to do the same (Col. 3:16). In this verse Paul uses the same two words that he employed in 1:28, those same two concepts that are especially the work of the pastor, and broadens them out for all of the Colossian believers. He says that what is the pastor's work (in particular) is the work of all (in general). What was his work, par excellence, was the work of all to a lesser extent: "Let the word of Christ dwell within you richly, with all wisdom teaching and nouthetically confronting one another."

This passage, together with Romans 15:14, enjoins the duty and sets forth the qualifications that are necessary for fulfilling this duty. Three things are associated with nouthetic confrontation by the people of God. The first of these is a rich or full knowledge of the Word of Jesus Christ. "You are filled with knowledge," he told the Romans. Writing to the church in Colosse, he said, "Let the Word of Christ dwell within you richly." Knowledge of the Word of the Lord Jesus Christ, therefore, is an essential qualification for this kind of confrontation. This is crucial. It is central, basic, fundamental to everything else. A man simply does not know *when* to confront another about *what* unless he knows the Word of God. The knowledge of sin, for example, is through the law (Rom. 7:7). Unless we know the law of God, we do not know what it is to sin against that law. And, of course, we do not know how to help a man who has sinned against that law unless we understand the gospel of our Lord Jesus Christ and the sanctification that comes through the use of the Word by the Spirit. So a rich, full and complete knowledge of Christ's inscripturated Word is essential. If then we have a growing knowledge of the Word of Christ, increasingly we shall be able to help one another.

But more is required than mere knowledge. In Colossians 3:16 he says, "With all *wisdom* let the word of Christ dwell in you richly." You must use that Word with wisdom. This is *how* to do it. "Wisdom" speaks not of *what* to do but of *how* to do it. There are people who know the will of God but they do not know how to confront another person about it. Wisdom is fuller than knowledge. In fact, in the Scriptures it is even more than the wise use of truth, more than a kind of common sense about *how* to use the Word of God. As it is used in the Book of Proverbs, wisdom is a rich word. But the word does, at the very least, embrace the element of practical or common sense. Knowing how to handle truth in relationship to individuals in this context certainly seems to be a prime emphasis. Wisdom here means using the Word in such a way that we heal rather than hurt, unite rather than drive further apart, bring to repentance rather than provoke to wrath. We spend much time teaching biblical data (as indeed we should), but how little we teach the wise ways in which to use those data. Wisdom involves not only knowledge of the Scriptures, but also knowledge of the person in need. It involves the ability to adapt the Word to human situations without changing it or compromising. It means sizing up problems, situations and persons. Wisdom in Colossians 3:16 is the right use and application of the Word in counseling another person. This wisdom comes from God through the Scriptures and their regular use.

In Romans 15:14 there is a third qualification. Not only do counselors need to know the Word of God and how to apply it to needs, but they also must be properly motivated to do so. They must want to confront someone in the first place. We need that kind of motivation, because otherwise we can think of plenty of excuses for not doing so. It is not easy to confront another person about a problem in his life. Embarrassment might be involved, or fear of receiving a negative response. There is often doubt about whether you might do more harm than good. Such things easily get in the way, along with many others. There is also a selfishness in the sinful heart that it takes grace over a life of Christian living to wash out.

So then, there is a third element necessary. This element is mentioned in Romans 15:14. There Paul says, "filled with all knowledge and full of *goodness.*" Paul might be talking about the personal life of the individual when he mentions "goodness" but I doubt it. I think he means by goodness the attitude of goodness (good will, warmheartedness or concern) toward another person. Goodness is outgoing love toward another. Either way, the two are really interlaced. A good man will be outgoing in love toward others; his goodness will spill over like a cup that runs over. He will be a man filled with the Spirit who is a well of water overflowing to many others. A good man will not keep good things to himself; he will be well disposed toward other people. He will be concerned about the household of faith. His own heart will be torn to pieces when he sees the lives of others in shreds. He feels the bruises that another receives. Because of his good disposition, he must reach out to help a brother in trouble. God has put within him a goodness toward others. This is the *why* of it all.

So, then, three things are needed: the motivating power of good will toward others, a rich and full knowledge of the Word of God, and wisdom to know how to help a person to meet his problems in Christ.

In the light of what we have seen so far, let us turn to a passage that says all of this in very plain and pointed words. Because of its great importance we must consider the passage in some detail. It is found in the sixth chapter of Paul's letter to the church of Galatia. At the beginning of chapter 6 Paul says:

"Brethren, even if a man is caught in any trespass, you who are spiritual restore such a one in the spirit of gentleness, looking to yourself lest you be tempted. Bear one another's burdens and thus fulfill the law of Christ. If anyone thinks he is something when he is nothing he deceives himself, but let each one examine his own work and then he will have reason for boasting in regards to himself alone and not in regards to another; for each one shall bear his own load."

What is the import of these words? First, notice that Paul is addressing Christians: he says "brethren." That is important for our consideration because we have been discussing the common assistance of one brother for another that makes a church a warm, vital, healing and growing community. Instead, many congregations are riddled full of holes with power leaking out on all sides. But those leaks can be plugged! The people of God, themselves, can plug every hole and heal every wound. A church may become a powerful unity in which each member grows toward the other, speaks the truth in love, and realizes that he is a member of the others in that body. This is the way that Paul started churches, and this is the way he wanted them to continue. His words in Galatians 6 are aimed at fostering such unity and power.

Notice secondly Paul says, "If any of you catch another brother in a trespass"—in the act of sin. Possibly his words could be understood as teaching that the brother himself is the one who is caught (entangled) in the sin. It really makes little difference in the end. Both things, of course, would have to be true on either interpretation. But probably Paul means that you have caught him redhanded, in the act of sin. He pictures one Christian stumbling upon another who is involved in sin, somehow crushed under a load of sin; it has become such a burden that he seems incapable of lifting it.

Probably it would not take us very long to make a list of people that we know who are like that. We all know somebody like that, don't we? Every one of us knows other Christians who are involved in all sorts of sinful activities. Whom are you thinking about right now? Isn't there somebody in particular who comes to mind? At this very moment you may be thinking about someone you know; perhaps someone in your own church. Possibly he has been involved in this sin for a long while. Maybe you've prayed about it. Probably you have mentioned him to other Christians, at least to your husband or to your wife. You may even have gossiped about him. We all know someone like that. Paul assumes that we do. He assumes that you and I are going to run into this problem regularly. He assumes it will be so much a part of our Christian experience that he feels compelled to give directions about what we must do when we run into this problem. As you think about all of those people, you know that you can't avoid the consequences of such knowledge.

"All right," you say, "so it's going to happen. What do I do then?" That's the question. I want you to notice thirdly that Paul says God holds you responsible to help that Christian brother or sister who is in sin. But if God holds you responsible, you must not walk by on the other side, as the priest and Levite, leaving your brother lying battered in the road like the man who fell among thieves on the road from Jerusalem to Jericho. You must not! You must not walk by, says Paul; he will not let you become disengaged.

We shake our heads in disbelief when we hear about a dozen people hanging out of apartment houses in New York to watch a woman chased up and down a block, being stabbed again and again over a half-hour period, and finally slain before their eyes while not one of them does anything to help.

Not one called the police; they just watched, disengaged. We shake our heads when we hear of a crowd that booed a potential suicide who was persuaded not to jump from the top of a building. We shake our heads in disbelief asking, "How can people be so callous?" Yet you and I, brethren, in a church of Jesus Christ, stumble across each other day by day, caught in sin, crushed under loads and burdens, but we too only watch and gossip. We walk on the other side and say, "It's none of my business." Well, God has made it your business! He will not let us worm out from our responsibility quite so easily as we might like to.

We must not walk by hoping that the person in sin somehow will extricate himself from that situation. Often he cannot easily do so at this point. He may have become so deeply entangled in such a mess that he just doesn't know which way to turn. Sometimes even his attempts to get out of it worsen the problem.

For example, take a Christian husband and wife who started out their marriage quite well. Everything was going fine. They had Bible study and prayer together regularly. They were attending church regularly, and they had a deep fellowship with one another. Communication was about as wide open as the ocean. But then, little by little, piece by piece, day by day, week by week, year by year it began to narrow. She said something, he cut her off (gave her a short reply, perhaps), and she told herself, "That's the last time I'll raise that issue." So communication was narrowed. Later he did something she didn't like and she chewed him out, so he promised himself, "I'll not mention that anymore. I'll just do what I want about it on my own." And so it went. Little by little communication narrowed until soon it disappeared altogether. What communication is left is on the most superficial level. They talk about who is going to use the car when, and that sort of thing. Family chit chat on the least common denominator is now the most significant communication going on in that home. When things have gone that far, usually even attempts to rectify the problem on the part of either party only drive them farther apart. Even good will is misinterpreted. The fact that they try and yet fail and that their attempts to get things straightened out drive them farther apart shows that matters are in a condition where the help of a third person is needed. They need somebody to step into the situation and help them out of it. They need somebody else to take the two wires that have snapped and reunite them. They are unable to do it alone. That is the sort of circumstance that Paul is talking about in Galatians. So you can't walk by on the other side and say, "It is none of my business; they must get it straightened out by themselves." God says that it is *your* business to help. If, in His providence, you run across a believer who is caught in sin, it is your duty and your responsibility to help him. God Himself has made it your business. As a matter of fact, it is His providence that has brought about the occasion itself.

Neither can you pass off your responsibility on some marriage counselor or psychiatrist down the street. There are some who like to do just that. Even pastors do this at times. You can't say, "Well, you see this is a very difficult marriage problem. There is not much I can do in a situation of this magnitude; you need professional help," and feel very righteous about avoiding the situation. You see, God won't let you do that. Paul says in the passage, "Now, brethren, if you catch a man in a trespass, you who are *spiritual* must restore such a one." You who are spiritual. Who is that? "Well," you say, "that's the cream of the crop—the elders, or at least the most pious Christians in the church. Since that is who should get involved, that lets me off the hook. I do not claim to be an exemplary Christian."

But no, that isn't what these words mean at all. There is no such thing as a nonspiritual Christian; the very concept involves a contradiction in terms. Who then is this *spiritual* man? Every Christian is a spiritual man; that is who he is. If he isn't a spiritual man, he isn't a Christian: "If any man has not the Spirit of Christ, he does not belong to him," says Paul (Rom. 8:9). The second chapter of I Corinthians makes very plain who is spiritual and who is not. There are only two kinds of people in the world; not three, only two. There are people without the Spirit of God and people with the Spirit of God. Paul calls the latter a spiritual man. He is a man who has the Spirit of God. He is a Christian; one who has been regenerated by the Holy Spirit, who believes in Jesus Christ, and who possesses the Spirit of God in his life. He is a man in whom the Spirit dwells. That is a spiritual man. Some spiritual men are more holy than others, but they are all spiritual.

There is also a *natural* man, Paul says. What is a natural man? He is just a plain natural man. He has nothing but the sinful nature with which he was born. Nothing else has happened to him; he has never been changed. He is just what he is by nature. He is just a plain, natural, ordinary, common sinner. He was born a sinner, lost and condemned and headed on his way to hell. Unless the Spirit of God comes into his life and changes him, he will continue to be a natural man, a man who has only a sinful nature and nothing more. As a result, he cannot discern the things of the Spirit of God because they are spiritually discerned. If you were to turn on the television, you could prove that there are pictures and sound bouncing all around your room. You don't see or hear them apart from the receiving set. Turn it on, and you can hear them and see them. Natural men are just like that. The things of God are spiritually discerned, and until a man has the Spirit of God, he cannot understand or appreciate the Bible. Biblical truths are bouncing all around, but he neither sees nor hears. Paul says, "Eyes have not seen, ears have not heard the things that God has prepared for those that love him; but they have been revealed to us who have the Spirit of God." Spiritual men have the Receiver.

So what is Paul talking about in Galatians 6? He is not contrasting two kinds of Christians (top-dog Christians who are to do the work of counseling and lower totem-pole Christians who are not). That isn't what he is talking about at all, because he never talks about Christians that way. What then is he talking about? He is referring to *Christians* as over against *unbelievers;* that is what he is talking about. So if God says, "You who are spiritual (Christians)," you can't throw this work off on some unbeliever down the street who has a shingle hanging out that says "Marriage Counselor" or "Psychiatrist." This is a matter for Christians to get involved in and *Christians alone.* That is the whole point: spiritual men must restore fallen spiritual men.

Why? Because the problem is sin. The fallen believer has been caught "in sin." His problems have come from disobedience to the will of God. Unbelievers cannot help to extricate him from sin. No pagan is rich in the knowledge of Christ's Word; no pagan has the wisdom of the Holy Spirit: no pagan is motivated by Christian goodness; he simply does not possess those qualities that are necessary to restore a fallen Christian brother. So his counselor has to be a Christian. Also, the Name of Jesus Christ is at stake before the world.

I have also mentioned that you cannot leave this problem to the preacher or to the elders alone. The word "you" in the phrase "you who are spiritual" is plural. He is saying, "all of you who are spiritual are to do this." This is a task for all of you; it is not only the job of the elders. To be sure, counseling is the preacher's job, and perhaps *primarily* his job; but it is not his job *alone.* It is also the job of all.

But you may say, "I believe it, but it sounds frightening. That is a fearful responsibility." Right! Fortunately, in this passage God also tells you what to do and how to do it. He gives instruction about how to restore a brother. He does not say avoid him, gossip about him, complain about him, gloat over him, but *"restore* him." That is the first point. There is all of the hope in the world in this verse. The words "restore him" show that the possibility of restoration is always there. A Christian brother is never in circumstances from which he cannot be restored by the Word of God ministered by a believer in the power of the Spirit. There is no Christian who has gone so far (whom God has left in this world[9]) that he is beyond restoration. We have here a mandate that is possible to fulfill. It is possible for one brother to "restore" another, or God would not require him to attempt it. God also assumes that you will be able to help restore him. Therefore, He calls upon all of you to become involved. If you believe in Jesus Christ and you daily are working at becoming the kind of Christian that you ought to be, you can do it. Even though you now may be clumsy or tactless, even though there is much to be desired in your own life, if you prayerfully and humbly begin you will find that God will help you and will increasingly use you to help those in more difficult situations. Your own life will grow too through counseling others.

God does not want bad relations among brethren to dangle at loose ends; He wants erring brethren restored. How this may best be accomplished must be discussed some other time. Note now that He wants the problem solved. He wants the loose ends tied together so that power does not continue to be sapped from the Church. He wants the Church to run smoothly like a piece of machinery that is well oiled. As the love of the Spirit is shed abroad in the hearts of the believer, it smooths out the work of the Church.

"Restore," he says, but specifically what does that mean? The word is a specialized term that means to "mend," to "mend something that has been damaged in order to make it useful again." It was used, for example, of "mending" damaged nets. It was used in medicine for "setting" broken bones. Here is a brother who has been beaten and bruised and bat-

---

[9]Cf. However "some are asleep" (I Cor. 11:30), and, "if anyone sees his brother committing a sin not leading to death, he shall ask and God will for him give life to those who commit sin not leading to death. There is a sin leading to death; I do not say that he should make request for this" (I John 5:16).

tered by sin, lying along the road. Your task is to do something for him. It may be true that he is a frightful looking mess; his bones may be sticking out in all directions like a hat rack (as Mark Twain once put it). But you can help him; by your words you can set his broken bones. That is your task. God knows that we shall all fall. That is why He has provided the right kind of help for those who need help. That help is found in the Scriptures. The picture here is of somebody who is caught under a load, perhaps an avalanche, of sin. In verse 2 Paul wrote, "Bear one another's burdens and thus fulfill the law of Christ." Let love move you to help the man in the middle of the road who is crushed down by a great rock that has fallen upon him. You come along and size up the situation. You must lift the load; pry loose the rock and pull it up off him as he wriggles out from under it.

You "bear" this load, pick up this burden that is crushing him down, and help him out from under it *in order to restore him.* You are not to help him run away from his problem. No. You are not to carry his share of the work for him. That isn't what bearing another's burden means; rather it means helping him out in his time of need *so that* (notice verse 5) he may now return to *bear his own load:* "for each one shall bear his own load." You help him in such a way that he may no longer run away from his problem or run away from his responsibility. The solution is not to shift his responsibility to you; rather, the solution lies in helping him once again to carry his load of responsibility. You restore him to usefulness in the kingdom of God. That is the biblical picture of counseling.

There are so many broken down, beat up, bruised and staggering Christians who are not carrying their own loads of responsibility. You see, that is what is wrong in the church. That is why the power has leaked out. But if we begin to pry up the rocks and pull Christians out from under them, and then help them to shoulder their packs and carry their own loads of responsibility in the church once again, the power can be restored. That is what "restoring" means—mending so that broken limbs become useful again. The restoration of a brother means making him useful to the kingdom of God once more. That is the goal; that is the reason for restoring him. It means restoring him to his place in the church. Now he may carry on the work that God has called him to do.

But finally, notice the word of caution appended to the passage: restoration must be carried on in the spirit of meekness. "Meekness" is the same word that is used in the fifth chapter of Galatians, where Paul listed it as part of the fruit of the Holy Spirit. Only the Spirit of God can produce meekness. Obviously, then, we can see here one reason why a nonspiritual man cannot be called upon to restore a fallen brother. He does not have this meekness if it comes exclusively from the Spirit. But a spiritual man by the Spirit may help. You may be a diamond in the rough, you may not know what to do, you may feel as if you have six thumbs and five feet when going to help another person, but this is the key—if you go in meekness you cannot fail to help. If you recognize that but for the grace of God you might have been under that same rock, you will be of real help. And some day there probably will be somebody who will help you out. Already someone may have helped you from beneath a different problem. If you go in that spirit, knowing that all of us Christians are frail and sinful, and that anything that is good in us is the result of the grace of God, you will be of help. Jesus Christ came to die for our wretched sins on that cross; it is only because of that cross and because of His death that we are anything at all. In ourselves we did not have even the slightest inclination toward God. You must go in that spirit, the spirit of meekness, giving God complete honor and glory. You cannot go with any sense of pride, comparing or contrasting yourself with the fallen brother. Tell yourself, "There I am in principle; in my heart is every wicked and evil deed. What he has done, it is possible for me to do." The seeds of all sins are within sinners.

If you go in the spirit of meekness, you will recognize that you yourself might be tempted and you will be on guard lest you fall into temptation. Too often pastors (and others) have been caught in the same sins as those whom they counseled. Paul indicates why: they failed to counsel in meekenss, the kind of meekness that makes one so much aware of his own sinful potential that he "takes heed lest he fall" (I Cor. 10:12). Meekness, therefore, is the fundamental condition of all Christian counseling; indeed, it is, like the rest, a unique element in Christian counseling.

Let us sum up: the kind of counseling that we have been discussing may be structured, may be carried on formally by pastors and elders, but it also is an informal pervasive force among the people of God. In the plan of God for His church as He reveals it in the Scriptures, such counseling is the responsibility of every Christian. There is always a need for this kind of work. Quietly, silently behind the scenes, it should be going on all of the time. Every one of us is called upon to do this work.

Do you remember when I asked you to think about somebody who is crushed by a load of sin? You may have immediately made a mental list of several such persons. Well then, let me ask you this: doesn't that mean that you have some work to do? Doesn't that mean that there are some people that you ought to see right away? Is there someone who needs to be restored? It doesn't mean that you must become a busybody[10] but it does mean that if there is a rock on your brother's neck you must hurry to him and lift the burden. The whole church will profit as he stands up straight again and starts to carry his share of the common load. That is what the Church of Christ needs—doesn't it?

---

[10]Exactly not. Cf. II Thessalonians 3:11; Proverbs 26:17; 28:25. You do not need to look for problems. You will have enough to do handling those that in God's providence appear on the road from Jerusalem to Jericho.

How You Can Get the Most out of Counseling

How You Can Get the Most out of Counseling[1]

What goes on behind your pastor's study door? Perhaps this is more than an academic question for you. You may have been considering talking with your minister about serious trouble in your marriage, about an inexplicable feeling of deep depression, about the discipline of your children, or about some other problem that distresses you. You ask, "Can he really help me?" You wonder, "What would he expect me to do? How long would it take? What would it be like?"

I wish I could tell you step by step what to expect, but I cannot. It is impossible to predict what may happen. Almost anything might occur, and in some cases nearly nothing will. Clearly situations vary in ways that make all specific predictions hazardous. But much depends upon the concepts of counseling that your pastor has adopted (if any) and how seriously he follows them in actual practice. And, of course, much depends upon you, your motivation and willingness to obey God.

Some ministers themselves may be curious about what is going on behind other study doors. They feel a sense of dissatisfaction with their own counseling. Perhaps they have never seen another person doing counseling. For both, though principally for counselees, I hope to discuss a few things about counseling. Particularly, I am interested in assisting anyone who wishes to seek help to prepare to get the most out of counseling.

Take a Look at One Case

"How about your ironing?" With that question the initial interview took a turn. Before she could reply, Sharon Whit-

---

[1]This essay was originally written for publication in the *Presbyterian Guardian* under the title "Behind the Study Door," and appeared, in part, serially in the April, May and July-August, 1968 issues. It has been revised considerably for inclusion in this publication.

man's face registered the painful amazement that the two counselors sitting across the desk by now had come to expect. "How did you know?" she asked.

"There's no mystery about it," replied Jim, the counselor in charge. "Few women seem to enjoy ironing, and when they get as depressed as you they begin to neglect unpleasant household chores."

Sharon broke in: "I don't feel like ironing when I'm depressed; I just can't iron, even though I know I should."

The other counselor, a ministerial trainee named Bill, explained:

"That's exactly the point; you're caught in a cyclical problem. Once you get depressed over something, you don't feel like assuming responsibilities, so you let your ironing go. But when you get behind in the ironing, this bugs you and you feel worse. And the worse you feel, the less you want to iron, so the pile grows larger and you become more depressed. Before long this momentum snowballs to other responsibilities like dishwashing, cleaning the house, and making the children's lunches. The first thing you know, you are wasting away whole days irresponsibly lying around on the sofa—depressed, feeling guilty, and sorry for yourself."

Jim interjected: "How far has it gone with you, Sharon?"

What you are sitting in on is a small slice of what happens every week in the counseling room of the Christian Counseling and Educational Center of Hatboro, Pennsylvania.[2] Sharon Whitman—a fictitious composite of a frequently encountered problem type—is a Christian woman who will discover very shortly that she has become depressed because of her unscriptural ways of living. In her case she will find that failure

---

[2]The Christian Counseling and Educational Foundation was begun in 1966 for the express purpose of developing counseling procedures based upon biblical principles; and for the purpose of training ministers to counsel scripturally. The center is a service agency to the Church.

in handling anger (which she allows to turn into long-term resentments) is one of the basic patterns she must be taught to overcome by God's grace. Sharon came because she felt depressed. but that depression had developed from guilt arising. out of a long-standing inner feud that she had been carrying on between herself and her mother-in-law.[3] This recently had erupted into open hostilities. By neglecting her ironing and other duties (because she rightly felt guilt-depression over her sin), Sharon had turned a bad depression into a severe one.

The depression will lift slightly when she begins to reassume her responsibilities as a homemaker and mother, but she will find complete relief only when she finally confesses her sinful ways to God and asks her mother-in-law's forgiveness. Beyond that, Sharon will need to set about building a new Christian relationship between herself and her mother-in-law. In addition, she must learn to replace sinful patterns of response with biblical ones. Since the problem of resentment extends to many areas of her life, she will find it necessary to straighten out some matters at her church. These efforts may go a long way toward healing a grievous division among the women of the congregation.

From the outset, the help of Don, Sharon's husband, was enlisted. Don attended counseling sessions along with Sharon and stood by her in all of this. His help and encouragement were a valuable day-by-day adjunct to the weekly sessions and were a major factor in the dramatically rapid changes that occurred.

During counseling Don saw that there were areas of his life that needed attention too. The changes he made also strengthened their marriage. Because Sharon was willing to adopt biblical life patterns in obedience to God, she "graduated"

---

[3]Not all problems have an interpersonal base. Some, of course, develop from organic causes: e.g., brain damage, glandular or other chemical imbalances. There is also a gray area of problems that are of uncertain etiology.

from counseling in seven weeks. Sharon and Don were "debriefed" to help them understand the dynamics of their problem, how they were helped, and what to do in the future when new difficulties arise. The object of the debriefing session was to show them how to handle their own problems scripturally so that there will be no need for them to return for future counseling. They were taught God's ways of responding to life's problems and what the Bible says to do when they fail.

They will return for a six-week checkup, at which time if all is still going well counseling will be terminated. Over the counseling period they studied the Scriptures in relation to themselves. They took home written materials and a personalized workbook to which they may refer in future crises to remind them of the principles they learned in counseling.

I have attempted to sketch the course of a typical counseling situation as it might have taken place in the life of a type of Christian woman who complained of being deeply depressed. In her case, as so frequently, her depression was due to guilt—the guilt of long-standing resentments complicated by other irresponsible actions.

These subsidiary factors stemmed from failure to handle her initial guilt-depression properly. If she had sought forgiveness from God and man, the debilitating effects of guilt heaped upon guilt never would have occurred. Briefly, I shall discuss the principles behind that case later on. But first I want to talk about some of the ways in which counselees may prepare themselves for counseling.

Your Expectations Must Be Biblical

To begin with, you turn to a minister in time of need because you expect him to be able to help you solve your problems. You expect this from him because of his unique relationship to God and to the church. This is a scripturally justifiable assumption.[4] God requires the church to choose its teaching elders from among men of the highest spiritual maturity (Titus 1:5-9; I Tim. 3:1-7), whose understanding of the Word of God is "accurate" (II Tim. 2:15), and whose conduct sets an example for the rest of the flock (I Tim. 4:12; Titus 2:7).

So long as your expectations stay within these scriptural bounds and you demand neither omniscience nor perfection, you are on firm biblical ground. Within these same scripturally realistic limits ministers must ask whether they are fit to counsel. Helpfulness and effectiveness in counseling largely depend upon these preconditions.

You May Prepare Beforehand

Once one has asked for an appointment, what does he do next? The counselee may *prepare* for the initial interview. His objective ought to be to put the counselor in possession of the maximum amount of information as quickly as possible. One way that has been found helpful is to go prepared to answer the three following questions (I suggest that you write out the answers to these questions and take them with you):

(1) *What is my problem?* As clearly as you are able to do so, be ready to set forth the exact nature of the difficulty that led you to seek an appointment. You may find that the problem is complex, not simple. You may find it helpful to distinguish between long-standing underlying factors and the immediate occasion that prompted the interview. Consistently Jesus went behind the immediate or "presentation" problem to a deeper one. You have only to read the Gospel of John again in this light to see how this was His constant prac-

---

[4]Much modern counseling theory teaches otherwise. One professor taught us in a graduate course in pastoral counseling: "Never give advice. Nevet use your authority as a minister. Always ignore direct appeals for guidance. Your only job is to help the counselee help himself."

tice. The woman at the well (chapter 4) is an instance, Nicodemus (chapter 3) a second, and the man born blind (chapter 9) a third. Yet He never ignored the presentation problem.

(2) *What have I done about it?* Prepare to relate, as crisply as possible, in chronological order, the steps that you have already taken in an attempt to solve the problem (with any consequent results, either good or bad). Your attitudes toward others involved in the problem also may be considered; sometimes problems of wrong attitudes arising out of issues grow larger than the issues themselves.

(3) *What do I expect the counselor to do?* Do you want advice, support, information? Say so, explicitly. This may seem unnecessary, but note Jesus' question in Luke 18:41, "What do you want me to do for you?" Of course, Christ was not merely seeking information. His questions were calculated to help others understand the situation more precisely. This, too, is an important reason for formulating your ideas carefully at the outset.

Come to counseling with *hope.* Many persons seek counseling in a hope-against-hope attitude. They expect little and often (as a result) get what they expect. If the counsel is biblical, you have every reason to have genuine hope; God has an answer to your problem—no matter what it is.[5] Your expectations may have much to do with the outcome; they should be realistic but high.

Come to counseling only after *prayer.* If you ask for help with willingness to hear and to do the will of God as it is expressed in the Scriptures, you will receive more help than if you have not considered the matter prayerfully beforehand. You should look upon biblical counseling as, at least in part, the answer to prayer. Ask God for help as you seek counsel

---

[5]Cf. II Timothy 3:17. If your pastor does not give biblical counsel to you, you should insist upon such counsel. Also see: Jay Adams, *Christ and Your Problems,* Presbyterian and Reformed Publishing Co., Nutley: 1971.

from His servant. Ask God not only to help you, but also to help your counselor to help you.

Counselors May Follow the Same Pattern

If a counselee is not prepared to offer such helpful information, a wise counselor may ask these or similar questions. Christ elicited valuable information by the use of just such queries: Mark 9:14-29 (esp. vss. 16-18 and 21-22). Data derived from the answer to question 2 (What have I done about it?) often provides essential insights into faulty courses of action that, by becoming new elements of it, have enlarged and complicated the original problem. Such unscriptural responses to stress often indicate more deeply ingrained habitual response patterns that may characterize a basic personality "set" of the counselee as he comes for help.[6] It is important to try to discover these patterns at the outset, for they must be analyzed and corrected according to scriptural standards before counseling may be terminated successfully.

Do Not Settle for Too Little Too Soon

If the counselor's intervention is aimed at meeting the immediate crisis alone, he may help the counselee substantially,

---

[6]Scripture consistently notes the importance of habit patterns developed over long years of "training" (usually unconscious): cf. "a heart trained in greed" (II Peter 3:15) and "as is the habit of some" (Heb. 10:25). Note also Hebrews 5:13, 14; 12:11 for comments on the positive patterns that develop as a part of the process of sanctification. Old life patterns constitute one's "former manner of life" (Eph. 4:32) and must be replaced by new ones. The old man (old habit patterns) must be put off and the new man (new patterns) must be put on.

Paul suggests in Ephesians 4:22-32 that this relates to the whole man, and as examples mentions speech habits, attitudes, interpersonal relations, work, and other matters of the same nature. In the chapters to follow he extends the application of this principle to the crucial problems involved in several facets of life. Ephesians 4:28 speaks of the contemplated change in terms of the specific case of a thief who not only must give up the practice of stealing, but who also must develop new patterns of hard work.

but when the next crisis arises, the counselee is likely to find himself as helpless as before. The more fundamental problem of how to respond to trouble scripturally also must be learned. The counselor's objective will be not merely to patch up a bad situation, but to help the counselee learn how to "put off" the old man (sinful response patterns) and "put on" the new man (righteous response patterns), to God's glory. Counselees, therefore, should be ready not only to solve specific problems and thus gain immediate relief from them, but also to work on the underlying problems. If your counselor says that there is more to your problem than you thought at first, consider this carefully before discontinuing counseling. By all means, do not settle for too little too soon; ask God for all that you can get from counseling and then receive all that He has to give to you. Counseling (of the right sort) frequently can change the entire course of your life for good.

As counseling continues, it will become evident that sinful responses to trouble (patterns of self-centeredness, resentment, self-pity, worry, greed, laziness, blame-shifting, cowardice, and envy—to name a few) not only complicate problems, but in many instances are themselves problems beneath problems. The action is cyclical: bad response patterns develop; these patterns themselves give rise to new problems; often the new problems then are met with unscriptural responses, ad infinitum. It is important then for the counselee to spell out his answer to question 2 in some detail, whenever possible citing specific instances.

From the very beginning the focus of counseling should fall on the whole person, and not merely on the presentation problem. From the outset all counseling should aim at the growth of the believer in every dimension of his life. Problems must be handled specifically, concretely and in detail, but also should themselves become illustrations of and stepping stones to root out the deeper patterns which need to be replaced with biblical ones.

When Do You Need Counseling?

Growling to himself "What's the use?" John stalked out of the hallway, buried himself in a living room chair, and pulled a newspaper down over his head. All day long John Bickering had looked forward to this moment, and now *she* had blown it. It had been a long time since he and Nancy had known the joys that they experienced in the early years of their marriage. Somehow the marriage had grown stale. It was hard to remember just how the deterioration began, but there was no question now that things were in a miserable mess.

John was a Christian and he knew that this was no way for him to live. He knew that he was dishonoring Christ. He was deeply troubled about the influence that these conditions were having upon his children. He loved Nancy deeply, and wanted to start all over and try to make their marriage go, but he hardly knew how to begin.

That day at work (as usual) he thought much about the problem (it had been affecting his work adversely) and had reached the conclusion that something had to be done *now*. So he decided to have a heart-to-heart talk with Nancy in an effort to straighten things out. He knew that he was at fault in many ways and he was willing to change, but he felt that he needed her help and cooperation.

When he rang the doorbell that night, his heart was warm and full of hope. This would be the night when everything would start afresh. Nancy opened the door. Earnestly John said to her, "Nancy, you know the problems we've been having lately . . ." Before he could utter another word, Nancy spit back, "You're mighty right that we've been having problems, and if you don't begin to shape up, those problems are nothing compared to the problems that we're going to have!" It was at that point that John had turned on his heel and headed for the living room.

Nancy's day had been rough. The hot summer weather combined with her period and three squabbling youngsters had all contributed to her thoughtless outburst. She had been edgy, and John's reminder was only a spark to touch off the explosion. Actually, Nancy desired a reconciliation as much as did John. She, too, had thought much about the baneful conditions under which she and the rest of the family were living. It was only two days ago that she also had decided that she and John must do something about their relationship. Mentally she had chalked up tonight as the time when she would talk to him about it.

Now look what she had done! How could she broach the subject after ripping into him that way? "And . . . perhaps . . . yes probably, John himself was making overtures toward reconciliation when he came in the door," she thought as she stirred something in a pot. "Perhaps this was the answer to my prayers and I failed to see it. I've got to tell him I'm sorry," she said to herself as she put down the pot and headed for the living room.

"John," she said, "you know when you came into the house tonight . . ." Slapping the paper down into his lap, John retorted, "I know what happened when I came in the door—and I'd better not come home to anything like that again, or I may not come home."

Nancy wheeled about, stamped into the kitchen, picked up her pot and stirred furiously. In time with the beat of her spoon she muttered, "Now *he's* blown it; what's the use?"

The strange thing, as you noticed, is that Nancy and John were so close to and yet so far from making this marriage a success. They both recognized the need for changes, and both wanted things to be different. Both would be willing to do nearly anything necessary to bring about those changes. Both made attempts to initiate the change. Yet change did not come; instead, matters got worse and both are close to despair. What is the problem? Communication has broken down, and they need the help of a counselor who can reestablish contact and enable them to share their real intentions and motives with one another.

The question is often asked: when does one need counseling? The answer is: whenever his own attempts to solve or handle problems fail. And one of the most frequent signs of such failure is the breakdown of communication. In John and Nancy's case this breakdown has become so serious that even attempts to repair the situation lead to a more severe rift.

Therein lies the dilemma of the communication breakdown: communication is the one essential tool necessary to solve any problems, but when communication breaks down there is no means left to solve the communication problem. And unfortunately it is not long before any unsolved problem may be complicated by resulting in a breakdown in communication.

Communication binds people together; a communication breakdown separates them as the confusion of languages at the Tower of Babel so clearly demonstrated. There the problem was one of simple language failure. More serious is the failure of communication on the deeper levels of attitude, understanding and motive.

You Must Work on Communication

A wise biblical counselor will recognize that he must begin with the restoration of communication. He will first help you to reestablish communication with God. If you are not a Christian, he will speak to you of the communication breakdown which occurred in the Garden of Eden, where sin drove the wedge between God and man. He will recall how man and God walked in perfect communication before the fall, and he will point out the disastrous results that man's disobedience brought upon himself. He will show you how man hid from his Creator, feared God, clothed himself because he could no longer face God openly, and lied to his Maker. That was the first breakdown in human communication; and it was the result of sin. Do not be surprised, then, if your counselor may have some important things to say about your sin. Do not think that he has become sidetracked; he will be laying the groundwork for all that follows. Take to heart the Word of God as he shares it with you, and consider your own personal sin before a holy and righteous God.

The counselor also will tell you how the death of Jesus Christ for His people deals with that sin as well as all subsequent sins that they have committed, and how communication with God may be established by repentance and faith, and maintained by confession. Having dealt with that basic question, he will turn to the matter of communication on the horizontal level.

Counselors Will Require Biblical Reconciliation

In reestablishing communication, the counselor will want to bring you and other alienated parties together for counseling. Dealing with counselees separately only tends to perpetuate the suspicion, lies, and accusations that now separate them. He will want to help you and them to learn how to speak the truth in love to one another. Counseling may often begin with reconciliation in the spirit of Matthew 5 or 18. This may be difficult for you, but until reconciliation takes place it may be impossible to go further. More needs to be said about this later on.

A discussion of the Christian principles of communication explained in the fourth chapter of Ephesians might be one helpful way of opening the subject. Paul says, "Laying aside falsehood, speak truth each one of you with his neighbor, for we are members of one another" (vs. 25), and then goes on to explain what he means by this. We need one another as each of the parts of a body needs the other parts. All the parts work together in coordination only when truthful communication takes place.

Daily Solutions Important

But there are sinful roadblocks to such communication. Paul proceeds to deal with several. He commands in the words of Psalm 44, a nighttime Psalm, "Be angry, but do not sin: do not let the sun go down on your anger." Problems are solved when they are handled early. We cannot carry yesterday's problems into today. Each day holds sufficient trouble of its own. Moreover, anger harbored turns into resentment and bitterness that Paul insists must be put away. Each day that day's problems must be faced and settled before God and man. When the solutions to differences are kept current, communication problems do not result.

John and Nancy cannot extricate themselves from their difficulties because for years they have allowed resentments to harden within them. Not only has the sun, but many moons have set on their anger. With such built-in feelings toward one another, almost any act by the other person is likely to be misinterpreted.

After communication is finally restored, John and Nancy will have to learn to substitute biblical patterns of daily confession and forgiveness for the sinful patterns that have characterized their relationship in the past. They will have to learn to put off the "old man" with his resentments and bitterness and to put on new habits of daily reconciliation. Unless they learn to do so, they will soon find themselves caught in the same trap again.

A Reversal of the Past

But first John and Nancy will have to reestablish communication. Where can they break into the downward cycle that has developed? A counselor who follows Paul will advise them of the need for an immediate change on their part. There must be a reversal of the past. Until now, both Nancy and John have been driving one another away by accusations (often true) and counter-accusations. But Paul in Ephesians 4 stressed the importance of speaking words to one another that help solve the problems that have arisen, and that build up one another rather than tear down each other. Instead of working on problems, John and Nancy have been working on each other. They have become past masters in the use of unwholesome speech calculated to dice and cube one another. Such cutting remarks, that have been so much a part of the Bickering home, must cease. How can John and Nancy make such a transition?

Their counselor perhaps will recall the words of Christ about anger, in Matthew 5, and explain His solution to estranged relations.[7] There He stressed the importance and urgency of *reconciliation* by asserting its priority over worship. A Christian in the very act of worship, remembering that he has wronged another, must stop what he is doing and must go and be reconciled to his brother, before he returns to complete his worship. Unreconciled relationships affect worship adversely. You too may be asked to consider the implications of this passage in your own life. Jesus Christ will not permit brethren to remain in an unreconciled state.

Confession and Forgiveness

When one confesses his sin and asks for forgiveness and help rather than attacking the other person, he takes the first crucial step toward renewing vital communication. Talking about one's *own* sins and asking for help and forgiveness draws others close. Attacking them about their sins and failures tends to drive them away. There is a legitimate time for confronting another about *his* sin, but the time for that is after one has first dealt with his own sin.[8] One first must remove the log from his own eye so that he can see clearly enough to remove the speck from another's eye.

If the other person is principally at fault, nevertheless one still may confess any bad feelings and resentment on his part.

---

[7]"Therefore if you bring your gift to the altar and there remember that your brother has something against you, leave your gift before the altar and go your way; first be reconciled to your brother, and then come and offer your gift" (vss. 23, 24).

[8]Usually on a separate occasion. Confession to another must never be done in a spirit that accuses another of sin as it admits one's own sin.

Certainly he ought to confess the fact that until now he has not followed the Lord's injunctions in Matthew 5 or 18 for dealing with broken relationships.[9] Focusing upon one's self for the first time orients one in the same direction as the other person who also has been focusing upon him.

Thus the beginnings of communication can come about whenever a counselor has the courage to speak of the sin of communication breakdown and applies the scriptural principles of Ephesians 4. He will stress in particular verse 32: "Be kind to one another, tenderhearted, forgiving one another, even as God for Christ's sake has forgiven you." This verse teaches that even the way that we deal with our sin should reflect the redemption of Christ to the glory of God! Since preparation for counseling frequently involves matters pertaining to communication, it is important that these questions regarding communication, forgiveness and reconciliation be understood as early as possible.

Other efforts may be made to obtain the most from counseling; we could discuss many matters about cooperation and effort during the later counseling sessions, but such matters, of necessity, would be much more varied than we could discuss here. Hopefully, these few suggestions, however, may be of help to any readers who are contemplating counseling.

One final word: if you are not sure whether or not you need counseling—you *do*. You should discuss at least *that* question with your pastor right away.

---

[9]"Moreover if your brother sins against you, go and tell him his fault between you and him alone: if he will hear you, you have gained your brother. But if he will not hear you, then take one or two more with you, that in the mouth of two or three witnesses every word may be established. And if he neglects to hear them, tell it to the church: but if he neglects to hear the church, let him be as an heathen man and a tax collector to you" (Matt. 18:15-17).

Can Your Marriage Succeed Today?

Everywhere that we turn we hear this question asked in one form or another. We all have felt the increasing demands upon marriage made by the contemporary American culture.

In order to understand the pressures of modern society, take a look at what the automobile, to mention only one modern innovation, has done by providing us with a new mobility. The effects of the automobile are so sweeping that it has brought about a new form of community: the bedroom town. A husband who lives in a bedroom town does little more than sleep there. The better part of his life is spent in the city where he works. I was once the pastor of a church in a bedroom town in New Jersey. Many people in town commuted across the river into New York. They got up at an unearthly hour, left home before the children awakened to go to school, and drove off into the crowded streets along with thousands of others heading for the tunnels. When they arrived home exhausted from work and travel, often as late as 7:00 or 7:30, they ate a late meal alone. The older children, who ate long before, were by now already engrossed in homework; the younger ones tucked away into bed. In some homes dad hardly existed as far as the kids were concerned. Even mom looked upon him as a stranger. The pressures that such mobility has brought to bear upon marriage are enormous.

The automobile means that we no longer live in a village community. In the village everybody saw everyone else all of the time. A woman walked down the street to the general store and on the way saw and chatted with half of her neighbors. Villagers tended to hang around the streets, poked their heads out of windows to talk with a passing friend, and gossiped across the backyard fences. The men worked *together* on various projects, such as barn raisings or building homes.

---

[1]To a gathering at the home of Mr. and Mrs. Hugh Whitted (revised).

They went home for lunch. There was a community life. Even in larger cities, a generation ago there were block parties, neighborhood baseball teams, etc. That was just a very short while ago. Now nearly all of that has gone, except in a few very isolated places. But even in these places the automobile has changed conditions considerably.

The automobile has influenced the shape of the family. The modern nuclear family is frequently removed from in-laws and other relatives. It has become a smaller unit that must be self-contained in ways that were formerly unnecessary when close relatives lived nearby. Interdependence among kin is rapidly disappearing. The frequency and ease with which we move and change our locations is remarkable. Companies now transplant employees great distances at will. Families no longer send down deep roots. There are no built-in babysitters when a family is far away from relatives. There is just no continuity with the community or community life. Undertaking establishments, with their lineal dynasties, seem to be the only family units that stay fixed. Modern transportation, and primarily the automobile, has brought these new pressures upon the family, some of which at first seem to be unique. And these developments have appeared only during the last generation.

But the automobile is not our only problem. There are the pressures of very uncertain economic conditions. Everybody feels the economic squeeze in one way or another. Go down to the grocery store and look around for a few minutes. Look at the faces of the shoppers. They are grim and gray. People no longer have fun shopping. There used to be a time when most people enjoyed going to the grocery store, but that has changed. Today people shuffle stoically through the aisles. Over here is a woman faithfully clicking off the price of every purchase with a little plastic counter to make sure she is not spending two cents beyond her budget. Over there is a woman shaking her head as she reads the price label on a product— a price that has risen fifteen cents in the last two weeks.

Of course, on the other side of the picture, the motivational research people from Mad Avenue have done everything they can to trap you into every sort of impulse buying. So, shopping necessarily involves cold war with the marketer. As a diligent shopper you know that the cereals have been placed on bottom shelves, well within your child's eager reach. You find it hard to walk the full length of an aisle without running into a table filled with "sale" items strategically placed in the middle of the aisle. These items, of course, carry a special "one-day only" sign. "It's not on my shopping list," you say, "but it's such a bargain that I can't afford to pass it up!" Caught! You toss it into the cart and go your way with mixed feelings of guilt and triumph.

On the one hand pressures to buy, and on the other hand the recognition that the cost of living keeps going up, have put a strong squeeze on marriages. In the last year the Philadelphia area has been marked out as one of those in which the cost of living has risen most dramatically. The husband is forced into a double bind. Joe knows that he *must* somehow provide for his family in a day in which it takes more and more money to do so. Should he moonlight? This would help financially but . . . on the other hand, he is bombarded with injunctions to spend more time with the family. Which way should he turn? Often a small matter like that wind that blew you around on your way to the gathering here tonight will settle the question. The wind takes a couple of shingles off the roof and the repairman says that it is not only those shingles but all of them that must be replaced. The summer heat has curled them up like wood shavings; what you really need is a new roof. That means another $1500 - $2000. This sudden unexpected demand, along with other pressures and difficulties that impinge from all sides, pushes the decision. Dad knows he is mortgaged up to his ears and that he cannot take on an additional loan. So he feels he has no choice, he simply must get a second job or arrange to work overtime so that he can meet these new expenses.

Bill, Joe's next-door neighbor, is struggling with the same problem. He knows that the family finances are in bad shape. So he determines, "I'm going to get a raise; I'm going to be the most industrious man at work. I'll work nights if necessary, but I'm going to get that raise for my family." But the other side of that bind is that the more he tries to provide for his family in that way, the more he is owned by the company store. Before long he has sold his soul. His body and soul is at work, while his heart is at home. How can he pull himself and his family together again? He is torn apart while pushed from both sides, and finally concludes that he can't win. That's the way it goes.

Of course, there are many other factors that are working against the success of the marriage in our day. Consider, for instance, the effects of the pill. The pill has removed the age-old double standard. Now sinful women are free to be as promiscuous as men without fear of pregnancy. Why should not Mary run around a bit and work off her frustrations as some psychiatrists advise? She can become a glamorous person again. She can prove to herself that she still has the ability to seduce a man. Why not? In the long run won't she be a happier person . . . and perhaps even a better wife? After all, there probably will be no serious consequences like she once might have feared. The pill has taken care of that problem. Who's going to be hurt anyway? This is the kind of thing she is reading everywhere; even some of the women's magazines now feature this kind of advice. Of course, for a long while some psychiatrists have been giving this very sort of advice to men. Yet, while the pill supposedly has removed fear from illicit relations, the statistics show that the illegitimate birth rate is still rising. If abortion had not been legalized, the adoption agencies would have had a supply of babies far exceeding the demand.

The whole area of sexual relationships has been brought into question as the result of the pill. Pre-marital experimentation is now receiving encouragement from unexpected sources. Liberal clergymen in certain quarters have begun to advocate trial marriages. With the safety that the pill (and the more recent day-after-the-night-before abortive pill as a back-up) affords, why not experiment? Why not test compatibility (whatever that word means) and thereby avoid later problems after marriage? And, why not have some fun now that it is possible without fear? But there is a catch; sex without marriage inevitably causes problems. For instance, the guilt that is still associated with it stubbornly refuses to be erased by plausible arguments from expediency. A violation of God's law cannot be made right by a pill. And this guilt and suspicion also are carried over into marriage, exerting another heavy pressure upon an institution that is already hard pressed. And, as experimentation goes on in a new and more furious way, the frustration, the lack of trust, the lies, the deceptive life patterns and the broken confidences that grow out of it increasingly weaken the marriage institution.

Then, of course, there are all of the unrealistic marriage expectations that Americans have bought. The public has been sold an enormous bill of goods. The husband is to be such a good provider that he is expected to be able to provide everything, not only everything his family *needs,* but also all they may *want.* He must provide the best food, clothing, housing, recreation and an adequate amount of money and things in addition for his family to live according to the standards of the Joneses next door. Of course, the Joneses "next door" today are even closer than next door; they live in his living room on the TV. A good father must find plenty of time for each child, and he must give that time unstintingly. He must romp and play with his children, find exciting things for them and himself to do, be an outdoorsman, work around the house, etc. He must be able to work off all of his problems and frustrations by becoming an expert at golf or some other sport or activity where he finds proper recreation and (his physician says) proper exercise. He must save quality time for his wife, cultivate their relationship assiduously, regularly become involved in joint social activities (and find the money to do so), etc. In order to live according to these minimal standards and enjoy this nicely balanced life, it takes only about 48 hours a day. It seems that questions of priority and feasibility are never raised.

Joe's wife is expected to play what in many ways is an even more strenuous role. She must be physically attractive whether she has the natural endowments or not. Because she must be stunning, all sorts of accouterments may be bought to make her appear so, including a new crop of hair if she needs it. She has to be an expert cook. She has to be half engineer in order to control the dials, mechanisms and gadgets installed in her kitchen. She also has to find time for the children, who are increasingly thrown on her because dad is the missing person in the home. She has to be a Cleopatra in bed. She must know the facts about sexual compatibility. She ought to be intellectually alive and active; she must know about politics; she is to be up on the latest books; she will want to be aware of everything that is happening around her so that she won't go to seed by being *simply* a good mother and wife. She must be far more than that. All of her abilities should be developed to the full. All of these things are required of her today by the women's magazines, which, of course, she also must read. So, pressures upon her grow out of expectations that she sets for herself because of the standards and guides of modern society. Magazines, television and intellectual society around her have driven her to distraction; she has been almost totally distracted from her vital role as her husband's "helper" (Gen. 2:18).

Then, on top of all of this, there are the Hollywood and *Playboy* views of love, marriage and non-marriage that have begun to permeate our society. These philosophies quickly get down into the homes in a thousand ways. Hollywood, ever since its beginning, has taught a pagan philosophy of love. The philosophy is that love *happens.* Love is not something to work at; it just happens. Love comes full blown from the head of Zeus (or Aphrodite). It's the kind of thing that just is or isn't. It isn't something that you develop, it isn't something that grows, it isn't something that you work hard to achieve, and it certainly isn't something that you can *will.* It is something that happens. And when it happens, it happens in such a way that you know it has happened! It bowls you over; you hear music, see wonderful lights, or have a near psychedelic experience. Such love is wonderful, but what happens when that no longer happens? What happens when the happening is over? What happens after marriage when the sounds grow a little more cacophonous? What happens when feeling dies, the embers grow cold, and the lights go out? What happens to a Hollywood-type marriage based on feeling when the parties begin to experience the fluctuating character of feeling? What happens when one or the other begins to have growing *feelings* for someone else? When something begins to happen with the secretary down at work, when something begins to happen with the man next door; is that the signal for a change? If love is happening, what else should you expect to happen when the happenings change? In the *Playboy* philosophy, love is getting; it means getting what one can out of another person, using the other person as an object for love. It means grasping and holding and satisfying oneself by using another. And when he is through using that person, well fine, she's been used . . . up. That's it. When there is no more nectar in the flower, the bee must flit to the next, and the next, and the one after that. Hollywood has taught this, too, not only by film but also by the way in which so many of the stars themselves have been notorious flower flitters. If mom is to dress like the stars, style her hair like the stars, and make up her face like the stars, why shouldn't she also hitch her marriage to a star?

Madison Avenue also pressures marriages, in other ways. Advertising has its own code of ethics that underlies all of its marketing practices. You may read about it set forth very blatantly in a book by Ernest Dichter. *The Strategy of De-*

sire. Much advertising is rooted in the philosophy of hedonism. Motivational research people, like Dichter, have been saying that we ought to become out-and-out hedonists. Dichter thinks that it would be nice if the public were to accept this philosophy candidly and openly pursue pleasure as the goal of life. But he realizes that hedonism is still a rather bitter pill for many people to swallow openly, so he disguises it, thinly. The M. R. people disguise the truth just enough to help you justify your pursuit of pleasure. Then they unstintingly pour hedonistic values into your ears, your eyes, your nostrils and through every other gate. It innundates you in magazines, on billboards, over the television, and in newspapers. Everywhere you turn Madison Avenue is at you again and again with this hedonistic view of life.

Perhaps the most thinly disguised advertisements in a long time were the ones used by Pepsi a few years back. Do you remember Pepsi's campaign? A feminine radio voice would drum into your ears day after day and month after month, "Be young and fair and debonair, drink Pepsi." One of the ads in that campaign opened with these bald words, "Did you know you can buy sociability in a bottle?" That was about as open as any appeal could possibly be. It was a raw, flat motivational appeal. The motivational presupposition behind this campaign was that the Pepsicola company should not sell a drink; instead, it must sell sociability. According to this philosophy, you don't sell a soda, but social aplomb. You sell Pepsi by convincing people that all of the pleasures of being fair and debonair are to be found in a bottle of Pepsi. Well, Pepsi seems to have cut so much into Coke's sales that Coke had to retaliate with a similar campaign. Consequently, we learned next that "Things go better with Coke." (You can just see some young fellow, before popping the question to his girl, first popping a bottle of Coke into his back pocket as a kind of rabbit's foot!)

The assumption also is that you can buy happiness. Think of that; you can *buy* it, you can purchase it! After all, how else can you get happiness? If things aren't right, buy a bigger home, move out into the suburbs. Move into the same situation with all of those other young and fair and debonair suburbanites who drink Pepsi. All you need is a grill in your backyard like everybody else. Learn how to burn your hamburgers to charcoal out there, and you too will find happiness. More pressures; more pressures on *marriages*. Not only are there pressures to buy and spend—but think of the greater pressures that mount when Pepsi and charcoal and the suburbs don't really come through. Then what is wrong? It couldn't be Pepsi or Mad Avenue philosophy—no it must be that we can't make it together. We never were compatible. So happiness now is a new wife or husband! And that can be bought too, at the price of a divorce and the ruined lives of children and a guilty conscience.

Mad Avenue has taught us all to abhor obsolescence, which hypocritically was planned, of course. It is built into your automobile battery which dies one day after your three-year guarantee is up. Your automobile tires, two weeks after the final adjustment is past, fall apart, and your water heater lasts one month longer than its warrantee. We have come to accept and believe in this obsolescence. We don't patch up cars anymore; we buy new ones. You could probably keep one going for twelve or fifteen years, but who tries? Even the Volvo ads don't claim that many years, do they? The whole idea of obsolescence carries over into marriage in another way—if a wife becomes obsolete, grows a little too short for her weight, a little too difficult to handle, why not get a new model? Well, why *not* get a new one? Why not? After all, this is the philosophy; this is the way of thinking you have bought in other areas. Along with that philosophy goes another—the trial marriage. The advertisement runs: "You must be completely satisfied; otherwise you may return the unused portion and your money will be cheerfully refunded." If not "completely satisfied," why not similarly "return" a wife or husband?

And since Mad Avenue has drummed it into your ears for

so long a time, haven't you actually come to believe that you *deserve* the best? Or, at least, don't you deserve a little pleasure now and then? You've been such a hard-working husband, you owe yourself a little pleasure. You owe it to yourself to have some joy and happiness in this world. If she stands in the way, why not remove the roadblock; if she can't bring pleasure, then maybe somebody else can. This is the philosophy; this is the ethic that has been poured down our throats like Pepsi and stuffed into our mouths like ground beef. We bathe in it; indeed, we are swimming in it. Clearly our worst pollution, it is around us everywhere.

And really now, if you can buy happiness, why not? Our children have bought that philosophy, too, and we have helped to sell them on it! For instance, we taught them that you can buy your way out of the problems and sadness of life by popping pills, and it is obvious that they have taken us at face value. Though we haven't abused drugs in quite the same way, we set the goals and charted the course for them to do so. They simply pushed our premises to their logical conclusions. We taught them on TV. Mad Avenue said if you have any pains or aches, or if you simply have a tough problem, take a pill and compose yourself. Well, that is what they are doing. They are doing it so effectively that they have built a culture and an entire way of life upon this philosophy.

Why are we fussing? We taught our children that philosophy by our advertising and by public acquiescence in it. They have seen the shelf full of home remedies in our closets and bathrooms. They know that mom regularly goes to the psychiatrist to renew the prescription for her tranquilizers. They know that dad regularly takes that extra-strength pain reliever. Why shouldn't they take similar measures to get rid of the problems that this old, worn out, motheaten generation has handed to them? The problems of the bomb, of a world that can't get along together, of not knowing what standards to adopt about marriage and sex, and a hundred others like them have been served to them on a tarnished platter. And we've given them no other answer but *escape;* escape into fantasy, alcohol and drugs. Why in the world shouldn't they blow their minds then? We taught them to. They bought the philosophy, jazzed it up a bit and learned how to use drugs to get out of it all. They learned to turn us off as they turned on that world of colors and lights and music instead. Why not?

Well, some of them are beginning to find out the answer to that question; many of them far too late. But for each one that does, there are a hundred new ones coming on every day. The pushers are everywhere making new converts to get money to support their own $40 a day habit. And so the problem grows arithmetically and skyrockets. What drugs and the drug culture do to marriage is devastating. They lead to strains and horrors and fears with an intensity unknown before. The organic effects and the psychological instability that this life-philosophy will bring upon the next generation are fearful to contemplate. Add to this the new experimental ideas on marriage and communes that the hippie culture has developed, and you have what amounts to an ideological attack on marriage. What is marriage going to be like in another generation? Around us a generation is growing up dependent upon drugs, possibly deforming its unborn children as the result of chromosome breakdown. Situation ethics that has been taught by avant garde professors and liberal clergymen is being worked out in practice. What will be the outcome? Can marriage survive?

Other ideological attacks have been levelled against the structures of marriage for a good while. Consider Freud, whose views permeate modern thought. Somebody with a long-range rifle viciously picks off people right and left, and before the smoke has cleared people begin to say about the murderer, "wonder who did it to him?" Instead of, "Look at what he has done," you hear, "Look at what society did to him." We live in a society that has largely bought that ethic. It calls itself a "sick" (i.e., not responsible) society. Combined with the rest of these problems, look at the explosive force of this ethic that, in short, teaches that everything that I do wrong is somebody else's fault. Freud said to take an archeological expedition back into the patient's past (he's a patient; sick, not guilty, you note). See who did it to him. How did Grandma injure him? His parents? Society in general? The Church? It isn't his fault; it's somebody else's fault. And, of course, what they did to him isn't their fault either, because their faults are somebody else's fault, and so it goes, ad infinitum, like knocking down a row of dominoes. Ultimately, this blasphemous viewpoint casts full blame for man's sin upon God.

What are we going to do with this world and this society of ours? Are we going to be able to maintain the institution of marriage? Possibly not. Marriage as we have known it is finished; marriage for many is all but gone. We cannot maintain marriage successfully in this modern world apart from a radical change. Two changes must take place in order to save it. Those are absolutely essential to preserve marriage.

The *first* is the adoption of an absolute authoritative Standard. There couldn't be more confusion; there couldn't be more of a mix of ideas, values, concepts, and just plain question marks than there is today. To cut through the fog like a laser beam, modern culture needs a beam of light. Fortunately, that laser beam exists. Light that can penetrate the densest darkness is available. The One who was called the Light of the world has Himself provided light for the world. There *is* such a Standard.

The reason why there is such confusion today is because the generation before rejected that Standard. When the Light was extinguished, naturally, darkness came. Many theological seminaries abandoned and mocked the faith that they had been established to teach. One preacher summed up his seminary experience this way: "The first year," he said, "they threw out the Old Testament. The second year they threw out the New Testament, and the third year they tossed out the cover." Secular *and* religious leaders have been maltreating God's Word, undercutting it in every way possible, minimizing it, reducing it to man size, trying to make the Bible a laughing stock and an anachronism in the eyes of young people. As a result, in the minds of many youth they undercut the authority of God in society. The one Authority, the only Authority that can bring authority to all other areas of life is no longer accepted as the Standard.

You say that today the authority of government has gone. Why? Because it has no accepted authority from God underlying it. Authority in the school has gone for the same reason—God's authority backing it up is no longer there. Likewise, the authority needed to sustain marriage has gone as well. When you see authority disappearing, you can chalk it up to one cause: there is no longer a defined authoritative Standard widely accepted by our society.

There is a *second* factor necessary to preserve marriage. It is true that we need a Standard to tell us what a marriage should be like. It is true that we need an Authority to settle questions, to set goals and bounds, and to regulate the relationships and the functions of husbands and wives and children. But in addition, we also need a transforming and motivating power that can change us and make us capable of doing what that Standard requires and that can give us the ability day by day to grow in conformity to it.

As a Christian who believes the Bible and who time and again has counseled persons whose marriages are on the rocks, but who also has seen them changed, I am not just guessing or speaking theoretically about this. A power to change is needed, and that power is available. I *know* that Jesus Christ changes lives and makes marriages over anew. I know it because the Bible says so and because I have seen it happen just as the Bible says it would.

One couple who were on the verge of a divorce when they came, were dismissed eight weeks later, and their teen-age son said that they were acting like newly-weds. It was a new family; a new home. What he said is typical of what happens *regu-*

larly. He was wrong in one respect, however. They were not really acting like most newly-weds. Unfortunately many newly-weds build marriages on emotion. Rather, their new feelings were the result of a radical transformation brought about by the Spirit of God during eight weeks of earnest prayer and effort to conform to the Word of God. This time they had feeling based on a marriage, rather than a marriage based on feeling. All that we did was to point them to what the Bible says and then help them to structure their lives according to God's commands. God, by His Spirit, gave them strength and brought about the change. What a transformation it made! They trusted Christ and His Word and began to do the things that God required of them. And He gave them the power to do so. This happens all of the time when people repent of their sin, trust Jesus Christ as Savior and begin to mean business with God. But note carefully: salvation cannot be understood simply as another escape from pain and unhappiness—it is not a new drug. Jesus Christ does not simply give the greatest "high." Salvation must first and foremost issue from the recognition that one has sinned against a holy God, whom he has most heinously offended by breaking His law. One turns to joy and peace only when he turns *from* his sin in repentance.

It was refreshing to see a marriage that was far gone so joyously transformed. Both parties had been stiffarming hope when they came for counseling. They were holding hope at arm's length, saying, "I don't want to get my hopes up again, because if I do I know they'll come crashing down to the ground just like they have a hundred times before." Many people come with that attitude, and we know they do. They come as a last resort, thinking that counseling probably won't work. Often one of the parties wants the other to come *against* his wishes, or perhaps they both were pushed to come by a pastor. But when the Holy Spirit convicts them of sin, and changes their relationship to God, they also begin to see a change in each other, and hope grows again. Soon the arm begins to relax more and more, until finally instead of stiff-arming it, they embrace hope. Change generates hope, and from hope issues further change, as the Holy Spirit, using His Word, works in the lives and hearts of those whom He regenerates, and makes them His own. When the Holy Spirit gives faith to trust Christ, He also gives power to obey His Word.

How can a husband and wife settle differences if they do not have an authoritative Standard external to themselves? How can they? He says, "I think this." She says, "Well, I think that." They have reached an impasse. But when this happens to Christians, there need be no impasse. Both are basically committed to the fact that it is what *God* thinks that really matters. There need be no impasse because God has given a Standard that is able to equip His people to meet every situation that they may have to face in life (II Tim. 3:16, 17). In the Scriptures there are principles that cover every life problem. A Christian husband and wife together can find the joy and excitement of discovering these.

But apart from the power of God, real change is impossible. You know what you are like; you know how often you have failed—even when you tried the hardest (not to speak of all of the shattered New Year's resolutions). You know that there is no hope. Remember too the good intentions after you had that last big brawl? Remember how you hugged and kissed and determined that things were going to be different? Apart from a power greater than your own, you know you will continue to fail. You cannot obey God apart from the power of God; nor can you know His peace. But the same power that raised Jesus Christ from the dead can resurrect your dead marriage to newness of life and enable you to live for Him. God promises this to all who repent, and I have seen it work in lives to make changes that stick.

There is really no *other* hope. In this swirling, spiraling mass of confusion that we wrongly call modern culture, can't you see that marriage is doomed apart from those two factors? Is your marriage based upon God's Standard? Have you experienced the transforming power of the Holy Spirit that alone can enable one to live according to the principles that this Standard sets forth? Repent and believe the gospel, and the marriage that God requires can be yours.

Parental Sex Education

I was asked to speak about the general topic of counseling children about sex, focusing also upon two specific problems: the problem of masturbation and the problem of homosexuality. I might be able to branch out beyond these matters in the discussion period afterward if you care to have me do so. But my remarks at this point will be confined to those three subjects. The first of these is broad and basic, and must be discussed in detail. The other two can be touched upon only briefly afterward.

You are here because you want to teach your child about sex *yourself.* You want that privilege and you have, therefore, assumed that duty. Every privilege, of course, involves a duty. I commend you for your purpose. But let me warn you that you have undertaken a difficult task.

Being on Teaching Terms

If you are going to teach your child about sex, you must first be on teaching terms with him. You must know the prerequisites for effective teaching. You must be able to establish and maintain good communication with your child. You cannot teach him about sex, or any other subject for that matter, without such communication. In speaking about sex, if you don't have good communication you are going to find that he is likely to become embarrassed, clam up, blow up, or simply refuse to talk to you. Perhaps some of you already have discovered this. So, our first question tonight must be: how can we establish good lines of communication?

Taking Time

The answer to that question is very simple, yet it is difficult to do and profound in its effect. In spite of all of the

---

[1] An address given October 29, 1970, in the public high school, Quarryville, Pennsylvania (revised).

pressures of modern living, you must find time to talk to
your children. If you can't find it, you must make it! It does
not matter who you are, you cannot have good communication unless you work at it, and the way to begin is by taking
time to talk. Good intentions, kindness, gifts, privileges or
whatever else you like will not take the place of quality talk.
In establishing communication, there is no substitute. Some
parents foolishly suppose that it is possible to discuss an emo-
tionally charged subject like sex when they have not established lines of communication first by discussing other subjects. They sit down with their children and try, and to their
dismay discover they cannot. They do not know how to talk
to their children about sex because they simply do not know
how to talk to their children. They have not been working at
it. Learning how to talk to your child is an important matter
from every perspective. And certainly it is basic to sex education.

Listening

Communication is a two-way street; it means talking, but
it also means listening. You must learn to hear your child out
instead of cutting him short. You must learn to let your child
talk through a matter that is important to him. You must develop the habit of listening with genuine attention and even
eagerness. Sometimes you will think that what he is saying is
unimportant because it does not seem important to you. But
you must evaluate the situation from the child's viewpoint.
The basic question is whether it is important to him. You
must learn to consider a matter important whenever it is important to your children. Something should become important to you *because* it is important to your child. When he
comes to you eager to discuss some question and you give
him a halfhearted response (or no response at all), you close
down communication. If your usual response is "tell me
about it some other time," or "I'm reading now," or "I'm
sorry, I've got to go to a meeting tonight," you are teaching

your child that you are one person to whom he cannot talk. Soon you may find him coming to you less and less, and eventually not at all. When he or she was eager to talk and you didn't care enough to pay attention, you laid the groundwork for future communication problems.

If you truly were unable to talk at the moment, you might at least have said, "Look, that sounds like it's so important that I want to take enough time to talk to you about it in full; I don't have enough time now, so let's schedule our discussion for later on." But if you do, be sure you keep that appointment as faithfully as you would keep any business appointment. By failing to listen, you already may have begun to widen the communication gap and lessen your opportunity to talk to your children about sex or any other vital matter.

If you give them the idea that you are not interested in the subjects that are vital to them, children will not listen when you try to talk with them about sex. Because they do not believe that you understand what is vital to them, they will consider what you have to say to be out of touch. If, when they brought what they considered important matters you minimized them and turned them off, they will learn to turn you off.

So the most important first principle is that you must learn to respect your child by listening to him. This is not to say that his views are always going to be right or that every subject that he is concerned about is of the same importance, or that you can give unreasonable amounts of time to him. You will need to exercise judgment about these matters. You may have to help him to change his views and lead him to take interest in more crucial matters, but you will never be able to do so unless you listen to him. You must respect him enough as a person created by God to listen carefully to him even (especially) when you must reject his views.

If you think about it, you will see that the same sort of communication breakdown may have happened to you and your wife. You raise a subject, but perhaps she doesn't want to talk because you have introduced a touchy matter. So she cuts you off with a short answer. What do you say? You may tell yourself, "That's the last time I'll raise that issue." Similarly, when your child brings something up and you cut him off, he may learn to respond in the same way. He may say: "I'm not going to get stepped on by raising that question again," or, "This meant so much to me, but my parents don't seem to care; I guess I'll have to work things out for myself from now on." If this happens time after time, the area of communication grows smaller, and smaller, and smaller, until there is no space left. There are many parents and children for whom there is no longer anything significant left to talk about. Many young people have been functioning for so long a time *on their own* that when they are brought for counseling they indignantly take the position, "What business is it of my parents whether I do this or that?" But parents can expect nothing better when they fail to respect their children as human beings that God has made. Children have a right to come to their parents with matters they think vital and important.[2] You must learn to respect your child as a human being for whom God has made you responsible, by taking time to hear and discuss the things that are important to him.

Sex Is Only One Matter

Let us now turn to the next question. In order to talk about a difficult matter like sex, you must do so against the background of a growing number of discussions of difficult questions. You cannot suddenly plunge into a discussion of calculus with somebody who has never learned basic math. The way to learn to talk about difficult problems is to talk regularly about increasingly difficult problems, including sex. At each stage in a child's sex education you can talk to him about what he needs to know because you are able to build

---

[2]Cf. Deuteronomy 6:20; note how God expects parents to handle a child's questions.

upon the conversation levels of the past. He knows automatically that when you sit down in that favorite chair with that expression on your face, you're about to talk about something that is worthwhile and interesting because that has happened often before. Sex should not be isolated. Instead, it should be put in its proper place as one among other important subjects. When sex is isolated, when it is uncommon for dad to pull up a chair, close the door, and talk, already the discussion is prejudiced; the child becomes apprehensive about dad's strange behavior and is on his guard. Dad has made sex suspect. There are enough problems connected with sex in this world of sin, so that there is no need to add other complications. But that is exactly what you tend to do when you single out sex by making it the one topic you finally push yourself to talk to your kids about. If you haven't learned how to talk to them about other matters, you are not going to do very well by beginning with this difficult subject. So I'm suggesting, first of all, that if we spend enough time talking about serious and important matters of all sorts, the serious and vital matter of sex may be raised and heard more easily in that kind of context.

Taking Children Seriously About Their Sins

Many people avoid or lightly dismiss serious questions raised by their children. Not only do they fail to take their interests and problems seriously, but they also fail to take children seriously about their sins. Children like that come into our counseling sessions all the time. For example, a young girl had told her parents frequently, "I'm no good; I'm just no good; I'm stupid, fat, ugly and a complete failure. The world would be better off without me." Do you know how they handled that? They always replied with something like, "Oh, come on Susie, you don't know what you're talking about. You're a fine girl." So she was turned off.

One day Susie tried to take her life and her parents were shocked. They had anticipated nothing of the sort. When she came to our office with her parents, she was still saying the same thing and her parents were still failing to take her seriously. They didn't hear her yet; they had learned how to turn off unpleasant communication. They had learned to *minimize* her words by saying, "You don't know what you're talking about." We took her seriously by asking, "Susie, how stupid have you been? Tell us about your failures. What have you done about your ugliness?" and questions like this. Susie immediately took heart and counseling proceeded well. Instead of minimizing, parents must learn how to take their children seriously when they make such statements. One of the most important things in this world to human beings (whether they are children or parents) is to be taken seriously about their problems and their sins.

I do not know how many times a woman in the very first counseling session has said something like this: "Oh well, I guess I haven't been much of a mother," or, "I guess I haven't been much of a wife." Usually there is a little pause on each side of that statement, setting it off. This woman is watching and waiting to see if the counselor is going to do anything with her self-evaluation. It is almost as if she has let go of a little helium-filled balloon and she is watching to see if you are going to grab the string.

Whenever this happens we say, in effect, "Whoah, stop! (not usually with those words, though sometimes we might use them) . . . This is crucial." In other words, we grab the string, pull that balloon down and pop it. We want to see what is inside. We continue: "If you are not much of a mother, that's serious," or, "If you are not much of a wife, that's serious. God expects you to be a good mother and wife. Tell us how bad a mother (or wife) you are." Now we get one of two reactions immediately. If this is merely a "pious" statement intended to impress, she will back off quickly and say, "Now don't get me wrong; I don't mean to imply that things are *that* bad." But nine times out of ten that is not the response. Rather, there is a brightening of the eyes and a flooding forth of the story. It is like pulling the stopper: the whole story pours out. For the first time, perhaps, she knows that somebody is taking her seriously. Someone is listening to her own evaluation of herself.

The same is true of children. Why did the girl who had attempted suicide tell us her story that night when she hadn't told her parents? Her parents were still minimizing as she came into the counseling room. when she told us, "I'm just no good," they replied, "I don't know how she could say such a thing: she is such a wonderful girl." We had to stop them and say,

"Now although you may think that you know your daughter well, you don't know her life like she does. There is only one Person who knows her better than she, herself, and that is God. So we'd better listen to what she has to say. We'd better let her tell us what she thinks. Probably her evaluation of herself is dead right, but her solution to her problem was almost dead wrong."

When she saw that we were taking her seriously, the whole story came out, a story of terrible interpersonal relationships that led her down one blind alley after another until she threw everything up into the sky and said, "It's no use going on; the world would be better off without a person like me." She was doing many wrong things, but God's solution was to straighten those things out His way, not to give up on life.

We need to take our children seriously when they speak about their problems, about their sins, and especially when they make negative evaluations of themselves. When we do so about other matters, our children will be more likely to confide in us if they begin to get into trouble over sex.

Talk Is Not Enough

But when you talk to your children, you must remember that talk about problems alone is non-productive. There is much false talk about talk, just as there have been many false

ideas about listening (especially those ideas of Carl Rogers[3]).
I don't want to discuss listening tonight, but I do want to discuss talking. Talking in itself is not helpful. Talking must be
viewed as only a means to an end, and not an end in itself. It
must be used as a means for solving problems. The solution to
a problem ought to be the end product of talk. Otherwise,
talk only opens up more cans of worms. If, for instance, you
merely talk to a person with whom you have had a bad relationship, the talk serves only to tear the scab off the old
wound again.

It is true that bare talk may bring momentary relief, but if
nothing is done about changing the relationship, both parties
will go away and feel worse five hours later. For the moment
they feel better for having gotten it off their chests, but afterward they recognize that all that their talk did was to rehearse
the problem and re-emphasize its seriousness. It may even
have enlarged the problem. Talk always should lead to biblical solutions. Talk must be used as a means to find and imple-
ment God's solutions. Even when, as in giving sex education,
the purpose of talk largely is to convey information and attitudes, it also should lead to life and action that is based on
that information. Decisions may be made and courses of action often may be laid out as a result of a true discussion of
sex. Such talk, then, should not be merely information giving; it ought to be used as a means to an end, and never
allowed to become the end itself.

There Are Always Two Problems

Remember, when you talk to somebody, there are always
two problems that you must face: (1) there is the question
you are talking about, and (2) there are the interpersonal

---

[3]Rogers has been applauded for his emphasis on listening; yet that is
precisely what he does not do. Cf. Jay Adams, *Competent to Counsel*
(Nutley: Presbyterian and Reformed Publishing Company, 1970), pp.
87 ff.

relationships between the two people who are talking. The issue itself often is no larger than the dot that my pen makes, and can be solved easily. But the issue may not be solved at all because of the poor interpersonal relations that may be as large as my hand. Just as my hand covers a dot, so the interpersonal problem covers the issue, so that you are never really able to get to it.

Often counselees are perplexed because they cannot solve some very simple problem. They may have tried to do so for many years, but they could not because there was another problem covering it up, the problem of their sinful attitudes toward one another. Can you imagine two people fighting over an issue like this:

> "My wife leaves drawers out when she's finished with them; she won't close them. When I come around the corner, ugh! I get a stomach full of drawers!"

Can you imagine adult human beings fighting over this? Well, in one case they were. They were fighting like cats and dogs over that issue and they couldn't solve it. Why? Because the husband had not only had a stomach full of drawers, but he had also had a stomach full of his wife!

Take another typical problem or two: A man throws his socks on the floor and drapes his pants over the chair and his wife has to hang them up for him. She is furious with him. She thinks,

> "He has never grown up. He wants me to pick up after him the way his mother did. If he wants me to mother him I will, but if I'm going to play mother, he is going to have to learn to do what mother says."

The first thing you know, she is not only picking up the pants in the house, but she is wearing them too. No wonder they have never been able to solve that problem! People get divorces over whether the husband should take out the trash. Married people cause pier 9 fights over whether to squeeze the toothpaste tube in the middle or roll it from the end! Are they really fighting over trash and toothpaste tubes? Yes, they are, but also over much more. When he comes to see this, a husband may admit, "I don't love her any more, Whenever I see that toothpaste tube squashed in the middle, I think, 'That blasted woman has been at it again.'"

But you see, that is just the very point that must be made about talking with your child. How can what you say to your child about sex seem meaningful if your relationship to that child is wrong? The question of sex and its problems is certainly larger than the issue over the toothpaste tube, but if you can't even talk to him about tubes, how can you talk about sex? If the relationship is not right, there can be no fruitful discussion. So, you see, there are two factors in any discussion: there is the *issue* which is being discussed, and there is also the *relationship* (good or bad) between the people involved in the discussion.[4]

Admitting It When You Are Wrong

In order to establish good communication, you must be willing to admit it when you are wrong or have done wrong. There are very few parents who do that. All too few parents are willing to admit to their children that they have been wrong or have wronged them. When I speak to Christian school teachers, I find that they too have the same problem. They claim to believe in original sin, but I find that often they do not act as if they believe it. They live with their students from the time the bell rings in the morning till the time the last bell rings in the afternoon. Day after day, five days a week, year after year, they live with those same children. Yet, when I sometimes ask them how often they talk to their children about the things they have done wrong or confess to them that they have wronged them, I usually draw a blank.

---

[4]Counselors must learn how to sort these out. Often it is impossible to work on the issue until first the bad attitudes that are destroying the relationship have been dealt with.

But can sinful teachers live sinlessly in class? Of course not; their sins are apparent every day, and both the teacher and the class are well aware of the fact. They teach children to believe in original sin, but by their actions they belie their belief. "Well," they may say, "you don't really mean that I should tell those children I did something wrong? You don't expect me to apologize or something, do you? Wouldn't I lose my authority?"

What really builds authority? After all, if you teach a child that everybody is a sinner, that includes you as well as the children; there can be no double standard. You break down the authority for your teaching when you say one thing and do another. That means that if you have done something wrong, you must learn to own up to it. You never lose authority by admitting your sin. Children already know it when you have wronged them. A teacher gains authority and respect when he is willing to admit a wrong, confess it and straighten it out.[5]

And when you, as a parent, admit your wrongdoings to your son or daughter, you don't lose respect either. As a matter of fact, this is one of the things that might open communication for the first time. After all, you expect your children to confess the wrongs that they have done and to straighten them out, don't you? But where are they going to learn how to do this? What kind of model will they have and after whom are they going to pattern themselves if they have never seen it happen in their home? If instead, when their parents do something wrong the children see them trying to cover it up, what are children going to do? They too will learn to cover up; they too will learn to mishandle their sins in the same way that their parents do. Parents instead must teach them God's way: "He who conceals his transgressions will

---

[5]And, of course, make every effort to forsake that sin in the future. You cannot expect to use confession and apology as a means for justifying continuance in sin.

206

not prosper: but he who confesses and forsakes them will obtain mercy" (Prov. 28:13). They must learn to confess sin to God and man. The authority that God gave to the parent is not undermined at all by admitting one's sin: the parent acknowledges thereby that he too is under the authority of God's Word.

Sharing Your Failures

Similar to admitting sins is the painful experience of sharing your failures with your children. This really helps to open communication. You do not need to do this, of course, except when it is really necessary, but you ought to be willing to do it then. Here comes Johnny with his report card. The report card is a disaster! It has one C, two D's and four F's (and the C was a gift). Now, what does the parent do? Dad takes one look at it and bellows: "I never got grades like this when *I* was in school." Whether that statement is apochryphyl or true is beside the point. But even if dad has not had a convenient lapse of memory, his comments are not helpful and certainly tend to close communication. If but for a moment dad would pause in his wrath and disappointment and take three gulps (he'll probably have to take ten at first) and think back hard enough to remember some experience where he goofed in a similar fashion, he probably could help Johnny instead. And he probably could open an area of communication wide enough to drive a Mack truck through. If dad would report honestly at that point about his own experiences, he could be exceedingly helpful. For example, he could say to Johnny,

"Look son, it's not just that this report card disappoints me terribly; of course you know it does. But Johnny, let me tell you something about my own life. During the last couple of years in high school I started goofing off. I began running around with girls and not doing my studies. I just barely squeaked through my senior year with a report card nearly as bad as this. For a long while I had been looking forward to going to Johns Hopkins University. I had my heart set on going there, but when they took a look at my grades they said, 'forget it.' You know that I ended up at Podunk College.''

Relating an experience like that does several things. It causes some pain for dad, and the child knows that it does. Dad's pain shows the child that dad really loves him. Johnny thinks,

"He has been willing to share this difficult experience out of his past; he has been willing to embarrass himself because he loves me and is concerned about me. He must really think this is important."

The experience puts dad "one down" instead of "one up" on the child. This makes him very approachable for Johnny to talk to. It pries open lines of communication.

I'm not asking you to invent stories; doubtless, there are plenty of true examples from your past that you could draw on. But where you can, you ought to be willing to share your failures when it is necessary to help your child. That is one reason why in the Bible we read so much about David after his sin with Uriah and Bathsheba. He recounted that experience in the Psalms (Psalms 51, 32). There he tells us how his unconfessed sins affected him. His sin was "ever before" him; it dogged him day and night. He says that he staggered around like a soldier with arrows stuck in his back. He felt as if he was going to die. His tongue clung to his mouth. He experienced other anxiety reactions: his heart beat heavily, his loins burned, and his bones felt as if they were cracking with age. He was in utter misery until God sent Nathan, the Prophet. Nathan pointed the finger at David and said, "Thou art the man." Then David fell down on his knees before God, confessed his sin, and the joy of relief flooded into his soul. It was, he said, like standing in the middle of a crowd of people who were singing, shouting, and praising God. Toward the end of two of those Psalms he wrote (in effect),

"I shared this with you so that I could help you. Don't be a fool like me; don't be a mule that has to be dragged to confession before God. Instead, come quickly to God when you have done something wrong. Confess it, and receive forgiveness, relief and joy."

Because David shared his experience, those Psalms mean much to us. When we read them we reverberate. Sharing one's experience for the sake of somebody else can be effective. Well, dad and mom, you also need to learn how to do that. Then when you sit down to talk to your child about sex, he will listen.

If He's Confused and Embarrassed

But suppose you haven't been building confidence and establishing lines of communication gradually and haven't been giving your child the sex information that he can learn at each level. You need to recognize that he is going to be confused and embarrassed when you finally do determine to have a talk. If you remember back in your own life, maybe that was so for you; it was for me. Most of what I learned about sex came from my peers in the early days, and it was mostly wrong. Not only was the attitude toward sex wrong, but the facts were too. I got a terribly confused picture. I would try to piece together bits and pieces, but couldn't. One person would say this and somebody else that, and the two didn't fit together; it was like trying to make a picture out of pieces of jigsaw puzzles that came from six different boxes. And it was terribly frustrating. Today, there are still many youngsters like that. Many, who may be younger than you think, have a lot of pieces of the puzzle or the wrong pieces from some other puzzle. When you try to talk to your child, if you have been neglecting this question, more than likely you are going to find him confused and embarrassed. You must recognize this and try to make it easy for him to say, "I don't understand." You must not demand that he know facts that he has not yet been taught.

If you have neglected teaching him prior to this point, is there still hope? Possibly. Maybe a good way to begin is by admitting your previous failure and expressing your present desire to help. You might say, "Look, Bill, my mom and dad didn't tell me about sex in time, and as a result I was confused. I'm sorry that I haven't talked sooner to you." Putting together a couple of these principles that we have been talking about, you might begin with power and force by saying,

"I know that I have failed you, but I don't want to fail you any more. I'm sure there must be some confusion of the sort that I had. I'm sorry that I let you get your information in the wrong way. But I want to correct the situation now and sit down and talk to you and tell it like it is."

When Communication Has Broken Down

"If you are in the process of building communication this is okay," you say, "and it may do even if it is a bit shaky. But what if communication has already broken down, if the lines are snipped? What do you do then?" Of course, that is another problem, and here I can suggest only two possibilities. They are simply an extension of what I have just mentioned above. The Bible has an answer in Matthew 5:18 and Matthew 18:15-18. There Christ talks about reconciliation. The only way I know to repair communication lines is to do so directly. Confess your sin to God; ask Him to help you to change. Then, go directly to your children and admit the ways in which you have wronged them, ask their forgiveness and start to straighten these things out. If reconciliation takes place a new relationship then can be built. On this basis the lines of communication can be restored. The Bible says to take the log out of your own eye before you look for a splinter in someone else's eye (Matt. 7:3-5). Whenever you complain about another, first you must make sure that you have the lid on your own garbage can. And if your relationship with your children is bad, I don't see any other way for you to begin.

If two people are behaving like this:

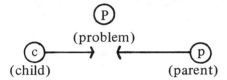

accusing each other, angry at each other, resentful toward each other and blaming each other over some problem, the question is how can you get them to do this:

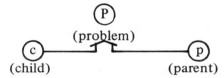

They have been attacking each other, but you want them jointly to attack the problem instead. Okay, how do you get them from this

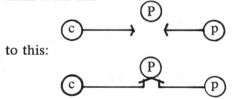

to this:

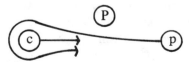

That's the question. Well, the answer is by doing this:

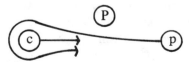

Let's say the child's arrow is pointing toward you. But if you extend your arrow line around the child it comes back and points at you too. If you want to get both arrows to point toward the problem, first you must get the arrows headed in the same direction. One way to get the arrows headed in the same direction is by also pointing your arrow toward yourself. You say, "Look, I did so and so, and I'm sorry." He can't disagree with that. He may disagree with everything else that you say, but there is one thing he won't disagree with—that you have wronged him. For the first time in a long while both of you are headed in the same direction. As a result, it may not be long before both of you are going to be heading in the direction of solving problems.

When you approach your child (or any other person) that way, you should spell out the specific ways in which you have wronged him and ask him for forgiveness. But don't stop there. Ask also for help and cooperation in building a new relationship. You do not want to drift back into the old sinful patterns again.

But if the situation is so far gone that even attempts at reconciliation make things worse or are looked at with suspicion or rejected, you probably need to seek the help of a third party. But be sure that the one you seek out is qualified to help on the basis of biblical requirements.[6]

Three Factors

Well, so much for communication. Next, I want to suggest three other important prerequisites. You must have the *desire,* the *conviction* and the *information* necessary to help. Recognize now that it will take time and effort and probably require study in order to be able to tell your child all that he or she needs to know about sex. There is much information abroad, some of which is wrong. You probably may have to read some books. You will have to think through some problems. You probably will have to analyze your child before you can share with him the right kind of information in the right way, at the right time, in the right amounts to meet his needs. This is not the kind of mechanical thing that you can do in one sitting and then run your fingers over your forehead and say, "Whew, I'm glad that's over." This is going to take repeated contacts over a period of time, some of these

---

[6]Cf. other articles in this volume that discuss biblical qualifications.

growing into long discussions, others only amounting to brief talks. It will take effort on your part to study and plan ahead. The questions kids ask sometimes are amazing. So you may have to do some homework, and you may not always have answers even after you have done your homework. They may drive you back to the books (or to your pastor or somebody else) to get better answers. Children come up with some astounding questions!

Not all of your problems may come from the child's side. It may be difficult for you to teach your child about sex because you may not feel too comfortable in talking about the subject. This difficulty may stem from your own background. You must change any wrong attitudes that you have acquired through poor training or bad sexual experiences. In order to do so you may need to study the biblical viewpoint to gain the biblical perspective of Paul in I Corinthians 7 and the writer to the Hebrews who wrote: "Let marriage be held in honor among all, and let the marriage bed be undefiled" (Heb. 13:4). Your own attitude toward sex must be wholesomely biblical. The attitude in which you teach your child communicates too. Sometimes it says more than your words.

So then you will need determination. You must do something difficult. Good determination brought you here tonight. Good determination will grow as you continue to come each week. But be careful. You may tell yourself, "Now I am in good shape; I went week after week to those meetings, and now I know all about it." But if you don't *do* anything about what you have learned, it is all time and effort down the drain. You must put legs to your learning; you must follow through with determination. God gives His people the strength and determination to do difficult things (cf. Phil. 2:13).

Convictions and A Standard

In addition to determination and correct basic information you need convictions before you can talk about sex. That is one of the amazing things about many writers; they make assumptions and take certain viewpoints toward sex, but they fail to tell you where these convictions come from. One writer thinks a practice is proper, another says it is wrong; one believes something is permissible, another declares that it is not. Who is to say? Again, let me ask, where do those convictions come from? You must face the fact that you are making value judgments all of the time. You do, you know, when you tell your children that sexual relations must be reserved for marriage alone. Now how did you come to such a conviction?

You'd better be prepared for that question. Young people today are questioning the values that you may simply assume to be true. They don't take things for granted and they won't let you take things for granted either. You need to have some solid convictions then, but where are you going to get them? Are you going to appeal to your opinions? Well, you might. Many people do. But then so will your teenager. If you do, all that you have taught him by that is to believe that each man is his own ultimate authority. Surely, you can't object then when he believes you and acts on this principle! He will say concerning your values, "That's your opinion; I live in a different era; I have different opinions." Are you going to appeal to society? Well, you can't any more. There might have been a time when the Christian ethic so permeated society that most people believed the same thing and even practiced it, at least outwardly. But that no longer holds true. The world around you today (and even that liberal clergyman in the church on the corner) is saying, "Promiscuous sex isn't so bad now that we have the pill." If your convictions are based on nothing more than what society says, you're in trouble. If your code is only what grandma taught you, or what you think is right, that is a very shaky base for your child's sexual education. She says, "Mom, you don't know society any more. You're out of it; you aren't with it."

What you need is a standard. Not using a standard is like trying to dial a correct telephone number by chance. If you do that, you may end up by dialing the zoo, the city morgue, and a thousand other wrong numbers, but the chances are that you will fail to get the number you want. That is a fruitless way to solve your problem. When you want to know a phone number, you go to the telephone directory; you use the standard. Your son asks, "How do you spell that word, Mom, with an ie or ei?" You can't remember, so you turn to the dictionary and there is the answer. You use the standard. Well, you also need a standard for ethics. And God, who has determined what is right and what is wrong, has given us an infallible one: the Bible. If your convictions are not based on God's Standard, you are in trouble. Young persons today are challenging everything; they want to know the source of your convictions.

I don't know where your convictions may come from, but I am thankful that I have a solid basis for mine; that I have an objective Standard. Because I am a Christian I know that the biblical revelation from God tells me what I must do and what I must believe. It is my Standard. It is relatively easy for me to know what to say about sex because I have a standard of faith and practice. I know what I believe and why I believe it. I have God's dictionary, God's telephone directory, to which I can turn for answers.

If you don't have this Standard, frankly, I don't know what you can tell your children. If you don't have the Bible as your Standard, as a Book that stands outside of yourself and other people, whatever you believe is subjective. Only a divine revelation gives you a timeless Standard so that your child can't say to you, "That's what *you* think" or, "That's just what *your* generation held to." You need an objective Standard that is not like that.

To take an example, I was asked to speak about masturbation and homosexuality tonight (and I do intend to get to these subjects). But opinions differ about these matters. There are people who say that homosexuality is determined by genes. Today there are people who say that homosexual relations are just as acceptable as any other way of expressing sexual desire. Homosexuality, they feel, should be allowed, and even encouraged if necessary. Men and women should be given full freedom to engage in such activity. Some churches that no longer follow the Bible even do allow such freedom. But I do not believe that they are right. I have convictions about that issue. And I have an answer for my child when he asks about homosexuality. If he doesn't ask, eventually I will tell him something of what God says about it; you see, I have convictions because I have a standard.

I don't have to flounder around and try to figure out on my own what is right and what is wrong about the question. If I did, I wouldn't get to first base. I have a Book that tells me that homosexuality is not sickness, but sin. This Book from God tells me that homosexuality is not due to genetic disposition, but to the choice of a sinful way of life. The Bible calls homosexuality an "erroneous" and an "abominable" way of life. I have something then that is clear-cut, straightforward, and unquestionable. I have convictions and something solid to base them on, and I am thankful for it. I don't have to appeal to my own authority; I point my children to the Word of God. You'd better discover where your convictions come from if you intend to instruct your child today, because he is going to want to know.

Masturbation

Assuming all of this, what about these two assigned subjects? Well, first of all, let us start by constructing a viewpoint (and I must take a *biblical* viewpoint because I cannot take any other) on the question of masturbation. So far as I'm able to read, there doesn't seem to be any direct reference to masturbation (as such) in the Scriptures. There is one verse that some people (especially Roman Catholics) have taken to refer to masturbation, but it is highly questionable that it does. It probably does not. So, if we do not have specific reference to the matter, we must turn to other broader biblical principles that will apply to this subject. One very important principle is found in I Corinthians 6:12 where Paul says: "All things are lawful for me, but I will not be mastered by anything." This is an important principle. It means that even those things that are right must not be allowed to get such a hold over a Christian that they become his master and he becomes their servant.

Anyone who has had anything to do with counseling young people, particularly young boys, knows that many of them are *trapped* by this habit. Masturbation can get such a hold on a child that it can almost drive him out of his mind. Let us remember, too, that today there are aspects of the problem that you and your parents didn't have to face. Children are maturing sooner now than they used to mature in the past. This means that the sex drive arrives sooner. They are maturing some time around the ages of 11, 12 or 13. And on the other end of adolescence, their schooling has been lengthened. They are now in droves going to college as well as to high school. There was a time when a sixth grade education was all that was necessary to get by, then it was high school, and now, college. Fewer are getting married as early as before; and so the unmarried period during which this desire is strong (and for males possibly the strongest) has been lengthened, causing intensified difficulty. It was bad enough for you to have to endure that period in an abbreviated form, but it is even worse for your children. Paul says that a Christian must not let anything gain the mastery over him. But, I have seen young people (even *Christian* youth) who are so tangled up in this problem that they hardly can think about anything else but sex all day long. And the more they engage in masturbation, the more they depend upon it, the more they want it, and the more they feed it. And the more they feed it, the more they are trapped by it. They are caught up in one big vicious circle. Masturbation can gain such a tenacious control over them that it saps their energies, takes their minds away from their studies, and sets them to thinking about sex everywhere they go and with every person they see. Masturbation is a serious problem, much more serious than many may think. Your children need your help in dealing with this problem.

Because of the little public and private discussion that is devoted to the subject of masturbation, you might forget your own adolescent problem and tend to minimize its importance. But just because the problem of masturbation is not discussed often in society does not mean that it is not an explosive problem. It is explosive and it is serious. And your child (particularly if he is a young boy) is likely to be having problems with masturbation if he has grown to puberty. And, as an additional complication, don't forget, in our society sex is used commercially on every billboard, in every magazine, and as a part of nearly every television program. Everywhere you turn, women dress provocatively because that is what the billboards, magazines and TV dictate. Young men have a terribly difficult time.

Now look at a second principle that is found in Matthew 5:27, 28. There Jesus said that it is not just the outward act of adultery that God is concerned about, but that God also considers the inward thought and consent of the heart to be adultery. A child who becomes tangled up in the masturbation spiral eventually cannot avoid becoming involved in this sin as well. It is true that in a very young child masturbation may be only exploratory, but it won't be very long until it gets plugged into fantasizing about sexual relations with imagined sexual partners. Jesus said that this is sin. Adultery of the heart, He said, is just like hatred, which is murder in the heart. To kill with a knife or a gun is not the only way to become guilty of murder before God. It is better for the other fellow of course, if you murder him only in your imagination, but it is no better for you in the sight of God. The same holds true for adultery. And there isn't any one of us here tonight who isn't a murderer in that sense. There isn't anybody here who has never said something like, "If I could just get my hands around his neck, I'd *wring* it." Maybe you haven't said it outwardly, but you surely felt it. Your son may be facing a similar problem. He looks at a woman and lusts after her in his heart. And for him this may be all tangled up with the question of masturbation. So if you are going to take a stand on this question, you must have some solidly-based biblical convictions to stand upon.

But specifically, what can you do to help? At least two things: (1) If you are a Christian you can explain the biblical basis for your convictions to your child. You also can explain the function of the organs of the body that are involved and how God expects them to be used properly. That is the first thing you may do; you can explain. (2) The second thing you can do is to talk through the problem to a biblical solution. Notice, you must not just talk, as I said before, you must also lend help. Realize how hard it is to break a habit that may have been established long before. Find out the facts about his problem (how severe, etc.) and give him the help that he needs. What he is going to need is some sort of structure. Of course, the power of the Holy Spirit in the Christian's life is a tremendously important motivating factor. But people who don't know Christ as Savior can't know anything about that. The Holy Spirit sets forth the need for structure in the Bible. He talks about "putting off" old patterns and "putting on" new ones. He insists on "discipline." He speaks of "training" (by practice) in godliness. He gives principles by which to guide our lives. And when the structure of these principles is translated into concrete action in the child's situation and his determination is to serve God in this matter, he will be on the right track toward breaking that habit and establishing instead the correct biblical pattern for his life.

One of the things the youngster needs is a very specific concrete structure adapted to his particular situation. Kids come for counseling in agony over the problem and beg us to help them to stop. They often feel so guilty that they plead, "Do something for me, help me some way." Well, there are all kinds of things that can be done to help. For example, you can find out when and where masturbation occurs most frequently. Is it after the child goes to bed at night while he lies awake for a half hour or so? If it is, then something might be done about how he goes to bed. He may be encouraged to exercise vigorously to tire himself out so that he will fall into bed exhausted. When his head hits the pillow he needs to fall asleep. If masturbation takes place mostly in the morning when he wakes up, you might suggest that he put his alarm clock across the room instead of next to his bed. Then the first thing he must do when he awakens is to get out of bed to get to that alarm clock. He should then begin the habit of making his bed.

Another young man who always engaged in the practice while in the bathroom found help by putting a big X made of masking tape in that area. This sign reminded him that he had promised God to stop masturbating, and whenever he saw it he prayed instead. There are many concrete things you can do to help your son or daughter. But the principle is that they need your *help;* that is the key point. When the structure is set up, you should agree to check up and remind them until the new patterns have been established. It would be desirable to start the day together by praying about the matter. Sin, the Bible says, must be fought daily ("take up your cross daily"). It is not good enough to lecture children about masturbation. The answer is talk—plus biblical action. The only standard for the first is Scripture, and the only sufficient motivation behind the second is the power of the Holy Spirit.

Homosexuality

What about homosexuality, the second matter that I was asked to discuss? The Bible is more explicit about this question. In many places God talks about it. In Leviticus 18:22, homosexuality is called an "abomination." In Leviticus 20:13 God says that when two Israelites were caught in this act they were to be put to death. In the New Testament, Paul tells the Romans that when men gave up God, God gave up men! As a consequence, those men who deserted God and His Standard and were deserted by God, wandered into shameful practices. And when he talks about these degrading passions and practices, he specifically talks about homosexuality. He says:

"For this reason God gave them over to degrading passions, for their women exchanged their natural function for that which is unnatural and in the same way also overturned the natural function of a woman and burned in their desire toward one another; men with men committing indecent acts and receiving in their own persons the due penalty of their error" (Rom. 1).

He calls homosexual acts "things that are not proper" (vs. 28). He says, "Those that practice such things are worthy of death" (vs. 32). We read about homosexuality also in I Corinthians 6:9, in Genesis 19, and also in I Timothy 1:10. In each instance, it is always considered a sin, not a sickness. In every biblical reference homosexuality is considered an irresponsible way of life, not an irresistible state that results from genetic factors. It is called an "error," a wrong way of life.

We frequently help homosexual people at our counseling center. In the last three years we have had the joy of helping a number to successfully break this habit. Without fail, in every instance, it began at an early age—sometimes very early. The practice may begin pretty much as it did in John's case: John and four or five friends have a garage that one of their families allows them to use for a clubhouse. So they start holding club meetings. All is innocent enough at first. Then somebody gets the idea: "Admission to the club from now on is going to be only for those who are willing to take all their clothes off." That is how John got started. Taking clothes off led to all kinds of other things; in John's case it was the beginning of a homosexual habit.

In other cases, an older person who has already acquired the habit may ensnare a younger person. You ask, "Why do effeminate-looking people so often get involved in homosexuality? Is it because of genetic factors?" Well, the effeminate aspects of the person may be genetic, but the fact that he got involved in homosexuality is not. It is the effeminate-looking person that the practiced homosexual is looking for.[7] He is the one he will seek to seduce. He is the one that he is going to entice. The Bible is clear: homosexuality is a *sin;* it is not a sickness. And that is why there is hope. What hope is there of changing genes? But God is in the business of dealing with sin.

Prevention is one important matter that you can work at as a parent. You can know where your children are and who they are playing with. You can keep closer tabs on them. You can be sure that even your own children at home do not spend a lot of time in the bathroom alone and naked with one another. There must, of course, be a full discussion of the question of homosexuality with your child at some point. But if he already has become involved, there is only one solution, the same one that I mentioned before. Bring the judgment of the Word of God to him. Seek to bring him to repentance and then help him to change.

Conclusion

I have said a few things about the kind of communication that is necessary for teaching a child about sex. I put the stress on communication because this is basic to a discussion of sex or any other subject. You must have this kind of communication with your child in order to tell him the facts of life. But even more important (though we have been considering the facts of life tonight) is that more difficult question about the facts of death. If you can talk about sex, then you also can raise that even more vital subject with him. The facts of death

---

[7]Contrary to many explanations of homosexuality, the choice of a partner that approximates (as closely as possible) a member of the opposite sex shows that the problem does not exist in a lack of interest in heterosexual characteristics, but just the opposite. Other factors are basic to the perversion. But note, interest in an effeminate person by another male shows his basic need and even desire (though warped) for a female rather than male.

really are central to all of the convictions that you must have and that you must communicate to your child. The facts of life and the facts of death are bound up together. Christian faith centers around that question. God sent Christ to die for my sins in order to solve that problem. He was born to die.

I, as a lost, guilty, rebellious sinner, deserved eternal punishment in hell for my sins, but Christ took that punishment for me on the cross. When God raised Him bodily from the dead, He thereby publicly declared that His justice had been satisfied by Christ's substitutionary death in my stead. I now trust in what He did for my salvation. And, as far as I am concerned, I do not know how a person who is not a Christian can really deal with either of these difficult subjects in a world of tremendous pressures such as you and your children are under today. I just don't know, apart from the Standard of God's Word, the message of salvation it teaches, and the motivating power of the Holy Spirit, how a person can go on. About that subject I shall be glad to speak to any of you later, if you would care to talk further.

Drugs and Your Child

During the 1960's an old but relatively minor problem became a new problem of major proportions for the Western world: the problem of drug abuse. Parents everywhere have become frightened over the potential destruction that such abuse could bring to their children. Christians are no exception, although drug abuse among members of the Christian community seems to occur less frequently than elsewhere. Because of the potential dangers, it is important for every Christian parent to study the question, to know the facts and signs, and to learn what to do about the problem.

The use of opium, heroin and marijuana is not new. But the indiscriminate and illegal use of these drugs by vast numbers in Western society is a wholly new phenomenon. Eastern countries have had the problem for centuries. India and Nigeria, for example, after long experience with the unrestricted use of products manufactured from the *cannabis sativa* (hemp) plant, from which marijuana and hashish are produced, have banned their sale and use. The opium trade of the orient has been well known for centuries.

Isolated individuals in the Western world have been known for drug dependence (Sigmund Freud, for instance, was dependent upon the use of cocaine in periods of depression). But drug use never became a matter of general concern until during the last decade. The use of these older "natural" drugs, together with the addition of a wide spectrum of new synthetic drugs that have recently become available, has quickly spread, so that the illegal production, sale, possession and use of drugs has grown almost overnight into a problem that has national and even international implications.

The natural curiosity of youth, coupled with the search of many young people for an experience and dimension in life that transcends the crass materialism of their culture, and the affluence, rebellion, distrust and basic disorientation of modern students, has given the various elements of organized

225

crime a strong incentive to exploit this rapidly expanding portion of the population by the organization of an amazingly effective world-wide operation for the manufacture and marketing of illegal drugs at huge profits. Psychedelic experiences in which the perceptions are distorted, have been touted among youth as mind-expanding and offering the most exciting "trip" in our modern culture.

Modern advertising, and particularly TV commercials, with which the youth culture of today has grown up, has pictured the use of drugs and medications as the sovereign solution to all of life's problems. Parents, too, with over-encouragement by some physicians and (especially) psychiatrists, have set a forceful example for their children by their widespread acceptance of and dependence upon tranquilizers (they outsell aspirin) and other mood-enhancing drugs as the prime means of coping with the complex problems of society and the ever-deteriorating interpersonal relations in families that are falling apart from the lack of a biblical foundation. Thus drugs have come to be used by our culture, either to give "kicks" to the user or to reduce his guilt and anxiety.

The influence of some early experimenters like Timothy Leary, who themselves have become dependent upon drugs, the widely publicized drug dependence of the Beetles and other rock musician idols, and the general distrust for an establishment that says "no," have also been potent factors that have combined to "turn on" English speaking youth. In Viet Nam and Korea the use of pot (marijuana) by American soldiers is widespread. Liberal theology, with its hollow promises and amateurish mimicking of political and social movements, has been found out. It does not challenge or speak relevantly to the under-30 generation because it is an echo. Like that generation from whose parents it took away the Scriptures and the gospel, and that it spawned without standard or principle, it has no program or eschatological *telos*. From such a sterile husk of Christianity young people are turning in droves to the oriental religions that offer a psychedelic religious

227

experience beyond the coldly rational or insipidly irrational approach of liberal theologians. In increasing numbers they can be encountered on the streets of San Francisco, Dallas, or Philadelphia evangelizing the public by urging them to try a simple chant that will enable them to obtain their heart's desire. Oriental mysticism and the transcendent experience go hand in hand with the effects obtained through the "trips" arranged by the use of hallucinogenic drugs, the "highs" of the amphetamines (or pep pills), and the dream-like Nirvana of the opiates (heroin) and marijuana. All these, and doubt-less many other factors, enter into the explosive situation that is currently spiraling beyond control. Only a virile, bibli-cal Christianity with truth spoken in sincerity and love can stem the tide. Only a powerful godliness that transcends mere form as the true vital experience in life can stand over against the psychedelic experience as superior.

Drug abuse involves the use of two classes of drugs: (1) those that are *addictive,* and (2) those that are *habituating.* *Addictive drugs* are those upon which a user may become "hooked" by becoming both physiologically and psychologi-cally dependent upon them. The body builds up a tolerance for such drugs and demands even larger doses in order to ob-tain the same effects. When one "kicks" (withdraws from) the use of the drug, withdrawal reactions occur. These reac-tions in some instances may be quite severe.

Habituating drugs are those drugs that (according to the present state of research are said to) cause psychological de-pendence only and do not cause physiological dependence in the user. There is no withdrawal period upon the cessation of the use of a habituating drug, although as a result the user may become tense, uneasy, depressed and irritable.

Within these two larger classes are several sorts of drugs:

I. The Addictive Class

   A. *Opiates:* Heroin, Morphine, Codein, Paregoric, Demerol (Meperidene), Methadone (the last two are synthetically produced) are the principal drugs in this category. All opiates are narcotics. A narcotic is a drug that relieves pain (produces analgesia), causes sedation and depresses. The analgesic properties of the opiates distinguish them from other sedatives, depressants and tranquilizers. Of these, heroin ("horse") has become the most popular because of its strong effects. Heroin wipes out fears and anxieties, brings on drowsiness and causes sexual responses (even to the point of orgasm). Heroin is sometimes sniffed, but more often "shot" (taken by injection). Thus opiate users often may be identified by the needle marks on their legs or arms. Heroin is illegally marketed and, therefore, may be sold on the black market at an enormous profit. It is not unusual for a user soon to have a $40-$50 per day habit. Theft and other associated crimes have increased markedly with the rise of drug abuse, since drug addicts who soon exhaust their own resources turn in desperation to robbery in order to obtain needed funds. Many themselves become "pushers" (salesmen) for the drug in order to obtain funds, and in this way the number of new users grows arithmetically. Female addicts often turn to prostitution in order to raise money for drugs.

B. *Amphetamines:* Benzedrine, Dexamyl, Dexadrine, and Methedrine are the principal "ups" or "pep" pills used by drug addicts. They are stimulants that cause excitement, euphoria, happiness and keep one awake. Amphetamines may be taken orally or by injection. Amphetamines impair judgment, make one reckless—heedless of himself and others, and if the user remains awake for two or more days, he may become subject through significant sleep loss to the same perceptual distortions that are caused by hallucinogens. Amphetamines may produce high blood pressure, accelerated or irregular heartbeat and even heart attack. Users of speed (methamphetamine or methedrine) may also suffer from liver infections, abscesses, abdominal cramps and respiratory disorders. They tend to become hostile, violent and even destructive toward others. Whereas opiates tend to relax, the amphetamines stimulate the user.

C. *Barbiturates:* Amytal, Barbital, Luminal, Nembutal, Phenobarbital, Seconal and Tuinal are the chief barbiturates on the market today. Barbiturates are sedatives that are taken in order to relieve anxiety, and may cause sleep. Sometimes they are taken by amphetamine users in order to counteract the effects of pep pills. By depressing the central nervous system barbiturates induce sleep; unlike opiates they do not relieve pain. Overdoses, particularly when used together with alcohol, can cause death. Barbiturates cause impatience and irritability, loss of balance, and slurred speech. Seventy-five per cent of all suicides by drugs involve the use of barbiturates. Withdrawal symptoms are severe.

D. *Tranquilizers:* Equinil, Librium, Miltown, Placidyl, Valium are used to help one cope with life by reducing anxiety and bringing on euphoria and a who-cares attitude. Tranquilizers cause the mind to filter out and reduce sensory information, keeping the user from being agitated by his environment. Thus, judgment is impaired. Inappropriate attitudes may result. Under some conditions tranquilizers may damage white blood cells. Dangerous severe convulsions may occur upon withdrawal. Tranquilizers have been prescribed with abandon by psychiatrists and physicians as if happiness and the solution to life's problems were contained in a pill. But dependence upon tranquilizers in order to cope with life is merely the substitution of one inadequate pattern of problem solving for another.

II. The Habituating Class

A. *LSD* (lysergic acid diethylamide), and other hallucinogens (including mescaline, peyote, psilacybin, DMT, MDA, belladonna and morning glory seeds). Hallocino-genic drugs are taken in order to "turn on" or "tune in" a whole new world of sensory experience. Because of their ability to distort sensory data by impairing percep-tion, users become entranced by the distorted world and think (erroneously) that they are having a deep, tran-scendent or even religious experience. Time and space and one's body and mind may seem to float; one may seem to be outside of himself; hallucinations and delu-sions occur. Depth perception is impaired; and there is a ten per cent chance of suicidal or homicidal attempts. Hallucinogens are deceptive: rather than opening up a new world by "expanding the mind" they dangerously close the mind to the true world around and distort much of the data that reaches the mind. Wrong decisions are made based upon faulty perceptual information that may lead to dangerous and foolish courses and action. The same perceptual distortions are experienced by users of hallucinogens as in those purported by persons who suf-fer from acute sleep loss (two or more days) and those who have been labeled "psychotic" or "schizophrenic."[1] LSD "trips" may last as long as eight hours. "Bad trips" can occur to any user of LSD at any time, and are unpre-dictable. During a bad trip the user becomes confused, anxious, depressed, and may panic. LSD is a very danger-ous drug that does not improve, but rather distorts per-ception, lowers intelligence, may damage the gene make-up, may bring about malformations in babies, and may possibly lead to leukemia, suicide or violence.

B *Marijuana.* "Grass" users claim that since marijuana is physically non-addictive and does not ordinarily cause

---

[1]These latter categories must be rejected. Cf. Jay Adams, *Competent to Counsel,* pp. 28-40.

such violent reactions as LSD and other hallucinogens, its sale and use should not be prohibited. What are the effects of "pot"? Usually one becomes "drunk." Three or four "joints" (marijuana cigarettes) bring about a pleasurable unawareness of time and space and may make colors seem brighter and the hearing keener; ten will lead to hallucinations. Reactions may differ from person to person. Reports include among the effects of "tea": depression, euphoria, confusion, hallucination, drunkenness, panic and fear, over-confidence, lack of self-criticism and judgment, loss of concentration, acute sensitivity to sound, dryness of mouth, enlargement of the pupils, and a floating sensation. Most of these reactions are also associated with LSD and the other hallucinogens. In current medical literature there are few defenses of marijuana. Instead, one reads about progression from marijuana to other stronger drugs, failures in school, loss of memory, inability to learn, listlessness and lack of initiative, and other undesirable results.

What should be the Chrsitian's position toward the abuse of these several sorts of drugs? I should like to suggest at least six fundamental responses that may be given to that question.

1. A Christian may not buy, sell, condone, use or possess any drug illegally. The principles of Romans 13:1-5 and I Peter 2:13-17 are explicit: in such matters a Christian must submit to the laws of the land. Simply as law-abiding citizens Christians may escape many of the problems that plague others who skirt the law. Christian parents, then, by both precept and example must stress the importance of obedience to God's authority granted to the state.

2. A Christian may not use any drug that is harmful to the body (or is likely to be so—cf. Romans 14:23) in proportions that may be harmful. His body is the "temple of the Holy Spirit" (I Cor. 6:19) and should be used in order to "glorify the Lord" (vss. 13, 20; cf. also Romans 12:1). God has not

given Christians an option about how they may use their bodies; their bodies, like the rest of themselves, belong to God (vs. 19), and must be used as He commands.

3. A Christian may not become addicted to or dependent upon a drug (I Cor. 6:12). While controlled use of drugs for medical purposes under some circumstances may be legitimate, habituation and addiction necessarily involve a "mastery" of the drug (vs. 12) over the individual. When addiction is likely to occur as the result of medical treatment, the use of other non-addicting medication ought always to be sought if available.

4. A Christian may not make use of drugs that distort his perception and thus mislead him to make wrong sinful responses. Erroneous data growing out of disperception may plainly lead to false judgments and actions. In I Corinthians 12:23, Paul observes that all things do not edify.

5. A Christian may not use drugs as a substitute for responsible action in the solving of life's problems. Drugs may not be used to relieve guilt and anxiety stemming from one's failure to handle problems God's way. Paul speaks disparagingly of those who "sear" (i.e., make insensible to pain) the conscience (I Tim. 4:2) and characterizes the attitude of those who are "past feeling" as antithetical to Jesus Christ (Eph. 4:19, 20).

6. A Christian may not rely upon distorted perceptual experiences and mastery by a chemical as a means of discovering truth or entering into a religious experience. Such an attitude shows rebellion against God, since it substitutes drugs for the study of the Scriptures and the true worship of the triune God. God seeks true worshippers, who "worship in Spirit and in truth" (John 4:23, 24). Truth and true worship are incompatible with the disperception experience. The principle behind the verse "be not drunk with wine, but be filled with the Spirit" also seems to apply (Eph. 5:18).

Pastors and other Christian leaders need to discover that

they have more to offer in helping drug dependent persons to withdraw and find independence from drugs than they might think.[2] The six reasons stated above are not merely reasons for drug abusers to abandon drug living. They also are good reasons for not beginning the use of drugs in the first place. The power of Christ to strengthen (Phil. 4:13) and the ability of the Scriptures to give us all of the information that is necessary to meet every life situation (II Tim. 3:17) are profound factors in helping drug abusers to withdraw. Christians themselves should undertake the task of helping drug-dependent persons (if necessary, in conjunction with a physician) rather than refer to a psychiatrist or someone else.

There are some things that you as a Christian parent can do to prevent your children from becoming involved in the illicit use of drugs:

1. You should prayerfully instruct him in the six principles stated above. Do not begin such instruction too late. Studies have shown that drug experimentation usually begins during the Junior High School age.

2. You should instill strongly in your child respect for the legitimate authority of the state.

3. You should instruct him in the harmful results of drug abuse and warn him about the subtle ways in which such drug usage may begin.

4. You should take to heart earlier comments pertaining to the example of parents in dependence upon drugs, and reevaluate your own practices.

5. You should know where your child is at all times.

6. You should know all of your child's friends and help him to acquire the proper friendships.

7. You should take time to establish good avenues of Chris-

---

[2]Centers (perhaps in churches or Christian homes) are needed to which young people who seek help in withdrawing from drugs may be sent for care during the period of withdrawal.

tian communication with your child (see comments elsewhere in this volume about this matter[3]). Perhaps no other factor is as vital as this.

Parents also may take various positive steps to help their child break away from the use of drugs (assuming that he has repented of his sin and wants to do so):

1. Speak to a trusted physician about the effects of the particular drug that your child has been using and the side effects and withdrawal symptoms that he is likely to experience.

2. Speak to your pastor and obtain his help. He will probably want to set up a weekly counseling program with you and your child extending over the next eight to ten weeks.

3. Insist that your child break off all associations with others whom he has known to use or sell drugs. He may need to write letters (don't suggest that he speak to them) to such persons, breaking off his relationship. Remember, "Evil companions corrupt good morals" (I Cor. 15:33).

4. Obtain and report the names of any known pushers (illegal drug sellers) to the authorities.

5. Be ready and available at all times to help your child over periods in which he may be tempted to return to drug use. Let him know specifically of your loving concern and availability.

6. Help him to schedule (he will need some rigid structure at first) a full and productive life in the service of Jesus Christ.

7. Help him to acquire new Christian friends. If he tells them frankly about his past problem and his present determination to remain off drugs and asks their help, possibly they can be of great help to him. Obviously, he should participate fully in the activities of a sound Christian church, particularly taking an interest in the youth meetings.

---

[3]"Parental Sex Education," pp. 195 ff.

8. Help him to see the biblical answers to the problems that may have been disturbing him. Good counseling from the pastor in conjunction with your own help should be of value.

9. Remember that talk that does not result in positive biblical action leading to solutions to problems is counter-productive. Always direct discussions toward God's solutions and agree upon as many as possible at each conference. Then, *schedule* the first step in taking the agreed-upon action. In structuring such discussions, the following agenda may be found helpful. Proceed by writing the answers to these questions:

(1) What is the problem?

(2) What does God want me to do about it?

(3) When, where and how should I begin?

POPULAR NAMES FOR DRUGS

acid - LSD
barbs - barbiturates
bennies - amphetamines (esp. Benzedrine)
blues - barbiturates
candy - barbiturates
cocktail - methadone substituted for an opiate
coke - cocaine
copilots - amphetamines
dope - a depressant
drivers - amphetamines
eye openers - amphetamines
footballs - amphetamines
goofballs - barbiturates
grass - marijuana
hard stuff - an addicting drug (usually heroin)
harry - heroin
hash - hashish, marijuana
horse - heroin

236

joint - marijuana cigarette
jolly beans - amphetamines
junk - any drug causing psychological or physical dependence
Mary Jane - marijuana
monkey - morphine
nimbies - bartiburates (Nembutal)
peanuts - barbiturates
pep pills - amphetamines
pink ladies - barbiturates
pot - marijuana
reefer - marijuana cigarette
seggies - barbiturates (Seconol)
sleeping pills - barbiturates
snow - cocaine
speed - Methedrine
stick - marijuana cigarette
stuff - drugs
sugar - cube of LSD
tea - marijuana
truck drivers - amphetamines
weed - marijuana
yellow jackets - barbiturates

Group Therapy - or Slander?

Articles recently appearing in national magazines have emphasized the rapid growth of a modern phenomenon known as The Group. These articles have given the general public a candid look at the procedures that are used at the more lavish and well-known centers in which group "encounters" are taking place (cf. the article in *Time Magazine,* November 9, 1970, pp. 54-58). These articles themselves should be the most potent means of discouraging Christians from participation in such activities. The fundamentally non-Christian purposes and character of the activities in question should be apparent to every instructed Christian. Shedding all principles and inhibitions (even those Christian virtues that are appropriate to normal everyday living), sinful men and women are encouraged to express their here-and-now feelings with abandon in whatever manner they may see fit. The then-and-there perspective to which responsibility before God is attached is perilously forgotten. Resentments and bitterness may be vented with vehement hostility; sexually erotic contacts are encouraged in stimulating and provocative contexts. Literally, there are no holds barred. The desperation of unbelieving psychiatrists (if they cannot be charged with more reprehensible motives) at least seems apparent in these attempts to rid their patients of their cultural and religious "hang ups."

It is not, therefore, with the more obviously extreme varieties of Encounter Groups, T Groups, Sensitivity Training Groups, Human Potential Workshops or whatever name a local variation of Carl Rogers' Esalen-based movement may assume, that I am concerned in this article. Rather, I should like to call your attention to the less spectacular and, therefore, potentially more dangerous backwash now beginning to

---

[1]Published originally in *The Presbyterian Guardian,* Vol. 40, No. 2, February 1971. This article has been revised extensively. The word "slander" is used in a nontechnical biblical sense.

240

appear in schools, industry, mental institutions, counseling centers, seminaries, and even in Christian churches. These groups have not received the publicity allotted to the national organizations, which they often reflect, but they also are growing with astounding rapidity. Because participants in these less spectacular groups do not ordinarily disrobe or engage in the more esoteric practices of others who are involved in the better known programs, they may suppose that they are participating in an entirely different activity. Preachers themselves, unwittingly, may adopt procedures that are based upon non-Christian presuppositions.[2]

In addition to the "Encounter" groups that are based upon the non-Christian idea that an uncontrolled release of emotion is desirable, there are other forms of group "therapy" that stress confession and openness (honesty). One example of the latter is O. Hobart Mowrer's Integrity Groups (the distinction is becoming blurred even here, however, since just last year [1970] Mowrer "discovered" the need for "involvement." That discovery has moved his confession groups closer to the Esalen movement. He now calls for shouting, crying, and "reaching out" to touch other members of the group). It is this latter sort of group, stressing confession in combination with elements of the encounter or sensitivity groups, that seems to be making a significant appeal to Christians. Seminarians and youth groups, for instance, are now being subjected to such group programs. Since it is impossible to describe the endless variations upon the several basic themes that run throughout these groups, it might be most profitable to gather together some important biblical criteria by which any local manifestation of group encounter or therapy may be

---

[2]Cf. the recent Reformed Ecumenical Synod Report on Race (Chicago, March 2-5, 1971): "That a model be prepared for facilitating attitude change ('mind liberation') . . . the teacher would encourage them to express their feelings . . ." p. 6.

judged. And since space here is limited, I shall then focus upon only one of these in depth.

Among the many trenchant issues that might be mentioned are the following:

(1) There is no biblical warrant for systematically unlacing another person and throwing his stuffing around the room in order to ventilate one's own hostilities in a selfish attempt to find relief for himself. It is really quite unnecessary to take other people apart or tell them off in the name of honesty and openness. Biblical honesty is of a different sort, and neither requires nor allows such activity. Consider James 5:9, 10; 4:11; Ephesians 4:27-32; Proverbs 10:12; Philippians 2:4; Romans 15:1-3.

(2) "Openness" of the sort frequently encountered in such groups is not a biblical concept. While believers should "speak the truth" to one another "in love," they must not be so open that they may feel free to discuss any and all matters, without distinction or exception, with anyone in any group. Ephesians 5:3, 12 seems pertinent to this problem.

(3) Christians must carefully select the groups with which they associate intimately. They may not so associate with any group indiscriminately. The Christian's relationship to the church as a biblical group bound together by the Spirit in the bonds of the gospel, the truth and the love of God, differs radically from his relationship to other groups. It is questionable whether it is even possible for a Christian to consider seriously participation in an encounter or therapy group composed of non-Christians on the basis of the membership of the group alone. On the other hand, there is also the necessity to demonstrate the need or biblical warrant for Christians to sponsor encounter and therapy sessions composed of Christians alone.

(4) The Bible does not suggest that people with unaltered sinful life patterns should be dealt with in such groups (apart from groups gathered together to listen to the proclamation of the Word). Indeed, Matthew 18 seems to require that prob-

lems be kept on a personal level if possible. II Thessalonians 3:14, 15 and I Corinthians 5:9-11 seem to be of relevance.

(5) Biblical wisdom indicates that one must not rely upon sinfully rebellious and biblically confused persons for counsel. On this matter, read Proverbs 13:20. Should the blind lead the blind?

(6) Such groups tend to develop divisive loyalties that do not serve the cause of Christ. The warnings of Titus 3:10 and Romans 16:17 are of importance in evaluating the tendencies of very "open" groups which, in order to preserve their openness, may find it necessary to become very tight-knit. Specialized groups can too readily be substituted for the proper group, the Church itself.

These and other similar issues may be raised about some of the groups to which many earnest Christians have been attracted in search of help. I cannot discuss them more fully here, but I do want to devote the remainder of this article to a serious objection that may be raised with regard to many of the confession type groups that are now beginning to appear under Christian auspices. That objection is that there is (unintentionally) a grave amount of gossip or slander sanctioned and carried on under the aegis of the Church

Slander and gossip are specifically forbidden in many places in the Bible (e.g., Titus 3:2, Eph. 4:31). Nevertheless, what happens in some groups is, in my opinion, nothing short of a violation of these divine injunctions. Members of the group are frequently encouraged to "tell their story" to persons who, until that moment, have no involvement or interest in their affairs. Yet now, before strangers, they are encouraged (sometimes coerced by group pressure) to reveal the details not only of their own foibles and failures (that sort of thing might be permissible under carefully controlled conditions), but also those of persons who have no means of knowing that their privacy is being invaded, who are powerless to stop it, and who are not present to correct the one-sided account that inevitably is given. Even in those groups in which one is supposed to concentrate upon his *own* sins (and this is by no means the prevailing approach), it is usually necessary to talk about others behind their backs in order to tell one's own story. It is hard for persons in such a group to avoid gossiping. Since our major problems in life mostly have to do with our relationships to others, it is nearly impossible to be "open" about ourselves and not involve others.

Can we dump our personal resentments and complaints on the table before strangers without slandering others? Specifically, should young people at a Christian college or seminary be encouraged to spill the beans about their parents, their brothers and sisters, their pastors, and other young persons back home? Should wives be provided opportunity to discuss the failures of their husbands behind their backs? Should men in a confession-oriented group disclose intimate details about their marriages and then declare to their wives that loyalty to the group supersedes the loyalties of the marriage relationship and, therefore, prohibits them from disclosing what they said?

A group context of this sort often encourages group members to make accusations and charges apart from the benefit of the safeguards of both the informal and official biblical procedures involved in reconciliation and discipline. When the group meets without these safeguards, it may operate as a kangaroo court. Without demanding adequate evidence or witnesses, without providing for a defense by the party whose name and character may be at stake, the group allows a member to make charges that it frequently accepts at face value. Judgment is given and action is often recommended on the basis of this one-sided information. In effect, in his absence and usually in complete ignorance of the fact, a brother in Christ who may be quite innocent of the charges is tried, convicted and judged *in absentia.* Great damage may be done as a result, since the group has failed to heed the warning of Proverbs 18:17, "He who states his cause first seems right until another comes to examine him" (Berkeley).

Talking to others who have not previously been involved in a problem about those who are is nothing less than the substitution of a human methodology for the divinely-ordained procedures outlined in Matthew 5:23, 24; 18:15-17. There God says that a Christian believer who is offended by another must go to him and attempt to bring about a biblical resolution of the matter leading to a reconciliation of the parties. (If he has wronged his brother, then he still is obligated to go and seek reconciliation.) Jesus specifically requires that the matter be kept in the strictest privacy: "If your brother sins, go and reprove him in private" (Matt. 18:15, NASV). Only reluctantly, when reconciliation cannot be achieved by private consultation, is one allowed to involve others—and then only one or two. These men are not pictured as members of a therapy or encounter group, but rather as counselors who should be "heard." If at length their efforts also fail, they become witnesses and official discipline is required. Only then does the matter become public, i.e., known to the Church (this probably means known to the eldership, who represent the church; not in the first instance to the entire congregation).

I do not want to convey the idea that I am opposed to groups as such. To oppose groups is like opposing motherhood or sunsets. God structured a group-type society from the creation. What I want to oppose is the abuse of groups. All sorts of group work may be biblical and, therefore, profitable. One of our tasks as Christians is to develop every form of group that is compatible with and, therefore, useful to the Kingdom of God. But it is also our task to detect and warn against every abuse of the group that appears.

There is a biblically legitimate form of confession group: such a group should be as large as but no larger than the group of persons who actually are parties to the offense. These may be as few as two, as in the examples given in Matthew 5 and 18. That is to say, a biblical grouping provides for the possibility of reconciliation and seeks it as its end. The group must, therefore, be composed of the estranged parties. Confession is wrongly conceived of when it is considered to be an end in itself. Unbiblical groups distort confession, making it a personal catharsis that occurs through ventilation. Confession rather must be seen as a means leading toward forgiveness and reconciliation. It is a loving act in which the other person is prominently in view, not merely one's self (Eph. 4:32).

Groups stressing confession in a non-reconciliation context often impede reconciliation. Ventilation temporarily reduces the pressure of the guilt of unconfessed sin and estrangement. The relief is temporary, to be sure, because in the long run ventilation increases one's sense of guilt. This is true since the original problem has not been solved by ventilation, the poor relationship has not been bettered, and now ventilation itself has added the guilt of gossip or slander to an already overburdened conscience.

The amazing growth of groups must be explained as a multi-factored phenomenon. For instance, new elements that characterize our modern mobile society, such as the virtual dissolution of village community life, have contributed to an acute sense of need for fellowship and friendship. After all, God made man a social creature who should find his fellowship in groups, like the family and the Church, that were ordained by God for such a purpose. There is nothing wrong with the people of God grouping together for worship, for mutual instruction and encouragement, for service and for fellowship. God Himself has endorsed and encouraged such grouping (Heb. 10:24, 25). It is not the idea of a group that must be opposed, but the distortion of the biblical idea. The problem with such therapy and encounter groups as I have described is that since they are unbiblical, they meet for the wrong purposes, they exist on the wrong basis, they operate with the wrong personnel and they use the wrong methods.

There is one note yet to sound: the Church has failed in large measure to help Christians meet their social needs and interpersonal relations in a truly biblical manner. It is time for the Church to begin to do so. The best protection against the baneful effects of unbiblical group activities is the blessing that flows from biblically oriented groups. This blessing will come only by making provision for all of those crucial social needs that God implanted in man. Many of these elements have been neglected. The Church must provide for its members more wholesome social contact, must preach, teach and encourage specifically the mutual ministry of all believers to one another in which the Spirit's gifts are used for the benefit of all, and finally must reinstitute both informal and formal discipline among its members for the glory of God, the welfare of the Church, and the reclamation and reconciliation of offenders. Encounter and therapy groups are not the answer.

The Christian School Teacher and His Disciples

The Christian School Teacher and His Disciples[1]

We talk about Christian *schools,* but what we ought to talk about is Christian *teachers* and *administrators.* It is the former about which I plan to speak tonight. The Christian school is no better than and, indeed, not different from its teachers, because at bottom the school *is* its teachers. You have heard James Garfield's definition of a school as Mark Hopkins on one end of a bench in a log hut and a student on the other. This definition boils down to the fact that only the teacher is crucial. For three and one-half years Jesus Christ taught twelve men in just such an environment so effectively that those men changed the history of the world. He demonstrated that the teacher is the school. And we as Christians should realize this above all others. Yet I find in talking to Christian school teachers, to seminary professors, indeed to all sorts of Christians, that there are very few who can articulate a biblical view of teaching and the teacher. What is God's definition of a teacher? What, according to the Scriptures, should a teacher do? What are his goals? What methods should he use? We are going to take a brief but pointed look at these questions this evening.

Jesus was the perfect Teacher. More frequently than any other word, the title of teacher was used to describe His work.[2] It was one of His own favorite titles for Himself. During the years of ministry prior to the cross He was a teacher, *primarily* a teacher. Teaching was His first and foremost activity. And the exciting fact is that this teacher of teachers had some very pertinent things to say about teaching. Moreover, this information is readily available to all in the Bible.

Turn first to Mark, the third chapter, verse 14. Here you

---

[1]This article was a speech presented to the Parent-Teacher Fellowship of the Christian School, Middletown, Pennsylvania (revised).

[2]Cf. Note at the conclusion of this article.

find the most basic principle of all: "He appointed twelve that they might be with him and that he might send them out to preach and to have authority to cast out the demons." This decision came at the beginning of the training of the twelve. It speaks volumes about Christ's educational principles. The statement outlines His essential goals and sets forth fundamental methodology. For three and one-half years the disciples were going to be taught, day and night, by Jesus Christ. Teaching, as He envisioned it, would involve living "with him."

Here, at the beginning, you will notice that the Lord Jesus *appoints* them as *His* students. The teacher sought out His pupils and accepted into His school only those whom He, Himself, had selected. Perhaps this principle of selectivity has too frequently been lost sight of—particularly in theological education. At their appointment, the purpose and methods that Jesus had in view, what He planned to do with these twelve disciples over the next few years and how He intended to do it, were also explained. He appointed (or chose) twelve that they might be "with him." That is the key word: *"with* him." You may say, "I thought He was going to *teach* them; I thought He was going to *instruct* them. And isn't that what He did? Don't we see Jesus Christ subsequently sitting privately with His disciples explaining to them in detail what He taught the crowd in general? Do we not read of His instructing them in important truths? Don't we see Him teaching, teaching, teaching His disciples?" Yes, we do. But teaching, as many people conceive of it, is thought of very narrowly. It is often considered to be merely that contact which takes place between a teacher and his students in which the teacher imparts factual information. Certainly, that is a large portion of teaching, and *nothing* I say here (please underscore that word) should be construed to mean that I do not believe in the teaching of content. We *must* teach subject matter; indeed, much more than is taught elsewhere. But there is also much more to teaching than the teaching of content. That is why the Bible does not say that Jesus appointed twelve that He might *instruct* them. He does not say that He appointed twelve that He might send them to class. Nor does He say that He appointed twelve that they might crack the books and take His course. That was all a part of it, but, note, only a *part.* There is a much larger concept in these words: "He appointed twelve that they might be with Him." "With Him!" Think of all that meant. Those two words describe the fulness of Jesus' teaching. Such teaching is full: rounded, balanced and complete. For the length of His ministry, the disciples were to be with Him to learn not only what He taught them by word of mouth, but much more.

"How do you know?" you say. "Aren't you possibly reading a lot into that phrase?" No, I don't think so, and I'll tell you why. The reason why I say that I'm not just reading my own ideas into this phrase is because in a definitive passage, Jesus Himself gave a description of teaching that accords exactly with this interpretation. In the sixth chapter of Luke, verse 40, He defines the pupil-teacher relationship, what goes on in that relationship and its results. Jesus says, "A pupil is not above his teacher, but everyone after he has been fully taught will be like his teacher." Now, did you get the full import of those words? He says, "Everyone" who is fully taught "will be like his teacher." Jesus did not say "will *think* like his teacher." That is part of it, but, again, it is only part of it. Jesus said that a pupil who has been properly (fully) taught "will *be* like his teacher." He will *be* like him, not just *think* like him. This passage helps us to understand the principles of education underlying Jesus' appointment of the twelve to be "with Him" in order to send them forth to teach. He was calling them to become His disciples (pupils) that they might be *with* Him in order to become *like* Him so that they might teach like Him.

But, did these principles work? Did their education really make them "like Him"? The evidence gives a clear answer to that question. After Jesus had risen from the dead and ascended into heaven, He sent His Spirit back to continue His work through the Church. In Acts 4:13, Luke gives us a view of how the enemies of the Church looked upon the disciples (now called apostles) who were the leaders in this work:

"As they observed the confidence of Peter and John and understood that they were uneducated and untrained men [that is, formally so], they were marveling and began to recognize them as having been with Jesus."

The evidence is now complete. Look at it: He appointed twelve that they might be *with* Him. He said that a pupil, properly taught, will be *like* his teacher. And in the course of time others recognized that the disciples had become, in large measure, *like Him.*

These data tell us some other important things about Christian education. First, Christ's words focus (as I said at the outset) squarely upon the teacher. He is the model and, therefore, all important. Secondly, Christians must not look upon education merely as the conveying of information. Because Christ certainly conveyed much information in His teaching, Christian teachers must do so too. Underscore that! Solid content is essential. But, if that is all that we intend to do in teaching, we have a very circumscribed view of teaching that is decidedly not biblical. It is not biblical because a truly biblical view of teaching takes into view the fact that the better a student is taught, the more he will become like his teacher in *every* way, not just in thinking and knowledge. He will *be* like his teacher. According to this view, the whole teacher teaches the whole student.

It might surprise you how often in the New Testament the principle of teaching another by one's life comes to the fore. Let us turn to a few passages. I do this, not because I want to take up your time, but because I want to impress you with the overwhelming emphasis in the New Testament upon this point. In I Thessalonians 1:6, 7, Paul says that the Thessalonians became "an *example* to all the believers in Macedonia and in Achaia." And then, he says, "You also became imitators of us and of the Lord" (vs. 6). Here the emphasis was upon their corporate example. In II Thessalonians 3:9, speaking about the unruly life and the undisciplined manner in which some people were acting, he says,

"You yourselves know how you ought to follow our example, because we did not act in an undisciplined manner among you, we did not eat anyone's bread without paying for it . . . not because we do not have the right to do this, but in order to offer ourselves as a model for you, that you might follow our example."

In I Timothy 4:12, Paul urged the young preacher, "Let no one look down on your youthfulness, but rather in speech, conduct, love, faith and purity show yourself an example of those who believe."

In the second chapter of Titus (we'll skip over some other similar references in II Timothy), Paul insists, "In all things show yourself to be an example of good deeds, with purity in doctrine, dignified" (vs. 7).

In Philippians, Paul could even say, "Brethren, join in following my example and observe those who walk according to the pattern you have in us" (3:17). Here his recommendation was not only "follow me," but also "follow those who are following me." And then in the fourth chapter of Philippians, he continued, "The things you have learned and received and heard and seen in me, practice these things, and the God of peace shall be with you."

Here is a clear expression of the principle of total education summed up in Christ's words "like him." In the last chapter of Hebrews, the reader is exhorted to "follow the faith" of those who have the rule over them. In John's third letter he exhorts Gaius, "Imitate that which is good, not that which is evil." There are a number of other important passages appropos to this matter, but these should be sufficient.

Surely you can see from these few samplings how frequently the New Testament acknowledges the principle of imitation. We do follow examples, people do become models for us. And when is this more true than during the formative years of a child's life?

Who has the most vital opportunity for exerting this molding influence? The Christian school teacher. "School teacher?" you say; "why not the parents?" Because once he enters school, the very best hours of a child's life go to the teacher. The choice waking hours in that child's life are in the hands of that Christian school teacher. When Johnny comes home he is tired and dragged out. He has had it, and so have you parents to whom he comes home. But in contrast, the school teacher meets him fresh (maybe not quite bright yet, but morning fresh) and at a time when the school teacher is fresh too. And during that day both the student and the teacher live upon the content that each provides for the other. The largest part of the best hours of the teacher's life that day is devoted to his students for whom he lives those hours under God. Hours on end during the school year, the materials out of which a teacher builds his life before God are furnished by his students, just as he furnishes his students with much of the materials for theirs. By "materials" I do not necessarily mean content (in the sense of subject matter), but rather, all of the things that (in a day) go into making up one's life: the circumstances, the studies, the problems, and the other situations that are presented chiefly by his classroom and his classroom teachers. There is another kind of content then: life content. It must not be neglected any more than one may neglect subject content.

Fellow students also exert a powerful influence upon one another. This very important dimension must not be overlooked, but I cannot talk about peer pressure here.[3] The

[3]The topic deserves full separate treatment. I hope to be able to discuss the subject elsewhere in the near future. It is inadequate to say so here, but perhaps one suggestion, pointing in the proper direction, may be helpful: peer pressure must be understood, challenged, channeled and used for the benefit of all and the honor of Christ.

point that I wish to make is that the school teacher lives his life in the context of those students, and the students live their lives in the context of their teacher (as a model). Because their lives are being lived out in each other's presence, they will influence each other, either in a Christian or in non-Christian directions. So when we select a Christian school teacher, we should ask some questions about what kind of person he (she) is, not merely what he knows about his subject. Holiness of life must be a prime qualification. A Christian school teacher must not be chosen simply because there is an opening that has to be filled before September. That is dangerous thinking. Time, effort and adequate funds must be expended to obtain the very best. School teachers must not consider themselves qualified merely on the basis of their professional training. Instead, they ought to say,

> "My qualifications must extend beyond an academic degree. Qualifications must extend to my quality of life. I must become the right kind of person before I am qualified to teach. When I am right in God's sight, then I shall be right to stand before His children. I must consider the kind of influence that I shall exert upon my students."

No wonder James wrote: "Let not many of you become teachers, my brethren, knowing that as such we shall incur a stricter judgment" (3:1). What a fearful thing, teachers, to think that *our* students are going to be like *us*. This thought strikes me day after day at the seminary. What Jesus says is true (they will be like me) whether I like it or not, whether I think about it or not, whether I operate according to this principle or not. The fact humbles me as a teacher.

I cannot just say, "Well, from now on I think I shall start teaching more than content. I'll try to teach students to be like me." I have been doing it all of the time whether I knew it or not. I have been influencing the lives of my students. As they go out into their ministries, they will do some things the way I did them; not only as I taught them verbally, but also according to the kind of person that I was.[4] Even when they did not want it to, my personality and life rubbed off on them somewhere, somehow. The more effectively I communicated, the more rubbed off. How important then that you and I as teachers consciously recognize this fact. How crucial too that you as parents do so. You cannot separate these two sides of teaching. You must not say, "We'll choose a teacher on the basis of his ability to understand and communicate subject matter." Yet, this is exactly what has happened all too often. A teacher might be ever so queer or crazy, he might have all kinds of personal quirks about him, his life may be a poor testimony to Christ, but some schools seem to think that this really doesn't matter. So long as he makes a profession of faith in Christ and knows something of his area, he is considered qualified. That is not a sound basis upon which to choose a Christian school teacher; not if we believe in the educational principle enunciated by our Lord Jesus Christ. Remember that principle reminds us that the student is *with* the teacher. That is to say, your children will be with that teacher day by day, hour by hour, year by year. Tremendous influences are exerted upon them as a result of that continued communal contact. In school they are learning far more than history, mathematics and science. Remember that when you select another teacher for your Christian school!

This principle of total education is simply a fuller reiteration of what the Old Testament taught about the education of children and is the very principle upon which our Christian schools are founded. This shows its centrality. I am referring, of course, to that great passage in Deuteronomy 6 that commands parents to teach their children. There God plainly puts

---

[4]Teaching methodology is affected radically by this Christian philosophy. At Westminster Seminary I teach counseling, for example, by taking students into actual counseling situations with me, so that they learn not only by reading but also by observation, participation, seminar and critique.

the responsibility for education upon the parent. By extension, parents must turn over this responsibility (during school hours) to the teacher. The teacher must accept the full parental responsibility enjoined in that passage.

Of what sort of teaching does Deuteronomy speak? We know that in that passage and in succeeding chapters, total life teaching is enjoined. This is emphasized, reemphasized and amplified as the principle upon which the teaching is to be based. There God lays upon the parents the task of teaching His commandments so that they will be passed on down through generations to come. They are to be taught to sons who must teach them to their grandsons. God says, "I am now charging you to write them on your hearts and impress them deeply upon your children" (6:6, 7). How is such a deep impression to be made?

> "You shall talk of them when you are sitting at home, while you walk on the road, when you lie down, when you get up; you shall bind them as a token on your hand. Wear them on your forehead as a badge, and write them on the door posts of your houses and your gates" (6:7-9; cf. also Deuteronomy 11:18-20).

That is truly total life teaching.

The house in which I live was once owned by a Jewish family. At the entrance, on the doorpost, there is a small metal box covered by a sliding metal lid. Inside is a parchment with part of the Ten Commandments written in Hebrew. This is the modern Jew's interpretation of Deuteronomy. Already in Christ's day the passage was taken too literally, as it still is. This important Word from God was misunderstood so that the Scriptures came to be used as a talisman or rabbit's foot. It was placed in phylacteries by the Pharisees and literally bound to their foreheads and wrists, as well as affixed to the doorposts of their houses. But that sort of thing was not what God was talking about. Rather, He was giving an important educational principle to His people. What He meant by His

258

directive was, wherever you are, whatever you are doing, in all of life (when you are standing up, sitting down, walking, lying, in your house, wherever you are), in every life situation teach the Word of God by your words and example as it grows out of and applies to each situation. God's commandments pertain to all of life, and the best way to teach them to your children is out of the milieu in which you and your children live. That is what total life education is all about. That is how the commandments of God may be taught most effectively at home, and similarly, that is how they must be taught in the Christian school.

At school most of a child's problems are generated by his peers and his teachers. Plenty of problems arise at home, but even more originate at school. During the school years the school becomes a large slice of his life and usually offers him the greatest challenges that he faces. In the problems, joys, failures, difficulties, successes, needs and heartbreaks of the school experience, it is of utmost importance for the teacher to know how to mold everything to the honor of God. It is in these that the Christian character of the man or woman is being formed. The teacher must learn how to make lying down, sitting up, standing and walking, as well as the very doorposts of the school speak of Jesus Christ. Yet this must not be done in a mechanical moralizing manner, but naturally and biblically. This will be natural only to that teacher who has a new nature and daily is living and growing according to it. Much of such teaching will be done by modeling.

What does all of this mean concretely? It means that a relationship is established and continues to exist between the teacher and your child. This relationship grows, changes, develops, is strengthened or weakened and will be more or less biblical. It will be either a loving (that is, responsible) relationship founded on God's law, or not. There is no dichotomy between teaching theory and practice. Theory and practice are necessarily integrated in the life of the teacher. The teacher teaches some theory all of the time by his or her practice.

Of course, it may not be the theory he wished to teach! If there is a feud between teacher X and teacher Y, the children in the classroom, no matter how young they may be, are usually aware of it. If every time that teacher Y enters the room of teacher X the latter freezes, don't think for a moment that those children do not notice. They learn from that experience. But what? Well, they learn that when you don't like somebody you try to avoid him or you act nasty toward him, or you simply freeze him out! They are learning that instead of seeking reconciliation immediately (as Jesus commanded in Matthew 5 and Matthew 18), you put off reconciliation as long as possible. They learn that instead of talking the problem through to a biblical solution, you talk behind his back about the one who has offended you. They are learning. Certainly they are learning. The teacher has given them a graphic, unforgettable example. Such "instruction" usually makes a stronger impression upon one's life than facts about the length of the Panama Canal. Children learn from their teachers just as they learn from their parents at home. The teacher truly is *in loco parentis.* In that classroom they are learning how to treat their future wives and children and husbands. They are learning. They are learning all of the time.

Take another example. Here is a teacher who believes in and teaches his class to believe in the doctrine of original sin. His class knows. therefore, that this teacher believes that we all are sinners and that we sin every day. Yet over a period of months that child has never once heard that teacher apologize to him or to the class or to anyone else. Never once!

What does he learn from *that?* He learns that you *talk* about doctrine, but that is as far as it goes. Sin is something that we are all involved in, but you must never think or talk about it in personal terms. You do not *act* on the basis of doctrine; it does not affect your life. You only talk about doctrine. You talk about it as the answer to a catechism question, but never as something that should change or determine behavior. It is fine to say the doctrine is taught in the Bible, but if it means a Christian school teacher or parent apologizing to a child—no sir, forget it! You can't tell me that a teacher who sins every day doesn't sometime, at least on crucial occasions, find it necessary to apologize to a class or a student. Are you afraid that you may lose your authority? Never fear. Of course you won't. On the contrary, you will only establish your authority as a Christian by apologizing when necessary. When you act according to the Christian principles which you teach verbally, you establish yourself as genuine and the Scriptures as practical. But when you fail to apologize, in practice you deny what you teach. Your behavior suggests that you do not really believe what you say you believe or that Bible teachings are unworkable. How will a child ever learn how to apologize if his parents and his school teachers never apologize to him? Where will he see the "with him" model he needs?

There is something wrong then, you see, with the way that we teach and the way that we live, not only in our homes, but in our classrooms. And what it all boils down to is this: we think we can teach the truth by reading the Bible to children and getting them to answer questions about it or by teaching them Bible content and letting it go at that. But that is impossible. Echoing Deuteronomy 6, John says that the truth has to be *done* (I John 1:6). Truth always must be lived. It will be lived and thereby effectively communicated to our children only by total life teaching.

Then there are times when difficulties come into the life of every school teacher, just as problems come to every family and every parent; these are crucial times for a class to learn. The class will be watching the teacher under pressure. They will learn from the way he handles (or fails to handle) his problems. They will learn a great deal more that day than 2+2=4. And what they learn probably will be more important too.

How do you handle your problems as a teacher? How do you handle your heartaches or sins? What do you do when life tumbles in or when you make a mistake? How do you hold up under stress or rectify an error? What happens to your relationships when people wrong you? Do you love your enemy and give him a cup of cold water? Do you pray for those who despitefully use you? Do you do good to them? Do you turn the other cheek and let someone take a second swat at you? From all of these responses children learn. The trouble is that in many instances they are learning the wrong things. This other side of teaching is fundamental.

In conclusion you may want to ask, "What must we do?" We who teach must look at our lives. We must always ask ourselves, are we qualified to be a teacher? The answer, of course, will be no. No, not any of us is qualified to be a teacher in the sense that Jesus Christ was qualified. But as we look at what He did and try to emulate Him, we shall become more qualified. We shall continue to fail as well as succeed. But at least there is one way in which we can be qualified: we can learn to handle our sins and failures biblically. And we can grow by His grace daily. In this, as a minimum, we can become a proper example. If we have taught how to handle sins and failures biblically, we shall have taught much. This is the key place in which to begin. Students must learn not only from our excellencies (this they may learn best from Christ's perfection) but, more often, they must learn from us God's way to handle our sins and our failures, because our excellencies are all too few.

That, then, is what we need in Christian school teachers: people who know that the Christian philosophy of teaching involves the process of discipling, and that discipling is becoming like one's teacher. When our Christian schools are fully aware of this, their full potential (possessed by no other) will begin to be tapped.

262

NOTE

JESUS AS A TEACHER

The word "teacher" *(didaskalos)* and its verbal counterpart *(didasko)* are used more frequently than any other terms to describe the preaching ministry of Jesus Christ. Indeed, they are used almost to the exclusion of all others. Three other words, *kerusso, evangelizo* and *diangello* combined occur only 18 times in the Gospels, whereas *didasko* occurs 41 times with respect to the preaching of Christ (plus once in Acts 1:1) and *didaskalos* 46 times; in all, a combined total of 87 references.[5]

In Luke the word "teach" (in noun and verb form) occurs 29 times with reference to the preaching of Christ. It occurs 26 times in Mark, 20 times in Matthew, and only 12 times in John. However, John uses no other term at all, whereas Mark employs one, Matthew two and Luke three.

The verb in all cases is translated "to teach" in the King James version, but the corresponding noun, "teacher" is (surprisingly) only once translated to (John 3:2). Elsewhere it is consistently rendered "Master." This latter rendering is arbi-

---

[5] "Chart"

The frequency of the usage of all terms
describing the preaching of Jesus Christ

	didasko	didaskalos	kerusso	evangelizo	diangello
Matthew	8	12	4	1	0
Mark	14	12	3	0	0
Luke	13	16	4	5	1
John	6	6	0	0	0
Total	41	46	11	6	1
		41			11
					6
Grand Total		87			18

trary and would be better translated in conformity with the verb as "teacher."

There is little question, then, that the primary scriptural word for the preaching of Christ is *didasko.* Since this is so, it is only proper that He should be called *ho didaskalos.* These two terms are found upon the lips of persons bearing every possible relationship to Him. His foes, His disciples, the Gospel writers, and He Himself use them.

The passages where Christ speaks of Himself as "teacher" are most instructive. They show Him adopting, approving, and recommending that appellation as a proper designation for His preaching. This cannot be said to be true concerning any other similar word.[6] In John 13:13 He says, "You call me teacher and Lord, and you speak properly, for so I am," thereby giving approval to the term. In Mark 14:14 He not only refers to Himself by way of approving the title, but recommends its usage by the disciples in addressing others: "Tell the owner of the house, the teacher says . . ." And finally, in Matthew 23:8 He appropriates exclusive right to the title: "But do not be called Rabbi: for one is your teacher."

The Significance of the Term "Teacher"

The significance of the word is clearly marked out in the New Testament in three references, one of which already has been quoted (namely, the last reference above). The other two are found in John 1:38 and John 20:16b: "They said to him, Rabbi (which translated means 'teacher')" and "She turned and said to him in Hebrew (Aramaic) 'Rabboni' (which means 'teacher'). In all three verses, the Greek title is used as the equivalent to the Hebrew (or Aramaic) "Rabbi" (or Rab-

---

[6]Jesus adopted other titles with reference to various aspects of His Person and work, but only "teacher" as a designation for His preaching ministry.

boni[7]). This title among the Hebrews was used very generally. Warfield says that in Christ's time it was "the simple honorific title by which . . . every professed teacher was courteously greeted.[8] It seems to have been used with respect to every public teacher whether he had studied to attain that position or not, and probably had nothing to do with academic degrees or standing whatever. It spoke of position or status acquired by doing.

One other interesting observation must be made in this connection. E. J. Young, in his mimeographed syllabus, *Old Testament Prophecy*, translates Joel 2:23 as follows:

"Be glad, then, ye children of righteousness, and rejoice in the Lord your God; for he giveth you the Teacher of righteousness.[9]

If this translation is correct, as it seems to be, it may well explain two facts. First, the title "Teacher of Righteousness" was assumed by the leader of the Qumram community. It is altogether likely that he borrowed it directly from Joel. In the Dead Sea Scroll commentary on Habakkuk, it is clear that the "Teacher of Righteousness" is there considered to be the fulfiller of prophecy. It is probable that he used the title to designate himself before the community as the fulfiller of Old Testament Messianic prophecy. Of course, it was falsely assumed by him, but rightly accepted by Christ. It would seem, therefore, that when Christ adopted the ordinary "honorific title" of the day and forbade its use to His disciples, He too was pouring a larger Messianic content into it. At any rate, His prohibition regarding its usage indicates that Christ lifted

---

[7]Although some distinction was originally made between Rabbi and Rabboni, the fact that this common Greek word is used to translate both indicated that at this time they were employed synonymously.

[8]Benjamin B. Warfield, *The Lord of Glory*, Zondervan, Grand Rapids (no date), p. 7

[9]Page 64. Cf. also the marginal reading of the NASV.

the title to such a unique level that it would have been improper or even blasphemous for another to assume it.

Conclusion

In summary, one significant conclusion may be drawn. Christ's sanctification of the word "teaching" as a description of His own preaching enhances the role of a teaching ministry and sets forth a high ideal for His disciples today.